PRAISE FOR *CHOOSING THE HARDER RIGHT: WEST POINT'S 1976 CHEATING SCANDAL*

"Destiny J. Ringgold, in her second book, *Choosing the Harder Right,* has taken on the tremendous daunting task of telling the story of her father's struggle in one of the most misunderstood and darkest period in the history of the United States Military Academy following the end of America's involvement in Vietnam. Destiny had her father and his records, logs, notes, and thoughts to learn about the details and characters involved on both sides of the situation and used her outstanding writing skill to flesh out the main and supporting characters to become as realistic as possible to the reader. I was asked to review a loose-leaf, unedited version of the book to see if I agreed that Destiny had captured me as I saw myself during that period; she had presented me better than I could have done and I'm sure she did the same for the other supporting characters. I think the book may be offensive to ones who think all liars, cheaters, and stealers should be eliminated from any of the military academies for any reason since they are at the academies at the taxpayers' expense—no exceptions to be granted. However, if you do not really know the reason for the struggle to stop the expulsion of cadets during this tense period, Ms. Ringgold's book will enlighten you and show you that justice did prevail."

—Colonel Arthur Lincoln, US Army (Ret.),
USMA class of '66

"Destiny has pierced brilliantly the complexity of the so-called 1976 West Point cheating scandal. These were turbulent, confusing, and challenging days. All there were tested in varied ways. Destiny's father was pivotal in confronting and correcting a massive injustice. His moral courage and steadfast determination against seemingly indomitable forces at last prevailed. He was, for me, always a profile in courage. Thanks to Cadet Tim Ringgold and many others our beloved West Point emerged from those dark days brighter, stronger, and more honorable. May this valuable work contribute to further understanding, reconciliation, and peace to all who suffered during those painful times."

—**Father Thomas Curley,** West Point
Catholic Chaplain, 1972–1977

"We live in an age where tribalism and polarization is the worst I have seen in my sixty-five years on the planet. These days, rather than falling into the feuding that seems so prevalent, I am on alert to discover ways to *care* for each other, to find common ground, to support generative efforts that seek to understand and restore. This work by Ms. Ringgold, born out of love and respect for her father, has the potential to deepen our understanding of what was transpiring in those cadet days so many years ago, when we were all twenty-something, trying to find our way. My hope is that the wounds carried by the men who navigated through those difficult days in the spring of 1976 can finally be healed. I would love to see evidence of this at our forty-fifth reunion in 2022, a gathering of all the surviving members of the *original* class of 1977. I believe there is an *esprit* in that direction that could be nurtured. This will require from each of us humility and a heart of forgiveness (a promise one gives to another not to resurrect or revisit past offenses). By God's grace."

—**Steve Hunt,** USMA class of 1977

"An interesting read and clarification of the difference between the honor codes of the Military Academy at West Point, New

York, and the Naval Academy at Annapolis, MD, and civilian institutions. West Point would do a lot for cadet anxiety levels if they would lessen the threat of tolerating the violation of the honor system while still upholding the honor system. Destiny, very much aware of the discipline and rigorous regulations, senses and accurately reports on the extreme anxiety induced by the Honor Code and the paranoia it causes at West Point, which sounded more like *Duty, Honor, Paranoia, Country.* As a Naval Academy graduate with twenty years of service as a Marine officer and now a practicing psychologist, I could feel the sense of urgency and anxiety."

—**Clifford R. Dunning** Ph.D., LMFT, LPC,
Lieutenant Colonel US Marine Corps (Ret.),
USNA class of 1961

"Destiny has reached into the past to retrieve a story nearly unknown to my generation. She has lovingly combined intricate research and hours of interviews into this retelling of her father's experience as a West Point cadet. As an ethics professor, the story is compelling because students can apply various ethical frameworks to the controversy to sort out the layers that make it so complicated; the actions by individual students, the administration, and the government provide endless opportunities for discussing how to best carry out justice in light of the scandal. However, it is Destiny's unique vantage point—and thus the signature on her work—that gives us the widest view of the scandal and the most interesting points to consider (and the greatest opportunity to really use philosophy). The context in which the scandal takes place—after the loss in Vietnam, after the Watergate scandal and Nixon's resignation—reveals not only a prestigious military school, but a nation, grappling with the dark side of all-or-nothing thinking. The scandal, and Timothy

Ringgold's role within it, reveals what happens when we ignore the opportunities presented by the uncertain, hazier, gray area of any situation. In our attempt to simplify what is complicated or to carry forward traditions—those habits and things that are known and comfortable to us—human beings often completely trample what is begging to be changed. And very unfortunately, it often takes something the magnitude of this cheating scandal to push people into *really seeing* and acknowledging the dark, sticky issue at the root of the perceived so-called problem. Destiny's scope of vision and attention to detail help the reader to see and understand that this cheating scandal is not only about honesty or academic integrity but is really about history catching up with a nation that would rather sleep through social and political issues that cannot be "solved" with black and white arithmetic thinking."

—Heather Coletti, Ph.D.

Choosing the Harder Right: West Point's 1976 Cheating Scandal

by Destiny Jennifer Ringgold

© Copyright 2021 Destiny Jennifer Ringgold

ISBN 978-1-64663-388-3

Published by

 köehlerbooks™

3705 Shore Drive
Virginia Beach, VA 23455
800-435-4811
www.koehlerbooks.com

CHOOSING
THE HARDER
RIGHT

WEST POINT'S
1976 CHEATING SCANDAL

A TRUE STORY

Destiny Jennifer Ringgold

VIRGINIA BEACH
CAPE CHARLES

For my Dad,
and all the cadets and officers affected by
West Point's cheating scandal of 1976

THE 1951
CHEATING SCANDAL

(twenty-five years before the events of 1976)

"The honor scandal was the worst experience of my life," he says. "I'm neither proud nor ashamed of my role. Fate chose me. I was bitter about that for a long time. But what embittered me the most was that neither Harkins nor my tactical officer—not a single officer at West Point—ever came to me and asked how I was. Not one son of a gun. And I was a kid. I could have been suicidal. I wasn't looking for a pat on the back. But not a single one of them ever said, 'Son, how are you doing?' Not one." [1]

—Ned Braun, former USMA cadet who was asked
to pose as a member of the cheating ring and turn
over the names of more cheaters, quoted in
Sports Illustrated, November 13, 2000.

I love to watch the rooster crow
He's like so many men I know
Who brag and bluster, rant and shout
And beat their manly chests without
The first damn thing to brag about

—Ernestine Ringgold

CONTENTS

JUNE 1976

JULY 1976

AUGUST 1976

SEPTEMBER–DECEMBER 1976

1977–1978

AUTHOR'S PREFACE

THIS BOOK IS ABOUT MY father, a career US Army officer, and his complicated relationship with his alma mater, The United States Military Academy at West Point. This also explained why I hadn't heard any stories about West Point from him until my senior year of high school when I was looking at colleges. He never once told me stories about being a cadet. He never attended any class reunions and never took weekend trips back to his college, even though we only lived three hours away. He volunteered nothing about his college experiences, until I asked.

Even though my father was an active Army officer, I did not grow up as a typical army brat, but instead attended Kindergarten through twelfth grade in the same civilian school district. I wasn't exposed much to Army life other than seeing my dad in uniform or visiting him at the Pentagon.

The first time I saw West Point, I was shown an environment of structure that I personally craved; it was like opening a present that I hadn't known I wanted. I immediately saw the allure. I did not have the same calling as my father, who knew he wanted to be a soldier since he was a boy, but I had the same serious ambition to do something meaningful, which led me to attend a similar school, Virginia Military Institute (VMI).

I did not graduate from VMI, but being a VMI cadet showed me the complexities of military schools firsthand. It is fascinating to compare my dad's experiences at West Point to my own experiences at VMI. There certainly were plenty of differences, but some very interesting similarities. We both had a similar love-hate relationship with our schools, not uncommon for most cadets. I, too, left and went back a year later like my dad did. I was part of the second class of women at VMI; when my dad returned to West Point the second class of women was entering West Point.

When I finally sat down to interview my dad with a microphone and computer, to hear about the 1976 West Point cheating scandal, I was in awe at the intricacies of the time period. From the mid 1960s to the mid 1970s, this ten-year period had a reputation for a generation of hippies, free love, and peace protests. It was most certainly a time for a national change in societal consciousness as our country was forced to question our values, beliefs, and what we stood for.

When my dad entered West Point during the summer of 1973, our country was divided over the Vietnam War. At the same time, many people were fighting for equality at home with the Civil Rights Movement and the second wave of the women's movement. Our nation felt betrayed by the Watergate break-in and President Nixon's subsequent resignation the following summer, in August 1974. It was a highly emotional and volatile time period, which assuredly influenced what occurred at West Point and the military at large.

Having been born in 1980, I joke that I was educated about this time period from watching *Forrest Gump* (1994). Forty-six years after the end of the Vietnam War, with our Vietnam veterans now our senior citizens, it is important to adequately summarize this time period in order to correctly paint the picture of what led to the events described here.

West Point was undergoing another layer of transition with the integration of women. Just months before the start of the cheating scandal, President Gerald Ford had signed the bill to open military academies to women. The three service academies: the United States Military Academy at West Point, the Naval Academy at Annapolis, and the Air Force Academy in Colorado Springs, were all forced to change their traditional all-male enrollment.

With the intricacies of the time and the evident need for the Academy to protect its reputation, it allows for the telling of a very theatrical story. It is my intention to illustrate my respect for the individuals, including my dad, who were willing to stand up against an institution when they saw something was wrong. Those that put their careers on the line, the numerous West Point law professors, including Captains Arthur Lincoln and Daniel Sharphorn, as well as the Catholic chaplain, Father Thomas Curley, are heroes in the story. To stand up in opposition to an establishment as powerful as the United States Military Academy, with all its alumni, enrolled Corps of Cadets, administration, faculty and the US Army, with its 174 years of tradition, was not easy, but was necessary to achieve a rejuvenation. The 1976 cheating scandal is historic because it was the largest cheating scandal of any service academy in history and was the catalyst that forced West Point to evolve.

Alumni like to think military schools do not change, that all graduates go through the same education and training. Though the essence of the school remains throughout the years, there are distinct generational differences. The school my dad attended was likely very different than the West Point in the 1960s or 1990s and is indisputably different than the West Point of today because of the changes Colonel Frank Borman's Special Committee recommended and Academy Superintendent, Lieutenant General Andrew Goodpaster, implemented in the aftermath of the events described in this book.

As the daughter of a man who was quoted many times in many newspapers, I can see the guts and courage it took to stand up and speak truthfully. I know he stood up for what he thought was right, and I know there was a cost he paid in having done so. Despite those costs, he always speaks highly of West Point and is proud to be an alumnus.

I wrote the story in first-person, told from the perspective of my father as the main character whose role was intrinsically unique. The book is compiled greatly from my dad's own personal journal entries from 1976, having been typed on a typewriter, which can be verified if anyone requests to see their authenticity. These journal entries were his recollection and interpretation of the situation. However, I did my best to match up the facts presented in the journal entries with the reporting in various newspaper articles.

The supporting characters are based on real individuals whom I had the honor of interviewing, as well as exchanging multiple emails: Lieutenant General Walter F. Ulmer, Jr. US Army (Ret.), Colonel Frank Borman, US Air Force (Ret.), Colonel Arthur Lincoln, US Army (Ret.), Dr. Peter DaRold, M.D., Major Michael Mamer, US Army (Ret.), Steve Hunt, Timothy Flanagan, Steve Verr, Major Robin Fennesy, US Army (Ret.), Reverend Thomas Curley, and Mr. Michael T. Rose, Esq. The stories of the supporting characters, Cadets DaRold, Mamer, Hunt, and Flanagan, are symbolic of the multiple experiences members of the Corps of Cadets had in living through the 1976 cheating scandal. Their names have been used with permission, but some cadet names have been changed. While my father's story is factual to his recollection, some creative license has been used in its telling, particularly with the recreation of private conversations.

West Point's Honor Code does not equip the USMA graduate to deal with the 'realities' of today's world. It is too idealistic, too absolute. Cadets are kicked out of USMA for actions considered 'honor violations' when junior officers would suffer no penalty for the same action. [2]

—Secretary of the Army Howard H. "Bo" Callaway,
a West Point graduate and Korean War veteran.
October 1, 1974.

CHAPTER 1
FROM STAUNTON TO WEST POINT

A GRAY MIST COVERED WEST Point on that January morning in 1971 as the radio reported a temperature of six degrees Fahrenheit. It was much colder than reported because of the strong winds that always blow through this portion of the Hudson River Valley, some fifty miles north of New York City. I was reluctant to leave the refuge and warmth of my automobile, with the heat on full blast, but this was the place of my childhood dreams. It was the college I aspired to attend after graduating from high school in May, four months from now.

I walked through the deep snow in my sneakers, which were getting soaked, towards Trophy Point and Battle Monument. Having grown up in Arizona, I was not used to this weather. The snow, still falling slightly, was already up to the mouths of the cannons that lined the walk. The wind was blowing fiercely, and I flipped my collar up to protect my neck and earlobes, looking very debonair. I was grateful I had a hat, even if it was only a LA Dodgers baseball cap.

As I stood at the top of the hill overlooking the Hudson River,

I realized I was not alone in this serene, almost sacred spot; a cadet was standing on the slope below me. Standing listless like a statue, he didn't move for a long time, peering off into the unknown mist. He seemed transfixed in the allure and majesty of our nation's oldest and most prestigious service academy.

Slowly reading the more than two thousand names immortalized on Battle Monument, I envisioned the men whose path—their glorious deeds and their valorous service—I was determined to follow. A transport tanker made its careful way up the ice-covered river. The ship's horn sounded out a warning for other vessels which echoed up the hill. I knew I was in awe of the school. I had grown up watching the movie, *The West Point Story*, and knew without a doubt who I wanted to be when I grew up: a West Point graduate and a soldier in the United States infantry.

I left my unknown companion and walked along Thayer Road by the Plain, the parade field, where men like Robert E. Lee, Douglas MacArthur, and Dwight Eisenhower had once marched as cadets. The landmark and awe-inspiring barracks became eerily visible as my exhale evaporated. I held my breath for a few seconds and took in the magnificence of the huge structure, knowing one day I would live inside one of the rooms within. The intimidating barracks was built almost two centuries ago and would continue to be intimidating after I was long gone. The stone-cold gray structure matched the gray uniforms the cadets wore as they proceeded to and from class in a continuous, determined manner. I was eager to be among them, wearing the uniform, and heading to class with the same purposeful mindset.

As I walked around West Point, along the Plain and past the academic buildings, I felt the power and nobility of the aristocratic setting. The gothic architecture and ample monuments gave me the feeling that I was walking among the gods themselves, with a hint of fear that comes with the awareness of a power so strong. I was made for an environment like this. I was strong, trim, competent, blinded with ambition, and chomping at the bit to be challenged. I knew I could create a life for myself that was rewarding and exciting, and surpass the limitations set in my childhood.

My family was not poor, but my three brothers and I grew up knowing that we had much less than our friends. We certainly had much less than our mom wanted us to have. Growing up with a feeling of lack can either create a defeated mentality or it can fuel a drive to succeed, as it did for me. I knew I was running as far and as fast as I could away from poverty and hopelessness and heading straight towards honor, duty, and achievement. The words from the Declaration of Independence rang true in my head: *We hold these truths to be self-evident, that all men are created equal, that they are endowed by their creator with certain unalienable rights, that among these are life, liberty and the pursuit of happiness.* I most certainly was pursuing my own happiness.

While my two older brothers were off fighting in Vietnam and my younger brother at home, I convinced my mother, who was alone raising us, about the value of attending the United States Military Academy at West Point. Founded in 1802, West Point was ranked among the top colleges in the country and considered the world's most prestigious leadership institution. West Point's mission was "to educate, train, and inspire the Corps of Cadets so that each graduate is a commissioned leader of character committed to the values of Duty, Honor, Country and prepared for a career of professional excellence and service to the Nation as an officer in the United States Army." West Point did not charge tuition but required a five-year commitment in the Army after graduation. If accepted, I would be the first member of our family to attend college. In fact, I was going to be the first high school graduate in our family, and my mother preferred having me in school rather than having a third son in Vietnam.

Ready to start this path of honor, duty, and achievement, at age sixteen I was too young to join the Army. Being too eager to wait, I persuaded my overworked mother to send me to a military high school, which would help me gain admission to West Point. West Point was a very competitive school; the more I planned ahead the better. The requirements to get into West Point not only included academic success, but an applicant needed extracurricular activities to show leadership, athletic ability, and personal ambition. All applicants were required to be between the ages of eighteen and twenty-two, not married, and without children. To be accepted into West Point, an applicant had to, by law, receive a nomination from the president, vice president, or a US senator or member of Congress.

In deciding what military high school to attend, my mother and I wrote to all the schools advertised in *Boy's Life* and *National Geographic*. We finally decided on Staunton Military Academy (SMA) in Virginia. I grew up in Phoenix, Arizona, so I would be far from home, but I would be on my desired path.

At Staunton, I quickly established myself at the top of my class while calming my mom's anxiety about the benefit of her added financial burden. Within six months, I was selected from among two hundred classmates as *The Outstanding New Cadet*, and as a junior was promoted to cadet sergeant. During that year at the commencement ceremony, I received the Conduct Award, a special award from the commandant of cadets for not receiving a single demerit, a feat I repeated the following year as a senior. Academically, my hard work paid off, and I graduated eighth out of one hundred and sixteen cadets with an academic average of 94.25.

During the fall of my senior year at SMA, I applied to West Point for the class entering in July 1971. Senator Barry Goldwater of Arizona, coincidentally a Staunton Military Academy alumnus, wrote a personal letter stating that he would be pleased to nominate me for an appointment. I was so incredibly pleased everything was falling into place. The following March, in 1971, West Point notified me that I was qualified to enter, but much to my bitter disappointment, Senator Goldwater had selected someone else. Each member of Congress or the vice president can have up to five cadets attending West Point at one time. I was one too many, so my admission was put on hold.

Discouraged, I enrolled at Arizona State University on a full Army ROTC scholarship. However, my enthusiasm for college life proved to be short-lived, as my hopes of a military career outpaced my academic achievement. With the war in Vietnam slowly winding down, two months into the semester I traded my four-year scholarship for a three-year enlistment.

Once in the Army, I found enlisted life a little duller and more tedious than I had hoped, but soon discovered that with a little effort, success came my way as easily as it had at Staunton Military Academy. I finished infantry and airborne training and enrolled in ranger training while waiting for a decision on my re-application to West Point.

The months crawled by as my anticipation to enter West Point increased. Finally, after nineteen months in the Army and two years out of high school, my nomination from Senator Barry Goldwater came through. My childhood ambitions became a reality when I reported to the United States Military Academy (USMA) at West Point on Monday, July 2, 1973, Reception Day— also known as R-Day—to join the *long gray line*, a phrase used to describe the graduates and cadets of West Point.

As part of the class of 1977, I took the Oath of Allegiance along with 1375 of my classmates that afternoon, affirming to "defend the Constitution of the United States against all enemies, foreign and domestic." We represented every state in the Union, along with several foreign countries. Upon graduation, our foreign classmates would return to their respective countries as officers in their armed forces, while the Americans would serve a minimum of five years active duty in the Army. We represented a cross-section of American society with a vast diversity of economic, social, and religious backgrounds. We were a serious, dedicated lot devoted to the ideals embodied in our motto: *Duty, Honor, Country*. Behind our gray confines, we thought we were isolated from society's complexity and the uncertainty of our times.

We were the first class to enter West Point after America's combat role in Vietnam had officially ended on January 27, 1973 with the signing of the Paris Peace Accords. The draft had been ended by President Nixon that same year, and American combat veterans were returning home. My classmates and I had applied to West Point during war time, and now entered it at the beginning of the post-war era. Not only that, but society had undergone a social revolution with the civil rights movement, women's movement, and anti-war movement that split our nation. It was not a popular time to serve in the military, but despite all the social changes, West Point remained as conventional and stoic as ever.

I was twenty years old, older than most of my classmates who entered right out of high school at age eighteen. I had already served two years in the Army, including a voluntary year at the Military Academy Preparatory School in Fort Belvoir, Virginia. I'd chosen to attend the West Point prep school in order to sufficiently prepare myself for the demanding coursework at the Academy. When my fellow plebes and I matriculated in the summer of 1973, we had no idea that our school, full of 171 years of tradition, would be tested to the very core and undergo a change in consciousness during our cadetship.

CHAPTER 2
THE HONOR CODE

WEST POINT'S MOST PRIZED TRADITION is its Honor Code, a seemingly simple premise that *a cadet will not lie, cheat, or steal, nor tolerate those who do.* The only penalty for a violation, or failure to report one, was automatic expulsion. In 1922, the Honor Code was officially made policy at West Point by General Douglas MacArthur who, at the time, was serving as Academy superintendent. "The highest standards of honor were to be demanded," Superintendent MacArthur wrote. "A code of individual conduct, which would maintain the reputation and well-being of the whole."

In wartime, the Army could be a life-or-death profession. Thus, the Honor Code was an integral part of the Academy's program to provide a deliberately stressful environment in which mistakes did not cost lives or compromise national security as it could in wartime. A soldier on the battlefield must trust the orders given by a superior or his comrades in arms.

Each incoming cadet signs the honor pledge in the mail before arriving on R-Day, vowing to live by the spirit, as well as by the letter of the Code. My classmates and I had the consecrated mandate committed to memory long before we donned our gray uniforms. If by chance we did not understand the sacredness and seriousness of the Honor Code, we plebes (first year students) were given a twelve-hour block of instruction of how the Honor Code was implemented within the Honor System. With the zeal, ardor, and idealism typical of youth, we set forth to maintain the standards of West Point by embracing the absolute, uncompromising Honor Code.

In addition to the sanctity of the Honor Code, cadets were taught the importance of working together, to *cooperate and graduate*. My classmates and I had to rely on each other for survival and literally became brothers-in-arms. We'd survived Beast Barracks together, the term used to describe the eight weeks of new cadet training in July and August, before West Point accepted us as plebes at the start of academics in the fall. The demanding academic and military lives of cadets caused the life you lived before to disappear as the relationships inside the academy became more important than those outside it. My closest brothers were four men that I depended on for survival, and we knew we would die for each other if needed: Peter DaRold, Michael Mamer, Steve Hunt, and Timothy Flanagan. We referred to each other by our last names, which was typical of military environments.

DaRold was our city boy, with a Long Island accent, kind demeanor and loyalty to a fault. He was my roommate plebe year and had become my best friend.

Mamer, known as *Moon Dog* for always making us howl with laughter, had a shit-eating grin showing off his perfect teeth. His sense of humor was always welcome, especially in an environment where seriousness was the attitude of the day.

Hunt was the straight and narrow cadet with a strong trust in authority. He grew up as a son of a career Army officer from the class of 1950 (half of whom served in Korea). He'd spent part of his childhood at West Point, from second to fourth grade. His dad was a company tactical officer and then a regimental tactical officer. Hunt was often around cadets who were invited by his father and his mother to their home nearby. His dad exemplified servant leadership both in his work and at home, which helped Hunt view military service as an honorable pursuit. His trust in authority was based on his personal experience being around his dad's Army peers and West Point cadets.

Flanagan was West Point through-and-through, having been born and raised on the West Point Military reservation, similar to Hunt. His father was also an alumnus, from the class of 1942. His father had served in WWII and had been seriously wounded in the Battle of the Bulge. Following his forced retirement for medical reasons, he'd spent the last part of his career on the commandant's staff as a permanent civilian serving as assistant operations officer from 1951 until his passing.

I was often told I looked like I was always thinking, which was partly true. I was certainly ambitious and determined to not let anything stand in my way, and I very much liked thinking things through before acting.

This intense bond with my classmates was often the most prized experience from attending a military school. Saddled with impossible demands on time, the five of us learned to rely on each other for moral support and encouragement to stay on task. Each of us learned that together we would make it, while alone, we couldn't. Bonds between classmates transcended time and distance, and we saw how alumni kept coming back to the Academy again and again.

DaRold, Mamer, Hunt, Flanagan, and I all came to West Point from different walks of life and parts of the country. All those differences disappeared when we lived in the same barracks, wore the same uniform, and marched toward the same laborious goal of graduating from a fast-paced, competitive, and extremely demanding school that allowed little freedom for an outside life. Thus, there were moments when our brotherhood was our life raft.

The complication of the Honor Code, unfortunately, was that each cadet was required to report a fellow classmate if there was suspicion of a breach. Due to the threat of toleration, a cadet had to set aside friendship and put duty first. It was incomprehensible to think of any of us reporting on one another; it would have felt like the greatest betrayal.

During our plebe year, our class, the class of 1977, was lectured by the honor chairman, Honor Captain Ronald H. Schmidt, a first class cadet (called a *firstie*) who was about to graduate in the class of 1974. He was the one man responsible for educating and training us on the scope and merit of the Honor Code. We, however, needed no training; we knew what the Code said and what was expected of us, but the chairman didn't see it that way. He told us that we had been reporting too many of our classmates for honor violations. He said our "ideals were set too high and should be toned down."

"That was bogus," DaRold whispered under his breath.

I shrugged my shoulders.

"I don't get it. I think the Code is pretty clear," Hunt expressed to my left.

Later that year, the honor chairman himself was accused of cheating on a test during class. To our astonishment, he was not dismissed despite the guilty verdict. He was, instead, allowed to graduate in June 1974, without being required to serve the mandatory five-year commitment in the Army. I assumed some of my classmates would have relished in receiving a free West Point education without the five-year military service obligation. The chairman's punishment did not make sense, especially since the only consequence for breaking the Honor Code was dismissal. That situation personally left me feeling uncertain and confused about how the honor system was run.

Two months after the class of 1974 graduated, President Richard Nixon resigned for the Watergate cover-up and was later that year pardoned by President Ford. What were idealistic young West Point cadets supposed to think about these two events? We came to realize the difficulty of reconciling our absolute Honor Code with an imperfect world. We found that within the honor system the pure and simple truth was rarely pure and never simple. We accepted the ideal of the Honor Code as our goal and continued to strive for perfection, but perfection was not an attainable goal.

TWO YEARS LATER: COW (JUNIOR) YEAR

FALL 1975

CHAPTER 3
THE ANNOUNCEMENT

"SOMETHING'S UP. WHEN HAVE WE ever had a full-blown assembly with the entire corps in one place?" DaRold asked, turning to me on my left.

"The administration and all the professors are present too," I said, nodding toward the captains sitting a few rows behind us, who were probably also wondering what was up.

"Maybe they're going to build an arcade on post?" Flanagan suggested with a smirk.

"Fat chance. I'm hoping it is more along the lines of eliminating any outstanding demerits, since I am still working off my slugs from last year from getting in trouble with you," I said, elbowing Flanagan underneath his left rib, which he fought off with his forearm.

"And why would the superintendent be that generous?" DaRold asked, his eyebrow lifted in question.

"I don't know . . . to build morale?" I suggested.

"You can't honestly still hold a grudge against me," Flanagan said. "As far as I remember, it was your idea to sneak out after

Taps and meet up with those two girls."

"Well, how could I resist two women pulling up and asking, *where's the party?*" I said, playing innocent.

"Do you even remember their names? Because I don't," Flanagan said.

"No, but I remember my punishment for having gotten caught. We both got sixty-six penalty tours. They gave you a twenty-two hour reduction for ratting on me, so they added your twenty-two to my sixty-six," I said with a stern face.

"Damn, you shouldn't have gotten caught," Flanagan said, clutching his side in laughter.

"I was your freakin' decoy."

"Yeah, you're right, man. Ha! I thank you for your service," he said, still laughing and slapped me on the back. "We still got caught and both punished—just you more than me!"

As Superintendent Lieutenant General Sidney Berry walked in and up to the podium, the sounds echoing throughout Thayer Hall died down as everyone faced forward to hear what he had to say.

"Gentlemen," General Berry spoke with strength and poise. His voice sounded crisp through the speakers. "I'm here today to address you as a whole. I'd like you to understand that what I announce today is something that I've spent the last few years fighting against."

"Oh no," Flanagan mumbled, like he knew what the general was going to say. I clearly didn't.

"I've done everything in my power to prevent this from happening." He talked with his hands, emphasizing his serious tone. "I took every precaution and every stand against this. On October seventh, President Ford signed into law a bill opening the three service academies to women beginning with the class of 1980, which will enter next summer."

"Booooooooo," an eruption of negative disapproval went through the corps.

"From the time of the first Congressional action in '72 to open the military academy to women until the final passage of the bill this fall, my predecessor, General Knowlton, officers, cadets, and I publicly opposed this action."

That comment silenced the audience. General Berry cleared his throat.

"That opposition was based on the fact that this military academy exists primarily to develop combat leaders, and national policy precludes women from serving in combat units. However, in May of this year, the House of Representatives vote of three hundred and three to ninety-six for the admission of women to the national service academies came as something of a surprise. Then, in June the Senate voted in favor of the admission of women."

He sighed as his eyes scanned the faces in the room of those wearing the uniform he himself had worn as part of the class of '48. General Berry's hands then gripped the side of the podium. He was clearly uncomfortable, even to the point of being distressed.

Murmurs broke out in the auditorium.

"I knew it. My dad was worried about this happening," Flanagan vented, shaking his head in disgust. "I thought it wouldn't happen during our years here, though."

"I know. Last spring in English class, I had to debate the future of women at West Point. I concluded it would happen someday, but that we'd never live to see it," I whispered. I, personally, was not disconcerted by this announcement. After growing up with three brothers, attending two years at an all-male high school, serving two years in an all-male infantry unit, and attending three years at this all-male institution, I wouldn't mind some females filling in the ranks. Women would certainly make our gray skies, gray buildings, and gray uniforms a little less gray.

General Berry cleared his throat again, resulting in silence and obedience from the audience.

"However, despite my objections, we have our orders: women

are coming to West Point. They will be entering our ranks next *July*. With this direct order," General Berry said, intentionally scanning the Corps of Cadets, "I tell you today, that we will do as instructed, and we will do so with honor, grace, and professionalism. Times are changing, and we must change with them.

"We intend to integrate women completely into the Corps of Cadets. Men and women will attend class, march, eat, and train together. West Point will not be divided into two institutions: one for women, one for men. During my visit to the Merchant Marine Academy, I found that women can do far more than I had previously thought. I saw women running, rappelling down cliffs, crawling under barbed wire, scaling walls, firing weapons, and patrolling right along with the men. Thus, there will be minimum necessary adjustments made for women cadets; where appropriate, they will undergo training equivalent to that of men cadets."

"So we are following the merchant marine's lead?" DaRold whispered to me.

"I guess so," I said, shrugging my shoulders.

"The presence of admitting women potentially expands the pool of qualified candidates—men and women—from which we select our outstanding cadets every year. This could raise the academic standards at West Point. Men and women cadets will learn to work together professionally—a good preparation for life in the army, and generally, in American society.

"Thus, I instruct you all to accept this change that is about to occur. July is closer than you think, and there is much work to be done. The past few months, I personally have devoted more time, thought, energy, and effort to preparing West Point for the admission of women than to any other single matter. As we implement these changes, I expect complete compliance from the faculty, the administration, and the Corps of Cadets. I will not tolerate any negative comments. We have to keep morale high. We are all soldiers. We will implement these orders to serve the best interests of the country, the army, the Military Academy, and the individuals involved. We will do this right, and we will welcome the first class of women to this school."

He paused and continued to look around the room. His stature commanded compliance, and I personally had a lot of respect for someone in his position. I thought he was handling this historic transition rather well. Likely, it was the cadets themselves that would be most put off by the incorporation of women, especially those who were here following the footsteps of family members.

As more dissatisfaction was being expressed among the audience, General Berry pointedly ignored them and went on. "So let me be clear, the time for debate has passed. Now is the time for positive thinking, understanding and support. I will not tolerate anyone speaking ill of this mission. If you do not agree with the decision, and you wish to resign, have your resignation on my desk first thing in the morning. But, if you choose to stay with the knowledge that the integration of women is just months away, accept this fully and completely or *leave!*"

General Berry knew there would not be a lot of cadets who would be moved to such lengths as resigning, even as a form of personal protest. With the knowledge that nothing truly stays the same, I was happy to have any of my classmates who were so opposed to this change that they would actually resign; good riddance to them. Despite a system that had been in place for almost two hundred years, I believed that women in the army deserved the same high quality leadership training as the men.

"This integration is happening. Hold your head up high. It's important that we do this well. Let's be the leaders and set the example for the other academies on how this transition is done correctly. Make me proud, cadets. Thank you. You're dismissed." With that, General Berry walked off the stage and out of the building.

We took our time getting up to leave. There were hundreds

of people ahead of us filing out of Thayer Hall.

Flanagan turned to me. "Ringgold, are you from a generation of West Point graduates?"

"No, I'm the first one in my family to go to college," I said. "In fact, I'm also the first one in my family to graduate high school."

"Oh wow. Well, I want the same experience my dad had as a cadet, no different," Flanagan said.

"I really don't have a problem with women entering, do you?" I asked.

"Absolutely. I won't be able to walk around barracks in my underwear anymore."

"Ha. That is something no one needs to see," I said.

"Not my Superman underwear? I'd be wearing it on the outside of our uniform if I was allowed to," he said with a straight face. "You know, every West Point cadet in our generation secretly desires to be Superman; it's a fact. We all want to be superheroes and save the world," he said, sounding very philosophical.

"You have your whole suit underneath your uniform right now . . . all you need is a phone booth, right?" DaRold asked, turning to Flanagan.

"Not all of it. I keep my cape in my bag," he replied.

"Well, maybe you'll have some luck with the incoming female plebes. I'm sure most of them want to date a superhero," I said, hopefully.

"No way. They're my kryptonite. I don't plan on going anywhere near them."

"I don't think you will be able to avoid them; there will be some in every company. Besides, I assume if any woman is hardcore enough to come here, then likely she wants to be her own superhero," I said, winking at Flanagan, and followed him out of Thayer Hall with DaRold behind me.

APRIL 1976

CHAPTER 4
THE CHEATING SCANDAL BECOMES PUBLIC

DURING THE PREVIOUS THREE YEARS, my friends and I had progressed through the rigorous responsibilities at West Point without any major problems with our Honor Code or its administration. A few of our classmates had been kicked out each year, but no one I knew personally. Our Honor Code and the Honor System did not come under the spotlight until April 6, 1976. That spring Tuesday, two months shy of the completion of our junior year, the Corps of Cadets was standing at reveille formation just before daylight. We were about to march to breakfast when random names were called from formation.

The one name that caught my attention: Cadet Peter DaRold. I had no idea what it was for, and from the reactions of the cadets around me, neither did they. Cadet Hunt was to my right, and I glanced at him, but he shrugged his shoulders.

Later that day, we were informed that it had to do with the previous electrical engineering take-home assignment, given on the third and fourth of March, which had been due just prior to spring break. Electrical Engineering 304 (EE304) was a required course for all cadets. The assignment had been given to more than 800 cadets, 823 to be exact. Attention was drawn when one electrical engineering professor noticed that a cadet had written on the bottom of his homework, with the full intention of honesty and disclosure, that he had received help from another classmate. The cadet who had given the help should have also written on his paper that he had given help. The logic was that if one cadet received assistance, then one must have given assistance, but no one self-reported having given assistance and was therefore guilty of giving unauthorized assistance on graded homework. Thus, the head of the department was notified, and then, to find the culprit, the electrical engineering professors were directed to compare answers, which led to the awareness of widespread similarities.

When the assignment had been handed out, we had been instructed to complete it individually. I had completed the assignment by myself, but I was also fully aware it had been a challenging assignment. I kept thinking about my friend DaRold and wondering if he was guilty of collaborating or if it had all been a misunderstanding.

This particular EE304 take-home assignment included ten mathematical problems, requiring the use of a computer, and one essay question. Two other take-home assignments in EE304 had been given earlier in the semester which had encouraged teamwork, setting a precedent for students to rely on each other to help complete assignments. This third take-home assignment was the first and only one identified as individual work.

On that day, April 6, academy officials announced that 117 cadets, all members of the junior class, were referred to the eighty-eight-member Cadet Honor Committee for investigation for cheating on the assignment. Out of the 117 cases, fifteen cases were quickly dropped, one cadet resigned, and the remaining 101 cases were referred to the Cadet Honor Committee for full Honor Boards hearings beginning on April 12.

The Corps of Cadets was organized into four regiments of nine companies each, totaling thirty-six companies of over 4000 cadets. First and Third Regiment took classes together, as did Second and Fourth Regiment. The accused were from all four regiments and most companies.

When a cadet is charged with an honor code violation, the process starts with a hearing, called an Honor Board, made up of thirteen fellow cadets, twelve of whom have voting rights and the thirteenth held by the honor captain. For a guilty verdict, all twelve members have to vote unanimously, otherwise the charges are dropped. With a guilty verdict, cadets are encouraged to resign, essentially to save face with their reputation and careers. All cows (juniors) and firsties (seniors) found guilty of an honor violation, and separated from the Academy, are required to serve two years in the army, starting at the bottom as a private, rather than as a second lieutenant upon graduation. Those given a guilty verdict are allowed to appeal to a board of officers, a five member group, and given free military counsel or permitted to hire their own civilian lawyers for a second hearing.

A few nights later, on Friday, April 9, I went to the pay phones in the basement of Thayer Hall and called my mother. I wanted to assure her that I was not involved. I was afraid she would hear something on the news and worry needlessly. Also, the stress was unnerving as the cheating scandal unfolded the past week, and I needed someone to talk to on the outside.

"Tim, I'm glad you called. Of course I've been worried, and I can hear that you are upset. You have absolutely nothing to do with this, right?"

"All the mistakes I made on my engineering assignment are my own, Mom," I said, teasing.

"How can you joke about this? Your future would be on the line if you were involved. The scandal looks serious. There have been reports all over the news about this."

"Yeah, it started with one hundred and seventeen of my classmates, but it seems to be growing."

"I've been seeing articles in *The New York Times* about this. I cut them all out. I have them right here; hold on." I heard rustling on the other end and a soft clang as she put the phone down on the table.

"Okay, one article in *The Times* from yesterday quotes one of your classmates who has been charged, saying that 'they had been held incommunicado for up to fourteen hours awaiting interrogation by the subcommittee teams.' That sounds serious."

"It is, Mom," I said, taking a deep breath and letting it out slowly. "West Point takes the Honor Code very seriously. The Honor Committee is working overtime investigating right now, to get this all straightened out. It's a big deal."

"Well, what exactly happened?"

"Well, I've heard that the Electrical Engineering professor went to the commandant about the graded homework that should have been completed individually. The fact that so many students apparently collaborated should have been a sign that it wasn't a reflection of the student body, but rather a reflection of miscommunication."

"Oh, I see. That's sad. And you're telling me you had absolutely nothing to do with this?" My mom said, still needing reassurance.

"None, Mom. I'm just not convinced that my classmates deserve to be thrown out for this."

"So that's what would happen if they're found guilty?"

"Yes. Cheating, including collaborating on homework, is an honor code violation and the only punishment is separation from the Academy, and one of my friends is being investigated: Peter DaRold."

"Oh no. Peter was your roommate plebe year, right?" She sighed deeply.

"Yes, he was, Mom. I have no idea how much trouble he's in.

I don't think it's fair. The whole thing just isn't sitting right with me. It feels so blown out of proportion."

"That may be true son, but what can you do?"

"I have no idea."

"You truly need to keep your nose buried in your books right now. You're almost done with your junior year. I wouldn't risk drawing attention to yourself."

"I know, Mom. I will. It's just not that simple. There's so much responsibility here that we all have moments where we take shortcuts, even unintentionally. Some cadets are kicked out on insignificant charges."

"I read about that kid, the plebe, who was charged with lying because he had been confronted by some upperclassman outside of the mess hall. He'd said his parents had been in a car accident to cover up the fact he was crying."

"Yeah, that's Cadet Steven Verr."

"Is it true that cadre had been starving him as part of his harassment?"

"Well, likely so. I remember feeling hungry most of plebe year myself. It's a traditional form of hazing, to toughen up new cadets," I said.

"So was there intention to lie?"

"Probably not. He was probably just hungry which is likely why his case was overturned by the superintendent. A cadet can get kicked out for lying, even something small like that. Sad, but true."

"West Point sounds like a scary place," mom said.

"Well, right now it is. The Honor Code is supposed to guide us, to protect us, but right now all of us feel the fear of being accused of a violation. It seems to be looming over our heads rather than supporting us. I'm most concerned right now for Pete."

"Son, the last thing I want is for you to be involved in this scandal. It's all over the news. Since it does not involve you, I would stay clear out of the way. Let the situation play out. Likely the Academy will come up with a solution in the best interest of all who were involved."

"I hope so. I have been overhearing my classmates condemning those accused. I just can't help but feel that any one of us could be in this situation."

"But you're not, and I would steer clear of the drama and just focus on your academics. In a few months, you'll be on summer break. Stay focused now and just bide your time."

"You're right, I know. I have plenty to do and certainly have exams to study for. I'll call you again soon, okay Mom? Love you."

"Love you, son. Thanks for calling."

I hung up feeling a little less burdened. This was a tricky situation, and I certainly didn't want to get caught up in any of it. I couldn't help but feel that if I had the opportunity to help my classmates, I would, especially Peter DaRold, who I considered a brother.

CHAPTER 5
THE VIETNAM WAR
AND GENERAL KOSTER

WHEN I WAS FOURTEEN YEARS old, my oldest brother Christopher left home to fight in Vietnam before graduating high school. He was determined to serve our country, and my other brother Mike, four years my senior, wasn't far behind him. Chris was a ground combat medic for a year, from 1967 to 1968 with the First Cavalry Division. My brother Mike had been a door gunner and crew chief for UH-1 Huey Iroquois attack helicopters, and he even volunteered to stay in combat an additional year after he finished his first deployment.

President Johnson had sent the first combat troops to South Vietnam in March of 1965, and the number of troops being deployed each year increased. The draft had been reinstated that year, forcing males between the ages of eighteen and twenty-five to join the military. Draftees formed one-third; the other two-thirds were volunteers like my brothers.

Part of me wanted to be over in Vietnam too, fighting alongside my brothers. I was itching for adventure and to make a difference. I knew I wanted to be an infantry soldier, and I tried not to judge the draft dodgers, especially as the number of body bags returning home increased. I knew my brothers could come home that way, too, so I felt compassion for anyone that did not want to participate in the war.

The Vietnam War personally affected every American. It was called *The Living Room War*, unlike the Korean War, which had been censored. Every night, for a decade, we saw on the television screen what was happening in Vietnam. War is brutal and violent, and the truth was being shown on live TV. We saw the destruction from the comfort of our living rooms, and we heard the reports of death tolls for both the Americans as well as the enemy.

The Vietnam War caused multiple splits in American consciousness. There were those that supported the war and thought we could win, primarily the older generation who lived through and fought in World War II and believed in military strength. The younger generation, being forced to fight a war they personally didn't believe in, created a lot of controversy. The outbreak of student anti-war protests showed the collective opposition to the war.

Some who got drafted were legally able to defer their enlistment by attending college, being married with children, or being physically or mentally unfit for duty. Others burned their draft cards or were imprisoned for non-compliance, like the boxer Muhammad Ali, who was a role model for men who did not want to fight, the conscientious objectors. According to author Tom Valentine, "Local draft boards had an enormous power to decide who had to go and who would stay. Consequently, draft board members were often under pressure from their family, relatives, and friends to exempt potential draftees." Political leaders who had influence were able to protect their family members from being drafted. Another option for those that did not want to participate in the Vietnam War, but did not have a legal reason to defer, nor a political connection, was to flee to Canada or Mexico.

Oftentimes any lack of support for a war was viewed as a lack of support for the military. I knew that mentality was too black and white and that you could support our troops while at the same time argue against the war.

Our purpose for fighting in Vietnam had not been clear and purposeful. During President Kennedy's first speech as president, he mentioned the Domino Theory. He vowed to continue the military support for South Vietnam, to prevent the overtake of communism. The fear was that if Vietnam became fully communist, the surrounding countries like Cambodia, Laos, and others would fall to communism as a result, like dominoes toppling.

On March 31, 1968, the Viet Cong's Tet Offensive on their Lunar New Year, during Johnson's presidency, showed our opposition's military strength. The North Vietnamese and Viet Cong infiltrated South Vietnam and took many cities with surprise attacks. The Tet Offensive was politically successful for the North, shocking, and a major turning point of the Vietnam War.

For years, because the amount of North Vietnamese deaths was much larger than American deaths, we Americans thought we were winning the war. However, when Walter Cronkite, the CBS News anchor Americans admired and trusted, reported after the Tet Offensive that we were losing the war, we believed him over what we were hearing from our own president. In fact, our whole trust in the administration came fully into question when President Nixon attacked Cambodia and Laos, rather than ending the war as he had promised during his campaign in 1968.

Near the end of my second year at West Point, on April 23, 1975, President Ford declared that the war was over. A week later, South Vietnam fell to the communists. We, as a country, did not know how to process the loss of Vietnam. For us in the army, the loss was more troubling. We were the strongest military force in the world after World War II, and we were taught that we won every battle in Vietnam, yet we still lost the war. The guerilla warfare was a completely different way of fighting than the army had been trained. We had to learn how to fight on their terms, which was brutal and costly. However, it is estimated that over a million North Vietnamese and Viet Cong died, compared to around 58,220 Americans who lost their lives.

It was the Americans who decided that the price was too high for the war to continue. It was a bittersweet end. We were the Baby Boomers, a generation that was traumatized; our country was ashamed, hurt, and shocked by the defeat in Vietnam. Not unlike our World War II veterans, our combat troops came back physically, emotionally, and mentally damaged. However, our society did not welcome them with open arms. Many were spit on, cursed at, shunned, and labelled as *baby killers*. Returning home was likely almost as traumatizing as the war itself. The psyche of the USA was wounded and angry. And just like our soldier forefathers, the Vietnam Veterans didn't talk about what had happened; they obviously didn't want to relive the events. In some ways, the silence about the war perpetrated a sense of shame. To this day, I have yet to hear firsthand the experiences either of my brothers, Chris or Mike, had while over there. Though, I was well aware they had been to Hell and back.

At the time I entered West Point in 1973, all of my professors, and I mean every single one of them, were Vietnam veterans. They had seen combat, and whether they realized it or not, they were scarred by the war—physically and emotionally. Here they were stationed at West Point, after the war ended, training the next batch of soldiers and wondering, *What, exactly, was the point?* The Academy was in turmoil because our country was in turmoil. The Vietnam War had ruined the army; it was not a popular time to serve. So much money and manpower, with a great loss of life, had been spent on the war. It touched everyone's lives. America was heartbroken. No one was unaffected by the war, and that was especially true at West Point.

The Academy existed, in part, as a living and breathing entity with its own values and tradition. As much as it stood separate from society, much like a monastery, in a world of its own behind the gray stone walls, it was nevertheless influenced by the changes in society. The staff, faculty, and administration who ran the school were looking for a sense of purpose from the defeat while at the same time in charge of training the officers who would fight future wars. As Army officers and Vietnam combat veterans, our role models were in a quandary. It was a time of individual and national reflection, which absolutely affected the foundation of how West Point was run.

Additionally, prior to my entering West Point in 1973, the superintendent, Major General Samuel Koster, was forced into early retirement. He had been charged with trying to cover up the My Lai Massacre, a charge that was later dropped. My Lai was a horrendous event in which 350 to 500 innocent South Vietnamese civilians were murdered by American troops. Doubtless, there were other tragedies that should not have occurred in Vietnam, but this event marked the *moral nadir*, the worst point of the war, and helped increase opposition to the war at home.

To complicate matters, one of General Koster's sons was a classmate, a member of the West Point class of 1977. General Koster's involvement was an embarrassment to the Academy. His prompt retirement prevented him from receiving a third star, and he was demoted to a one-star general. His replacement, Lieutenant General William Knowlton, had the monumental task of finding a way to get West Point functional again. He was superintendent during my plebe year, followed by Lieutenant General Sidney Berry my yearling (sophomore) year.

CHAPTER 6
MEETING WITH THE
UNDER SECRETARY
OF THE ARMY

ACADEMICALLY, MY FIRST TWO YEARS were unremarkable. I was more interested in sport parachuting—I made over 100 jumps plebe year—and other extracurricular activities. Beginning my third year, I committed myself to making the dean's list.

True to my word, I put my nose in my books and hit the ground running academically. On Sunday, April 11, I decided to study my nuclear physics rather than go to the movies as I usually did. Space, time, and length dilation was more important than *The Return of the Pink Panther*. Nuclear physics often challenged me to the point that I could think of the same problem for over an hour, contemplating the answer. Just as I began to study, I heard a knock on my door. I looked up. It was my company's first sergeant.

"Ringgold, the under secretary of the Army will be here on Wednesday for a routine visit. I need to find volunteers. Are you available?"

"Sure. Is there anything I need to know about the meeting?"

"Not that I know of. I just need to find a few cadets available."

"Got it. I'll be there," I said without hesitation. I didn't mind volunteering because it would get me out of class early that day.

The next day, Monday, the Honor Code Committee, made up of eighty-eight members, began the laborious process of the Honor Board Hearings. By now, over a hundred of my classmates were being charged, more than 10 percent of my class. It was quickly becoming the largest cheating scandal in the history of the Academy.

On Wednesday, I left class a few minutes early, as planned, and stopped by the hostess office for some coffee on my way to meet the under secretary of the Army. The hostess office is a popular place for upperclassmen to gather, and I often transitioned between classes there. Since classes were not yet out, it was not as crowded as usual. I overheard two of my classmates talking about the honor hearings as I poured myself a cup of coffee, leaving it black as I always did.

"If they separate all these guys, we'll have a better chance for stripes next year. Maybe I'll make company commander," said the first cadet.

"Don't you know it. The GAP (great American public) will love it. It ought to make our degrees really worth something," the second cadet said.

I stood there, sipping my coffee and listening, and grew alarmed at what they were saying. My own classmates were hoping to use the misfortune of our other classmates for their own benefit. I couldn't hold my tongue.

"Don't you two feel any compassion for our own classmates?" I interrupted.

"We weren't talking to you, and if you haven't noticed, West Point is a very competitive school. There's nothing wrong with us benefiting from their poor choices," the second cadet shot back.

"You or I could be in their situation," I said.

"If I'd cheated, then I would deserve to get kicked out, but I wouldn't be stupid enough to get caught," the first cadet said, convinced of his own logic.

"And up to this point, you've never done anything dishonest in your life, eh?" I said, disgusted and looked him straight in the eye.

"I know the difference between right and wrong," the first cadet matched my glare.

I chose not to continue debating. I easily saw the futility in it and left. I chuckled to myself recalling Thomas Paine's quote: *arguing with someone who's renounced the use of reason is like administering medicine to the dead.*

I walked over to Mahan Hall, where the engineering and English courses were taught. The small room, where we were expected to meet and wait for the under secretary of the Army, was too small to be a classroom, but held ten chairs in two rows of five and a small table. I sat down in the middle of the front row as the rest of the cadets arrived.

"Attention!" The colonel ordered. The other cadets and I shot up to show respect. "The Honorable Norman R. Augustine," he said as the under secretary of the Army walked in.

"Thank you, gentlemen. Have a seat." He turned to the officer. "Colonel, would you mind leaving us. I want to make sure all the cadets here today speak frankly and do not feel any pressure to give the Academy a "clean bill of health," he said.

"Yes, sir. I'll step out and leave you all here to have a leisurely discussion," the colonel said, closing the door lightly behind him.

The under secretary turned to us with an air of casualness. "This is one of my routine visits to the Academy and was scheduled before the current controversy. This is an informal meeting, so please feel free to speak up. The ten of you have been selected completely at random."

There were a total of ten cadets present, five yearlings (sophomores) and five cows (juniors), including me. Under

Secretary Augustine leaned against the small table at the front of the room, facing us. He smiled at each of us individually. "I visit West Point a few times a year to check in. I'm here to support you, so how are things going?"

Silence followed the question, so Mr. Augustine waited a few minutes and asked again.

"Women will be entering in a few months. This is a monumental undertaking. Are any of you excited about the reality of women being here?"

He got a sort of chuckle from everyone.

One yearling spoke up. "I know we're not allowed to complain about the changes being made. I'm just happy that I'll be part of one of the last all-male classes."

"That's understandable," Mr. Augustine replied, nodding as his eyes scanned the faces of the cadets.

"I'm indifferent," one yearling said. "I grew up with three older sisters. My mom and my sisters can all be as tough as nails. I'm sure the Academy won't have trouble upholding tradition. Just because women are entering doesn't mean the school has to change all that much."

Like a violin string wound too tight, a little tension was felt throughout the room. It was definitely less common to accept or even welcome the integration of women to the Corps of Cadets. Tradition was tradition and being forced to open the ranks to women was not welcomed by the vast majority.

"I like your viewpoint. I assume the majority of cadets are against this integration." He looked around as most everyone nodded but hesitated to speak up. "Now, aside from this historic change, I know that there have been some fellow cadets charged with cheating. What are your thoughts on that?"

"I think it's necessary that we uphold the Honor Code. One combat officer must always be able to trust the word of another. If they cheated, they should be punished," a classmate said.

"I agree. It is a tribute to the strength of the system that the charges were even brought forth at all," a yearling chimed in.

I sat silent, just taking in the comments. I wondered how many of my classmates shared the opinions of the two cadets at the hostess office. I wasn't eager to get into another petty disagreement.

"This appears to be quite different than the cheating that took place in 1951 when ninety cadets, including thirty-seven football players, were separated from the Academy for cheating. They were blatantly copying answers," he shared. "The main difference seems to be that cheating in '51 was organized to pass information, whereas the EE 304 assignment appears to be a series of separate incidents?"

Some cadets shrugged their shoulders. I sort-of knew there had been a cheating scandal in '51 but was not aware of the facts.

"And do you feel it was understood that the take-home exam was to be completed individually?"

"It was not an exam. It was a homework assignment," said one cow.

"I see." Mr. Augustine seemed content with our discussion, and that there wasn't much more to be said, so the meeting seemed to be coming to a close.

"And you, Mr. Ringgold," Mr. Augustine said, pointing at me with an openhand. He could read my nametag since I was sitting directly in front of him. "What do you think about the current cheating scandal?"

I cleared my throat, caught slightly off guard. I wasn't sure I wanted to share my thoughts; it was apparent to me that my viewpoint differed from the majority.

"Sir, I'm not convinced that any of those being charged with cheating actually did anything wrong."

"Why is that, Cadet Ringgold?" Mr. Augustine looked intrigued.

My throat tightened slightly, as if telling me not to say anything more. "Well," I cleared my throat. "The fact the violations appear so widespread tells me that it's likely not a problem with my classmates, but with how the homework assignment was administered. The Honor Code is an ideal, a model for all of us to aspire to. I know of no cadet who does not fully support its principles; I certainly do. We try, but cadets are not perfect," I said, as my mind drifted to DaRold. "We make mistakes like everyone else. I would guess then that the cadets did, more or less, what the rest of us have done at one time or another," I said, taking a deep breath and letting it out slowly. I wasn't sure how my comments would be received.

I knew they wouldn't be taken lightly. I wasn't willing to easily condemn those being threatened with expulsion over a trivial homework assignment. More than 10 percent of my class was under investigation and the numbers were growing. I hoped the administration would take an adult look at the irrational thought of throwing out possibly hundreds of my classmates.

"I don't cheat. Why should they?" a cow recoiled.

"Right," the under secretary replied. "Thank you all for speaking with me today. I hope the rest of your year goes smoothly."

The meeting came to an abrupt halt, and I walked out of the room feeling a bit unsettled. Mr. Augustine didn't react, and no one said a word as we left the room. Well, he did ask me my opinion, and the Honor Code required an honest answer. In addition, the under secretary had started the meeting by telling us to speak freely.

I walked outside Mahan Hall and back to the hostess office. Luckily, I caught the last few minutes of *Happy Days* on television before heading to lunch.

In the hostess office, I picked up *The New York Times* from April 7, 1976 and found the article "New Cheating Case Erupts at West Point" by James Feron. What caught my attention were the last two paragraphs.

Two years ago Capt. Michael T. Rose, then an assistant staff judge advocate in the Air Force, charged that legal practices at the nation's service academies violated constitutional guarantees in maintaining conduct, honor, and ethics codes.

Captain Rose, who later resigned under pressure, said after a two year study that academies' disciplinary systems fostered unfair expulsion, high attrition rates, and the fostering of a contempt for the law that, he said, leads to "justification of undesirable military practices."

I wondered if Captain Rose was right, if the administration of the Honor Code needed to be analyzed. I shrugged my shoulders. What role did I have in any of this, other than having compassion for those being charged? Where did my duty lie? Not truly knowing the answers to these questions, I was well aware of this premonition that somehow, I was going to be involved.

CHAPTER 7
THE HONOR CAPTAIN

THE HONOR COMMITTEE CONTINUED ITS hearings, called honor boards, day and night with no end in sight. Almost daily we received an update on the proceedings, usually during breakfast or dinner formation. By the end of the second week, forty-nine cadets had been exonerated, but fifty-two cadets were convicted and asked to resign. Two cadets resigned immediately, but the rest hoped to complete the semester before their appeal could be heard by a board of officers. Presumably, they too would resign after receiving academic credit for the semester.

I passed a leisurely Easter weekend at West Point by watching our varsity baseball team lose a double-header. Our lacrosse team fared much better by coming from behind to beat ranked Ohio Wesleyan. Easter Sunday, April 18, I went to the payphones in the basement of Central Barracks and called home to give my Mom the latest update on the week's events.

"I'm happy to hear that some of your classmates had been exonerated," she said, sounding relieved.

"Me too. The school seems motivated to investigate as quickly as possible." I sighed. "I participated in a meeting with the under secretary of the Army on Wednesday. I told him I felt compassion for my classmates, and that they likely didn't do anything wrong."

"Son, you need to be careful there. This is not your battle to fight."

"Mom, I know, but it was a privileged conversation. I chose honesty over convenience. After all, I only gave him my honest opinion when he asked for it. But don't worry, nothing is going to come of what I said." I reassured her. "I told him the truth and hopefully the administration will see that this is not a problem we need right now."

"I sure hope you're right, honey."

"How's everything at home?" I asked, feeling very far away.

"All is well here. I completed another painting. It's of two boys, one light haired and one dark, like you and John, carrying fishing poles and heading toward the river. To the left there is a sign nailed to a tree that says, *No Fishing*. What do you think they're going to do?" she asked mischievously.

"They're going to go fishing."

"Of course they are," she said.

The afternoon of Monday, April 19, I rushed back from class to Central Barracks to change for softball practice. We were not in season yet, but as the company intramural softball coach, I was determined to have a winning team. On my desk was a note directing me to report to Cadet Wayne Adamson, the chairman of the class of 1976 Honor Committee. I wondered if I was being called to testify for DaRold's case. I hadn't seen DaRold in over a week and desperately wanted to know what was going on with him. When I arrived at his room, Cadet Adamson was seated at his desk reading *The Philadelphia Inquirer*.

I tapped on the already open door and stepped inside.

"I'm Cadet Ringgold. I had a note that you wished to see me, sir," I said.

Adamson looked up from the paper.

I said, "I read the article 'The Shame at West Point.' I believe you were quoted in it, sir."

"I was," he said, looking down at the paper. "'The motto of West Point is *Duty, Honor, Country.* Honor is in the middle for a special reason. Duty and country hinge on honor and integrity. Honor is a necessity. You can't run an army unless the individuals who make it up have personal integrity,'" he quoted his own words from the paper. "Not bad, right? In the past week, I've had a lot of interviews. I'm trying very hard to keep the reputation of West Point intact."

I nodded in understanding.

"Do you believe in the Honor Code, Cadet Ringgold?"

"Of course, as every cadet here does."

"The Honor Code is the blueprint for how this school functions. It represents everything we stand for," Adamson explained.

I didn't disagree.

"I need you to come with me," he said, standing up.

"What is this regarding?" I asked.

Adamson didn't respond, but left the room, so I followed him. He led me down the hallway through barracks to an unoccupied room.

"Ringgold, go in and sit down," he said, leaving me.

A few moments later, Cadet Adamson returned with another cadet.

"Ringgold, this is Cadet Mark Irwin, the Honor Committee chairman for your class."

Without saying a word, Cadet Irwin nodded and sat down in front of me.

"Why don't you tell us what you said to the under secretary of the Army last week," Adamson began.

I paused and looked up at him, still standing. So this wasn't about DaRold. "I don't know what's going on here. As far as I'm concerned, anything that was said in that meeting was privileged information."

Cadet Adamson fumbled through some papers he held, as Cadet Irwin silently took notes. Finding what he was looking for, Cadet Adamson began again. "Did you say that everyone had, at one time or another, violated the Honor Code?"

I cleared my throat and looked him dead set in the eyes, prepared for defense. He was a senior and I was a junior. With two years in the Army before I entered West Point and at age twenty-two, I was likely older than he was. "I've already told you my conversation with the under secretary was private," I said.

"Cadet Ringgold, you seem to have a misunderstanding about what we're doing here," Adamson replied.

"Do I?" I asked. "You haven't told me why I'm here."

"Let me assure you, so there is no misunderstanding. You are *not* under investigation for an honor violation. In fact, that would be the last thing we'd want. Did you say that 'cheating is widespread?'"

Even though those were not my words, I knew that's how they were being interpreted. If I said *yes*, then I could be accused of toleration, an honor violation. I was in a catch-22. If I said *no*, then I could be accused of lying, also an honor violation.

"Do you know of any cadets who have cheated and not been investigated?"

I didn't answer.

Adamson sighed. "I'm trying to understand your position, and why you would say such a thing to the under secretary, so please just answer my question," Cadet Adamson said.

I remained silent, my mouth closed tightly and kept my intense gaze. I was not trusting these cadets, nor going to say anything else that could be misconstrued.

"I have six signed statements here in my possession." He shook the papers in his grasp. "They all imply that you've witnessed widespread cheating, so have you?"

I continued not to answer. *Six signed statements, but I'm not under investigation?* I thought to myself.

"Do I have to order you to answer my questions?" Adamson persisted.

I continued to say nothing. So much for confidentiality. Even though this prick was a firstie, I had no intention to give in. He was not going to intimidate me.

"Cadet Ringgold, as your cadet superior, I'm giving you a direct verbal order to answer my questions. If you fail to, I'll report you for a major violation of regulations. Do you understand?" Cadet Adamson demanded.

"Cadet Adamson, I have already given you my answer. I do believe in the Honor Code, as every cadet here does. My conversation with the under secretary of the Army was in private."

"Then, Cadet Ringgold, you are required to report to the commandant's conference room at 0800 hours tomorrow morning. If you have no questions, you are dismissed."

I nodded and pushed back my chair, which scraped against the floor. I stood up, straightened my gray jacket, and walked out.

CHAPTER 8
MEETING WITH THE
LAW PROFESSOR

AFTER I LEFT CADETS ADAMSON and Irwin, I took a walk, trying to piece together what had just happened and what I should do about it. I had done nothing wrong, that I was very clear about. Then the question was: what did they think I had done? Likely, they thought I had tolerated violations of the Honor Code, which was crazy. They were not going to find any evidence to prove that. Had the current cheating scandal knocked the Honor Committee so off balance that they felt compelled to investigate anyone who questioned the present investigations in order to vindicate the system?

I was obviously under investigation. That is the only thing *six signed statements* and the commandant's conference room could mean, which is where the Honor Committee holds its Honor Boards. That had to be it. They were trying to see if I violated the Honor Code, if I had witnessed other cadets breaking it. The thing was, though, I hadn't been formally charged with anything, so technically I had nothing to worry about. Why then did I feel so nervous? Because I'd admitted that cadets at West Point are human beings and thus are not infallible? Because I took West Point cadets off the pedestal and made us human? Was that a crime?

I decided to go to the library to study. I didn't want to talk or see anyone until I got a sense of control back. The library, however, was useless in my frame of mind, so I didn't stay long and went back to the barracks. My roommate, Cadet Randall, was in our room when I returned. We'd spent the past week avoiding each other. All room assignments are directed by the administration, and if we'd had the choice, we wouldn't be sharing a room.

"All those being accused should be thrown out. They are a disgrace to our school," Randall argued, sounding like the cadets I had overheard in the hostess office.

"We don't know that. Each case needs to be weighed on its own merits since all honor violations are not the same," I argued back. It felt like I had to defend those being accused, but it was more than that. "You know as well as I do that some cadets have been expelled for such trivial acts as asking a roommate how to spell a word for his research paper or taking a dime left in the coin return of a pay phone. Remember Cadet James Conner? He got expelled for lying about how many push-ups he'd done. Said he did twenty push-ups when he'd really done eighteen. Doesn't that sound ridiculous to you?" I asked, feeling I had made my point.

"Ringgold, they clearly cheated on the assignment; the collaboration is huge!"

"You don't know that! Or do you? Are you telling me you have firsthand knowledge of cheating that you've not reported? That's toleration. Besides, you are talking about our classmates who we have served side-by-side with the past three years. How can you so carelessly want to throw them out?"

"This cheating scandal is a disgrace to my school. West Point represents honorable people. I would've hoped that our classmates would have taken their cadetship more seriously," Randall said, clearly convinced of his own bias.

"Are you kidding me? For the whole year, up until that one assignment, we had been encouraged by our EE professors to work with our classmates. That was the first assignment we were told to complete independently! Collaboration was bound to happen! I can't believe you immediately group those that worked together as now being dishonorable and not good enough to go to *your* school. That sounds so black and white, it disgusts me. These are our classmates' lives we are talking about. They have invested themselves into this school as much as we have. You want their Army careers ruined over this?"

"It is black and white, Ringgold. There are good guys, and there are bad guys. Period."

"And which one are you?" I asked, appalled. "Life is gray, Randall. West Point is full of gray buildings under a gray sky, and we march around in gray uniforms. Neither you nor I know the truth of what happened and don't act like you do," I said, knowing my argument was falling on deaf ears.

"That's the system. You and I knew what was required before R-day."

"Minor transgressions should be dealt with less severely," I said. "At this point, though, we'll see what comes of the investigations. Looks like I may be grouped in with them," I said, sitting down with a sigh.

"You cheated too?" Randall asked.

His look of shock pissed me off, but I was venting so I didn't care. "No, but I met with the under secretary of the Army. I told him my opinion on the matter, and the next thing I knew the honor captain was interrogating me."

"Cadet Adamson spoke to you?"

"Yeah, and the vice chairman, Mark Irwin."

"That's not good, Ringgold. You shouldn't have opened your big mouth full of big ideas. You need to learn how to play the game. If you'd have only lied to those guys, you wouldn't be in this mess right now," he said, completely serious.

My mouth dropped open, but I didn't say anything. We should expel our classmates for unauthorized collaboration on a homework assignment but lie to cover our asses. The meaning of our Honor System was becoming very clear to me.

I looked down at my desk, thinking for some time. I noticed a crack in the grain and followed it with my right index finger. Everyone remembers the story of Catch-22. A pilot could escape combat duty only if he were crazy. If a pilot claimed he was crazy, however, he would be found sane because a madman doesn't know he's crazy. A deranged pilot couldn't possibly be taken off duty because he would never complain, so everybody flew. It seemed to me the Honor Committee had me in a perfect Catch-22. They interpreted my statement that "the cadets did, more or less, what the rest of us have done at one time or another," to mean that I was saying that cheating was widespread. Either that statement is a lie, which is also a violation, or it is the truth, which is a violation because it implies that I've had knowledge of unreported offenses and thus have violated the toleration clause.

It was obvious that I was screwed unless I figured out how to get myself out of this mess. It didn't take me long to decide my next course of action. I grabbed my hat, walked out of Central Barracks and headed for the law department in Thayer Hall.

★ ★ ★

"What can I do for you, Cadet?" Captain Arthur Lincoln, a law professor, greeted me respectfully.

"Sir, I need to speak to someone about a private matter," I said.

"Aren't they all?" he said, rhetorically. "Please come in and close the door behind you. What's going on, Cadet Ringgold?" he said, reading my nametag as it came into view.

I explained the meeting with the under secretary and the questioning by Cadet Adamson and Cadet Irwin.

"I'm not concerned that the Honor Committee would actually find me guilty, but I am concerned that my refusal to answer Cadet Adamson's questions could get me into trouble with the disciplinary system," I explained.

"Well, that's certainly a possibility. It is an ironic turn of events," he said, smiling. "I doubt this will come to anything," Captain Lincoln said, waving his hand through the air. "Until you are actually accused of an Honor Code violation, there's little I can do."

"What do you recommend I do, sir?"

"There is doubtless little you can do, but let things play out. Let them fix this and do the right thing on their own. Keep me informed either way. Let me know if the problem gets resolved or if the Honor Committee or the disciplinary system takes any action on you. Okay, Cadet?" He asked, holding out his hand for me to shake.

I grabbed his hand, appreciative of the support. "Yes, sir. Thank you for your time, sir," I said, a little relieved.

I left Captain Lincoln's office feeling less anxious.

Because my roommate and I weren't getting along, I tried my best to stay out of our room. The weather was cold and damp, and it rained off and on. What made matters worse was the radiator in our room was stuck on full open. With the windows closed, the heat was unbearable, symbolic of the tension in our relationship. With the windows open, the wind blew the rain onto my desk. As an alternative to the uncomfortable room, I headed to Grant Hall to get something to drink and socialize.

My friend Cadet Tim Flanagan was seated by himself in the snack bar when I walked in. I knew his company had been hard hit by the honor investigations. Eleven of the twenty-six juniors in his company, G-2, were under suspicion. Since his name hadn't been mentioned among those charged, I hadn't worried or bothered to check up on him. Likely, Flanagan hadn't heard about my situation, so I approached him.

"Hey, Flanagan, how are things?" I asked.

He looked up at me for a few seconds, debating. "You really want to know?" he asked.

"Absolutely, tell me," I said, sitting down across from him.

"Ringgold, it's about the scandal. There are a lot more of us involved. I think only six in the company weren't, but we didn't consider it cheating. We weren't really taking advantage of anybody. It was a tough assignment, and we were just trying to learn," he said. I could tell he was weighing my response, almost testing whether he could trust me or not.

I nodded in understanding. "You haven't been charged, have you?" I asked, suddenly worried.

"Not yet, but if they check those papers again, I'm sure I will be," he answered.

"Oh no," I said, processing the anxiety he must be feeling. "You know DaRold is in Transient Barracks. I haven't seen him since his name was called."

"Yeah, I know. Look, we didn't consider it cheating. We'd never have taken notes into an exam or looked over someone's shoulder. This was a take-home assignment. We were helping each other with our homework, like we'd been in the habit of doing. We didn't intentionally cheat," he defended, clearly knowing the seriousness of the situation.

Suddenly, I wished he hadn't told me. Flanagan was confiding in me, but he also knew only too well what he was telling me. He knew under the Honor Code I was required to report him or face expulsion myself, so why did he risk telling me?

"Flanagan, I'm so sorry," I replied, completely genuine, trying to rationalize that it wasn't cheating because it lacked intention to cheat, so there wasn't anything I needed to report. "I told the under secretary of the Army that I believed you guys didn't do anything that the rest of us haven't done at one time or another," I said, sympathizing.

"You did?" His eyes widened at that.

"I did. Now, because of what I said, the honor captain has been on my tail. I don't know what will come of it, if he is going to find a way to prove I had tolerated or not." I sighed. "It seems to me that the ideal standards of the Honor Code aren't so clear cut, and that it is so easy to accidentally violate the code. This is much more complicated than I realized. Good luck, man. I really hope that this gets resolved as soon as possible." I stood up and patted him on the shoulder. "Let me know if there's anything I can do, okay?"

I left Flanagan feeling powerless to help him. I thought long and hard about what he had told me. I wanted to believe him. I wanted to believe that it wasn't cheating, so there would be nothing to report. I thought about my own actions in the past and asked myself, how guiltless are we all? If the Honor Code is applied this harshly to every aspect of our lives, to our every thought and action, who among us is blameless? If we are all as perfect as the Academy would have us believe, there would be no need for an Honor Code, but we are not perfect. We make mistakes. We came to West Point to learn from those mistakes, to grow, but we can't do that now. To admit a mistake requires expulsion because there was no other penalty.

Out of my four closest friends at West Point, one was already being investigated and another one likely would be. I also felt haunted by the fact that Adamson had questioned me. *You are not under investigation for an Honor violation. You are not under investigation for an Honor violation.* Adamson's words ran circles in my head. I had this feeling that I would be seeing DaRold very soon.

CHAPTER 9
CADET STEVEN R. VERR
& CADET JAMES J. PELOSI

WHEN I GET STRESSED, IT is my natural tendency to withdraw into myself. The fear of getting kicked out of West Point was overwhelming. I knew I hadn't done anything wrong. I had always done my best to act honorably. To even have my honor questioned was bothersome. I can be honest to a fault and at the core a romantic, to the highest ideals. I would never have intentionally broken the Honor Code, West Point's most sacred standard. I also was wise enough to recognize that I was likely no different than the majority of my classmates—even those who were under investigation. My classmates and I had given so much to the Academy. That thought sent goosebumps down my arms. I had the sense there were going to be a lot of casualties before this scandal was over.

Just before 0800 the next morning, on Tuesday, April 20, when I was supposed to be meeting Cadet Adamson at the commandant's conference room, there was a knock on our door. As I opened the door cautiously, my first class honor representative, Cadet Michael Kasun, said "Cadet Ringgold. You need to come with me."

I rolled my eyes, sighed, and followed him to Cadet Adamson's room.

"Cadet Ringgold, you need to report to Cadet Carl Swanson's room, room one-thirteen," Cadet Adamson directed.

I looked at Cadet Kasun, who shrugged. With a stern face and complete annoyance at the cattiness of all of this, I walked to room 113. Cadet Kasun followed right behind.

"Ah, good morning, Cadet Ringgold. Well, it may not be a *good* morning to you, Cadet. You've been charged with violating the Honor Code for your statement made to Under Secretary Augustine," Cadet Swanson said, almost happily as if he enjoyed doling out sentences.

"Am I being accused of lying to Mr. Augustine?" I asked.

"Absolutely not. We believe you spoke truthfully," Cadet Kasun said. "But, clearly you witnessed cheating and have done nothing about it, otherwise why would you say such a thing to him?"

I felt the heat rise up my backbone. I was so close to snapping. "Are we done here?" I asked, in as much of a controlled manner as possible.

"We're done, but not finished," Cadet Swanson answered, clearly enjoying his position of power. "You'll be receiving a summons soon. It will say when to appear before your Honor Board."

I paused, processing what he'd just said, and then left them both to collaborate against me. I knew I needed to inform Captain Lincoln of the charges and secure him as my legal counsel as soon as possible; I needed a game plan.

"Sir, do you have a moment?" I asked, eager to speak with Captain Lincoln.

"Absolutely, Cadet Ringgold. Come on in. Has everything

been resolved?" he asked, squinting his eyes and examining me. "From the looks of you, I'd say not."

"No, sir. I've been charged with toleration."

"I see. Toleration is the most debated and most complicated part of the Honor Code. The Naval Academy's Honor *Concept* doesn't include toleration, but I digress. What evidence do they have against you?"

"As far as I know, none, except the statements from some of the cadets present during the meeting with Mr. Augustine."

"So essentially they have no evidence against you? They're just using hearsay?"

I nodded.

"Have they moved you to Transient Barracks yet?"

"No, not yet. I'm staying put until I am forced out of my room in Central Barracks."

Captain Lincoln shook his head, resigned. "Cadet, this isn't just about you anymore. We have bigger problems here."

"Sir?" I asked, not comprehending.

"The Honor System, the way it is being administered, has gone haywire. I've gone to Dean Smith asking for help to no avail. I've been reporting about the inconsistencies within the Honor System to the commandant and superintendent for months now, also without success. This has forced me to go to the media. Are you aware that I represent Cadet Steven Verr?"

"Yes, I knew that."

"Well Cadet Verr's conviction was finally overturned in March after he was in Transient Barracks for five months. He has continued to be harassed despite being returned to the Corps of Cadets *in good standing*. How Cadet Verr has been treated is a pure example of the breakdown of the Honor System. I have gone to the media with the facts, hoping that putting the truth out will force the Academy to fix what is broken. The publicity has drawn the attention of Senator Adlai Stevenson and Representative

Edward Derwinski of Illinois, Cadet Verr's home state. They've been investigating his situation here, which is good."

"Understood," I said, nodding.

"In taking on your case, I'll represent you to the best of my ability. If we do not succeed, we may need to go public."

"Okay." I wasn't sure what else to say. At this point, his lack of reassurance scared me, but at the same time I had to face the reality of what was happening. I could be found guilty and being found guilty of an Honor Code violation only meant one thing: separation from the Academy. That was the last thing I wanted, so I was willing to do anything that would prevent me from being kicked out.

The next day, I walked over to the library, since I didn't have a morning class. On my way there, I passed the larger than life-sized statue of World War II hero General George S. Patton, West Point class of 1909. At the base of the statue is carved Patton's favorite battlefield expression, which spoke to me that morning: *Pursue the Enemy with the Utmost Audacity*. Audacity is bravery, regardless of fear, and a willingness to take risks. I needed to remind myself of the strength in those words.

I went into the library and picked up *The New York Times*. There was an article, "West Point Cadet Faces New Charges; His Congressmen Demand an Inquiry," about Cadet Steve Verr. Cadet Verr was a nineteen year old Plebe from Brookfield, Illinois who'd participated in the 1974 Junior Olympics in Moscow which was impressive. In my own world as a second classman (junior), I truly had not given much thought to Cadet Verr's situation until recently when both my mother and Captain Lincoln spoke of him.

On August 14, 1975, Cadet Verr had been found crying outside of the mess hall after several days of not receiving enough food and feeling hopeless. Approached by two upperclassmen as to the reason he was crying, Cadet Verr made-up a story about his parents having been in a car accident to validate his tears. The cadet (Verr) was brought to the Rev. Thomas J. Curley, the assistant Catholic chaplain, who reported that Cadet Verr was practically starving. Accused of lying, the Honor Committee then found Cadet Verr guilty. The charge was overruled by Superintendent Lieutenant General Berry in March of this year, 1976.

It wasn't uncommon for upperclassmen to withhold food from plebes. I personally remember feeling hungry most of my plebe year, an unfortunate aspect of hazing, which officially doesn't exist at West Point. Unfortunately, Cadet Verr had spent five months in Transient Barracks, a modified version of solitary confinement, before his case was overturned. Once returned to the Corps of Cadets, his life did not return to normal. The account of Cadet Verr's experiences, after being cleared of the charge, was disturbing.

The article listed the multiple ways Cadet Verr had been harassed since he was reinstated to the Corps of Cadets. His mail had been opened, lost, or marked *return to sender*, a Federal crime in the civilian world that didn't seem to have the same consequences on campus here. Apparently, he had been pushed down a flight of stairs. His classmates had *Silenced* him, a shunning tactic used to shame and humiliate the victim where other cadets refuse to talk to him or acknowledge his existence. It appeared that many cadets were trying to get him to resign by making it hell for him to stay.

Back in March, I remembered reading a memorandum that went around barracks to the Corps of Cadets from Cadet Adamson, the chairman of the Honor Committee, the same firstie who had questioned me. The memorandum had mentioned that many cadets did not agree with General Berry's ruling that overturned Cadet's Verr's conviction by the Honor Committee. Adamson wrote that "while we have no authority or right to infringe on the human dignity [of individuals] we have the right to choose *who to speak to or associate with.*" It seemed Cadet Adamson had encouraged the use of *The Silence*. More importantly, the cadets that did practice The Silence were never punished for doing so.

Early in my plebe year, in September 1973, the Honor Committee, which Adamson now led, voted to officially end The Silence after the widely publicized case of Cadet James J. Pelosi. Cadet Pelosi had been found guilty of cheating because he took a few extra seconds to answer a quiz after being ordered to cease work. As part of the first new class to enter after his graduation, we were taught to literally drop our pencils, not put them down, but drop them within microseconds of hearing the *cease work* command or risk the fate of Pelosi. After his conviction was overturned by the superintendent, Lieutenant General William Knowlton, Pelosi was returned to the Corps of Cadets in *good standing*. However, Pelosi endured more than a year and a half of being harassed and shunned by fellow cadets, forced to live alone, and to eat alone at a table set for ten.

After Cadet James Pelosi's graduation, and the substantial negative press the Academy received because of his treatment, the Honor Committee, then headed by Cadet Captain Ronald H. Schmidt, decided to vote amongst themselves to eliminate use of The Silence. It is important to note that this was the same Cadet Schmidt who was later convicted by his own Honor Committee but allowed to graduate without having to serve a day of his five-year service obligation. There was no *official* ban on mistreatment of cleared cadets. In spite of the negative impact on the Academy and the poor example being set for the cadets— the Army's future leaders—the Academy took no steps to punish cadets for mistreating other cadets.

One had to admire James Pelosi's determination to stay at the Academy and graduate; I couldn't imagine the fortitude needed to withstand such adversity. There wasn't any formal consequence to shunning another cadet, so outlawing The Silence didn't technically make a difference. Cadet Pelosi's story had been so fascinating that a made-for-TV movie about him came during my third class year called, appropriately, *The Silence,* by screenwriter Stanley R. Greenberg, which aired on NBC.

Remembering the story of Cadet Pelosi made me shake my head in disgust. There needed absolute clarity of what constitutes cheating. More importantly, we needed to respect and honor the overturning of any guilty verdict by the West Point administration. The Honor Code must be respected both by those required to follow it, and those who enforced it. That should include obeying the orders of superiors, when the superintendent and the commandant chose to overturn a guilty verdict. In the Army, we were required to follow the orders of our superiors. Why wasn't the same true when a superior overturned a cadet-imposed verdict? To silence a cadet who had been exonerated seemed corrupt, a taking of the law into the silencer's hands, ironically, in the name of honor.

The *New York Times* article I was reading also mentioned the current cheating scandal and openly criticized the Honor Code, calling it "unworkable and the penalty too severe, especially for what are regarded by some as trivial offenses." So clearly, I was not the only one who had these thoughts. One cadet was quoted as having said, "The West Point Honor Code doesn't really develop integrity because it's based on fear."

I was beginning to realize the necessity of what Captain Lincoln was trying to do. Captain Arthur Lincoln, a 1966 West Point graduate and Vietnam veteran, was taking a clear stand in pointing out the Honor Code abuses, which made him something of a heretic among fellow graduates.

The article went on to quote a junior, one of my classmates, expressing that the current cheating scandal involved "300 to 400 of the nearly 900 second-classmen or juniors, who took the test." I frowned at the paper. First of all, it was hard to comprehend that as a reality. Second, I tried to picture half of my class not returning the next year, our senior year. It was inconceivable. The Academy relies on the first class to run the new cadet training program for the plebes, as well as oversee all their disciplinary actions.

I held my breath reading the last few paragraphs. They mentioned that during a meeting with the under secretary of the Army, a cadet had raised the issue of widespread cheating. Those were not my words, but that was clearly meant to refer to me. So, there it was in black and white, my confidential meeting with the under secretary of the Army that clearly wasn't so confidential. I was very aware of how unsafe I felt, as if there were landmines hidden in places throughout the Academy. So much for integrity.

On the evening of Monday, April 26, I went to Cadet Carl Swanson and filed a complaint on Cadet Adamson, the Honor Chairman, for lying to me about not having been under investigation. I also filed a statement on Cadet Irwin for tolerating Cadet Adamson's obvious violation. I would have liked to have reported the cadets who had violated the confidentiality about the meeting with the under secretary, but I didn't know which of them had done so.

MAY 1976

CHAPTER 10
FOUND GUILTY
OF TOLERATION

ON THURSDAY, MAY 6, I stopped in to see Cadet Michael Hodges, vice-chairman of the class of 1977 Honor Committee.

"Cadet Hodges, I'd like to know what happened to my statements about Cadet Adamson and Cadet Irwin."

"Cadet Ringgold," Cadet Hodges said solemnly, as if I interrupted him. "We think this situation was all a misunderstanding," he said, barely glancing my way.

"I see," I said. I knew it was bullshit. "Thank you for your time," I said sarcastically and walked out. Clearly, the Honor Committee had no intention of looking into my reports concerning the Honor Chairman, Wayne Adamson, and the Honor vice-chairman, Mark Irwin.

The following week, I was scheduled to appear before a subcommittee for my alleged violation. During the interval, I was approached by members of both the 1976 and 1977 Honor Committees and told that it had already been determined that I would be found guilty before a full Honor Committee. As a result, I requested from Cadet Irwin and Cadet Hodges that I be informed as to which members of the Cadet Honor Committee were to sit in judgment of me and also the names of any witnesses who were to testify against me. Both requests were denied. I concluded the Honor Committee proceedings would be little more than a kangaroo court. It came to my attention later just how much of a farce the closed-door hearing actually was when Cadet Adamson testified against me despite having not been present during my conversation with Mr. Augustine.

Trying to drum up some support about my potentially dire situation, I sat at my desk and composed a letter to my US Senator from Arizona. Barry Goldwater was a senior senator, in his fourth elected term, and a powerhouse. In 1964, he had been the Republican Party candidate for president against Lyndon B. Johnson. Senator Goldwater served on the Senate Armed Services Committee (SASC) which has legislative power over our military. I hoped he would use his position to help me and my classmates.

Senator Goldwater had not attended West Point but served as a member of the Academy's Board of Visitors which is similar to a trustee at a civilian institution. During my high school years, I'd attend Staunton Military Academy in Staunton, Virginia. In the history of SMA, there have been four graduates from Arizona: Barry Goldwater, Barry Goldwater Jr., Michael Goldwater, and me. When I had attended SMA, my mom had arranged for me to meet Senator Goldwater at one of his speaking events. I had worn my SMA uniform and had my picture taken with him. I was his nominee for West Point. I had no idea if Senator Barry Goldwater would do anything about my request for help, but this was me being proactive. I wanted to expose the Honor Committee and the Honor System. My classmates and I needed help, so I was asking for it.

Company E-2, U.S.C.C.
West Point, N.Y. 10997
May 7, 1976

The Honorable Barry Goldwater
United States Senate
Washington, DC 20510

Dear Senator Goldwater:

As a second classman at West Point from Phoenix, I feel
it my duty to inform you of the present state of affairs at the
Military Academy and to ask your help in resolving the situation.

You nominated me for the class of 1975 while I was still a
senior at Staunton Military Academy, and I subsequently was
appointed with the class of 1977.

At present, 50 of my classmates have been found guilty
by cadet boards of violating the cadet Honor Code and
recommended for separation from the Military Academy. I
know for a fact that the Military Academy is trying to quietly
dismiss my classmates for doing no more than each and every
cadet has done at one time or another in his cadet career.
Honor violations are not exceptions to the rule here. Cheating
is very widespread.

Last month, I was selected at random to speak with Under
Secretary of the Army Norman Augustine. At that meeting Mr.
Augustine asked me what I thought of the current scandal and
I told him that there was much widespread cheating within the
Corps of Cadets. For that statement, I have been brought up on
charges under the toleration clause of the cadet Honor Code.

I request that you, as a member of the Senate Armed
Services Committee and as a member of the Board of Visitors

for the United States Military Academy, consider conducting a full investigation into the current honor scandal. Given the opportunity, I would appreciate very much to give you the full details of the widespread cheating, coverups, and inside story of the scandal.

Time is of the essence because this scandal is affecting many of my classmates and myself. Next week, the first Officers Boards will begin deliberating on the future of the 50 already convicted.

I would greatly appreciate any help you may be able to offer in this most serious matter.

Timothy D. Ringgold

Cadet Cpl. Co. E-2

U.S.M.A.

The following Monday, I was ordered in a note left on my desk to report at 1930 (7:30 p.m.) and appear before a subcommittee for my alleged violation.

I put on my dress-gray uniform with shined shoes. I walked into the room, determined to rectify this situation, put an end to the nonsense, and clear my name.

Cadet Adamson, Cadet Irwin, Cadet Hodges, and a few other Honor Committee members that I didn't know, were present.

"Cadet Ringgold," Cadet Adamson gestured me in.

As I stood before them at attention, Cadet Adamson continued to address me. "You have been found guilty of toleration, an Honor Code violation."

"Excuse me, there was no Honor Board held," I interrupted.

"On the contrary, there was. We have a signed affidavit of numerous classmates as proof of your toleration."

"Who signed the affidavit and where is my copy?"

"Providing you a copy is unnecessary and nevertheless confidential. You are to be removed from the Corps of Cadets and moved to Transient Barracks immediately."

"Is there any other evidence against me?" I asked, my voice cracking.

"There was none needed," Cadet Adamson concluded.

I looked at each of the men at the table, with determination in their eyes, and I knew there wasn't anything I could do at this moment but hold my tongue. With my jaw set, I marched out of that room before my anger made me do something I would regret.

I didn't tell my roommate anything that was happening, about being found guilty of an honor violation. The next morning, when I returned to our room after morning classes, it was obvious. There was a tactical officer and a cadet guard waiting to escort me to Transient Barracks.

I put up my hand, palm facing him to prevent him from speaking to me. "So you're here to escort me to Transient Barracks?" I said, nodding. No need for him to answer the question. This was bullshit. I knew this was bullshit. My rage was bubbling under my ribs, but I kept it under control.

Ignoring my roommate, who was sitting at his desk, I took off my hat and put it upside down on my desk and breathed deeply to calm myself. I grabbed my duffle bag and threw my sweats, socks, underwear, deodorant, towels, razor, and bar of soap into it. I zipped it up and swung it onto my back. I stuffed my textbooks into my school bag, but they didn't all fit, so I left it unzipped on my desk. I reached for a handful of hangers of class uniforms, my shined shoes, but left the White Blouse used for parades.

I could feel the eyes of my roommate watching me, but I didn't say anything. Trying hard to keep my annoyance under wraps, I grabbed my school bag and kept my head high and walked out. With the guard tailing me, I walked straight past the looks and stares, determined to keep my dignity.

As I walked into Transient Barracks, I started to breathe again.

"Ringgold, what are you doing here?"

I looked over to the right of the room. "DaRold," I said and sighed.

"Not you too," said Cadet DaRold.

"Cadet Ringgold, you're to remain here until Lieutenant Colonel Cook meets with you," the tactical officer said.

"I want to speak to Captain Lincoln," I said, placing my things on the floor next to the empty bed.

"Not until Colonel Cook sees you. You're to remain here for now. If you have more things to get from your old room, you'll have to be accompanied inside Central Barracks at all times by myself or another guard."

I sat down at a vacant desk next to the mattress. The guard left the room, closing the door behind him. I turned to DaRold. He gave me a half smile.

"This is nuts, DaRold."

"I didn't know you were one of the ones being accused of cheating."

"I'm not. They found me guilty of toleration without a hearing, without witnesses. I don't even know *who* I supposedly tolerated."

"Oh geez."

Within minutes there was a knock at the door, and Colonel Cook entered. He turned to DaRold. "Mr. DaRold, can you give Cadet Ringgold and me a moment?" he asked, and DaRold started to get up.

"No need," I said, waving to DaRold to sit back down.

"Very well. Cadet Timothy Ringgold. You have been found guilty of toleration, an Honor Code violation. You have the right to remain silent. Anything you say can and will be used against you in a court of law. You have the right to speak to an attorney, and to have an attorney present during any questioning. Do you understand, Cadet Ringgold?" Colonel Cook sounded robotic. I wondered how often he had read the Miranda warning recently.

"Yes, and I would like to see my attorney, Captain Lincoln."

"And that is your right to do so. You have a right to request that your case be heard by a board of officers. You also have the right to resign. Since you are found guilty of an Honor violation, it will go on your record. You'll have a much better chance of getting a good post assignment in the Army if you resign, especially because of your previous two years served. Do you understand, Cadet Ringgold?" Colonel Cook asked.

"I understand." I knew it was unconstitutional and wrong that Colonel Cook was trying to dissuade me from appealing by threatening a poor post assignment.

"It is also my duty to take you to Colonel Rhyne's office."

Colonel Hal B. Rhyne was the deputy commandant. I didn't question Colonel Rhyne's desire to speak to me. Likely, he too wanted to convince me to resign. Too bad I was innocent and had no intention of doing so.

"Good afternoon," Col. Rhyne said. He sat at his desk and looked at me with the briefest of glances as I saluted him and then stood at attention in front of his door. "Has he been read his rights, Colonel Cook?"

"Yes, sir," Colonel Cook nodded, saluted Colonel Rhyne and left.

"So, Cadet Ringgold, do you understand your rights?"

"Yes, sir," I answered.

"Have you decided on your course of action, Cadet?"

"I am undecided, sir," I said, keeping it brief.

"It would be in your best interest to resign, Cadet Ringgold to save yourself the embarrassment of getting kicked out. You are in a precarious situation. You have already admitted to witnessing cheating; you are clearly guilty."

I didn't say anything.

"If the Board of Officers also find you guilty of an honor violation, it will be very difficult for you to get into another college," he said, looking straight at me, his left hand underneath his chin, his elbow on his desk, as he contemplated how to handle me.

I remained at attention with my eyes staring a foot above Colonel Rhyne's head.

"I have no intention of resigning, sir."

"Very well, but you might want to think about that long and hard," he said, sighing. "You are dismissed."

I walked out of Colonel Rhyne's office and headed straight to Captain Lincoln. Luckily, he was alone. I knocked lightly on the open door.

He looked up and recognized me. "Cadet Ringgold, what's wrong?"

"I have been moved to Transient Barracks, and I have been informed that they found me guilty of toleration in a secret Honor Board hearing. How can they convict me without a trial? Don't I have to be present and have witnesses testify against me?"

He let out a long, slow sigh, looking puzzled. "Is that so? I hadn't been informed of your Honor Board hearing,"

"Sir, I was just informed. There was no Honor Board or actually I was told there was, but I wasn't told about it until after I was found guilty."

"Based on what evidence?"

"None, sir, except the signed affidavits from some of the cadets who were also present during the meeting with Under Secretary Augustine, but I haven't seen the affidavits."

"That sounds about right," Captain Lincoln said and shook his head.

He had an array of papers on the desk in front of him. He picked them up and began to stack them neatly. "It can't be very comfortable being in your position. The Honor Committee has been convicting cadets without due process. The Honor Committee, regrettably, has been acting without a conscience. I highly recommend not answering any more questions from anyone on the Honor Committee. Ninety-five percent of the convictions here are based on self-incriminating statements."

"Understood."

"Our point of power right now is to go public. I'd like to share your story with the media, if that's okay with you, but there will be a cost in doing so. It is *fight* or leave. If you are in agreement, I'd like to set up some interviews for you. Are you willing to speak to the media?" He asked, looking directly at me.

I felt the heaviness of my devastating situation. "I am willing, sir."

"Excellent. As you know, there are three news stations on television: NBS, CBS, and ABC. I'm going to get you on one of them, and when I do, everyone will know your story. Are you just sticking your toe in the water or are you all in?"

"I'm all in, sir."

"I'm glad to hear that, but it wouldn't be fair if I didn't explain the consequences of going public. You see, the Honor Code is only one code here. The other one is *thou shall not rock the boat.*"

"Yes, sir, but what do I have to lose?"

"Okay, then. I'll be in touch shortly about the interviews. There are a lot of investigations going on right now within the honor boards. We will appeal your conviction, and I will represent you before the Board of Officers. For now, hold tight. This is a fast-moving train. Stay focused on your academics and keep your head held high. As soon as I receive your file, I will let you know. I'll be in touch, okay?"

"I'm grateful, sir. Thank you," I said and left, heading straight back to Transient Barracks.

CHAPTER 11
TRANSIENT BARRACKS

I WALKED INTO MY NEW room to find a few more cadets present than when I'd left.

"Ringgold, you know Brian Fraser?" DaRold asked.

I nodded at them and then became disheartened. "Moon Dog, I didn't know you were accused too," I said, addressing Cadet Mamer.

"Can you join us, Ringgold? We're discussing a game plan." DaRold's Long Island accent was enhanced by the fact he was deliberately speaking slower. He sounded tired. I wondered how much he had been sleeping the past two weeks.

"Yeah, sure," I said, walking over to the guys. The group was huddled around one bed. I leaned against the closest desk to the left of DaRold. He appeared to be leading the group.

"Fraser, Ringgold and I have been friends since we roomed together plebe year. You can trust him."

"Okay, good. We need all the help we can get," Fraser said. Fraser was the nerdy type, with thick dark glasses that reminded me of the ones they sold at the post exchange we called *birth control glasses.* His glasses only enhanced the worry in his eyes. He was clearly stressed, possibly bordering on panic.

"The investigations keep increasing. Before we know it, half our class is going to get investigated," Moon Dog said. His straight brown hair, which was normally clean-looking and parted to the side, was disheveled.

Even DaRold was looking less put together than he normally did. His five o'clock shadow was in, and his bloodshot eyes betrayed his calm demeanor. This scandal was taking its toll.

"Tension is running high throughout our class. Everyone is afraid of being caught doing something. Anything. There is a bit of paranoia going on," Fraser went on.

"And rightly so," said DaRold. "Anyone know how many have been kicked out or resigned so far?"

"Yeah," I stepped in. "Whether it is accurate or not, I read in *The New York Times* a few days ago that out of the hundred and one charged: three have resigned, forty-nine were acquitted and forty-nine are still waiting to be tried," I said.

Everyone nodded in understanding. The numbers had grown.

"It pisses me off how the media keeps referring to the homework as a quiz or an exam. It was a homework assignment!" Moon Dog exclaimed.

"I agree. That's how they dramatize it," I added.

"And now there have been cadets charged with trying to influence the Honor Board votes. They'll need to create more rooms in Transient Barracks to accommodate us all."

"Seriously," Moon Dog said.

"It isn't *innocent until proven guilty* here. That's why they separate us from the rest of the Corps. They treat us like criminals, and the administration tries to convince us to resign to save face," Moon Dog said, disgusted.

"Are any of you being pressured to resign?" I asked, my recent conversation with Col. Rhyne fresh in my mind. "I was told that if

I resigned, they would send me back to the Army, and I'd be given my first choice of assignment," I said, with a smirk on my face.

"That's bullshit. How can anyone promise that?" DaRold said, stunned.

"That's part of the administrations' manipulative charm," I said. "Have any of you had your Honor Board Hearing yet?"

"None of us. We're still waiting to be tried," DaRold explained. "But the fact we have already been separated from the rest of the Corps makes us look guilty."

"We've got to turn this around somehow. I don't want to get kicked out. My parents are going to kill me," said Fraser.

A few grumblings showed everyone had the same concern; it did matter to us what our parents thought. I remembered from Beast Barracks, the eight weeks in July and August when we were trained militarily before academics began, being asked, *"Plebe! Why are you here? Why are you at my school?"* with a firstie screaming in my face, demanding an answer.

It was a question every plebe was asked at one time or another, and a lot of the same answers were heard. Some were here because they wanted to wear the uniform. Some were here because their father, uncle, or grandfather went to West Point. Some were here for the tuition-free education.

Wearing the uniform becomes routine after a while. Trying to please someone else, like your parents, by attending West Point may have gotten you to West Point, but it is hardly the reason why anyone stays. And most importantly, the education received at West Point is anything but free. Every graduate not only has an obligation to serve, but has to surrender to the system, including the Honor Code. Being a West Point Cadet is about self-sacrifice, commitment, and a belief in the system you serve. So whenever I was asked *"Why are you here, plebe?"* I gave the same answer over and over: *"I want to be an Army officer, sir!"*

I likely knew how my mother was going to react if I got kicked out, and I had some idea how much my life in the Army would be impacted, and neither was good.

"What can we do except admit we made a mistake and hope that we can appeal a guilty verdict?" DaRold said, without enthusiasm. "Did any of you realize that you were cheating?" he asked.

"Not exactly," Moon Dog said, pausing. "I talked to my roommates about the math problems, only because I wanted to make sure I understood them correctly, but I hadn't thought to notate that I'd gotten help. I hadn't realized that discussing the problems was cheating. It was a homework assignment, no different than others we've been given. I'm so baffled by this whole situation. I'm not sure what to do."

"There is a strength in numbers," DaRold said. "There is no way that they would kick out half of our class. That'd be stupid. What would they do next year with only four hundred firsties to run Beast Barracks and Plebe Year?"

"Right, I agree. I don't think they'll kick out half the class. They are more likely to sacrifice a few dozen to show that the Honor Code is strong and well," Moon Dog said.

"But there is strength in numbers," DaRold said again, thinking. "We have to work as a team and prevent more cadets being thrown out."

"Well yeah, working as a team is what got us into this mess," Fraser said.

"You're right, DaRold. There is strength in numbers," I said. "And it's a fact the Academy is not going to kick out half our class. Honor violations are commonplace; we all know the truth of it. It would be unjust to punish a few while letting all the other Honor Code violators off. If we keep stressing the fact that every cadet makes mistakes, then I think we have our answer," I said. Who would have thought I'd use my own words expressed to Under Secretary Augustine to fuel my argument now?

"Yeah, either the Academy will realize they need to kick out everyone or change the system?" DaRold asked, looking right at me.

"I wrote my senator, the one who nominated me to go here. I recommend you guys do the same. I also talked to Captain Lincoln. He's putting his career on the line by getting the message out about how corrupt the Honor System is. I think we need to follow his lead. I've already given him my word that I'll give interviews and tell my story," I said.

"Wait, Ringgold. You're in here for the same reason we are, right?" Moon Dog looked baffled.

"Not exactly. I was charged with toleration and apparently found guilty, but they didn't even have the decency to give me an Honor Board."

"What?" Moon Dog said, a shocked look replacing his features, matched by Fraser's stunned look. "So if you have already been found guilty, are you leaving soon?"

"That I don't know," I said, honestly, shrugging my shoulders. "I spoke with Captain Lincoln, and we're going to appeal the charges. I have every intention of fighting this. We know there have been problems with the Honor System. We all know cases of classmates expelled over trivial nonsense, and we also know cadets who've committed egregious violations yet remained in the Corps and graduated. The system is broken. If we don't fix it now, it will only get worse. So, I think the game plan is to blow shit up," I said, convinced, looking each of the guys square in the eyes. "If you're willing, put yourself out there in the public eye," I said. "Tell the American public what's going on here. I, personally, plan to do just that."

"Right, so we need to blow this up, so they realize the only way out of this mess is by kicking out everyone or changing the system and allowing everyone to stay," DaRold summarized again for emphasis.

"Exactly," I said.

"So how do we make that happen?" Moon Dog asked. "None of us, at least none that I know of, brought notes into a test. None of us passed around answer sheets during an exam, and none of us were copying the paper of the classmate next to us during a test. *That* would be cheating, but that's not what went on here."

"I get it," I said. "We make mistakes. When I was in the Army before coming here, we trained and trained to learn from our mistakes and to get it right, so we don't make those mistakes on the battlefield. Shouldn't we be allowed to learn from our mistakes?" I said. "We need support. Ask your congressman for help. Spread the word that the Honor System is not working. Talk to the newspaper reporters and give interviews. Talk to the Law professors. Get your families talking to the press," I said.

"You really think that is going to work?" Fraser asked, his eyes widening in thought, looking very owlish.

"What do we have to lose?" DaRold said, with a look of exasperation. "I'm in."

"So that's the goal then, to make this as big as possible so they'll realize they can't kick out everyone, so they might as well keep us all?" Moon Dog said, still processing.

"Well, that certainly sounds interesting," Fraser agreed.

"I'm going to make some calls tomorrow. I recommend you do the same thing. Let's get this crisis out in the open and hope something good comes from it," I said, determined and ready for action.

That evening, my first night in Transient Barracks, I was visited by both my company tactical officer, Major Aloysius Greenhouse, and his boss, the regimental commander, Colonel Arvid West.

Major Greenhouse arrived first and made himself at home behind an empty desk. He was calm, low-key, and appeared far more interested in DaRold's *Playboy* magazine than discussing the growing cheating scandal. After a while, he left and returned a half an hour later with Colonel West. I tried to inform Colonel West and Major Greenhouse of what I'd learned from my classmates, that in fact honor violations at West Point were widespread. Colonel West made it clear he had no interest in what I had to say; he just wanted me gone—the sooner the better.

CHAPTER 12
BLOWING SHIT UP

THAT NIGHT I HAD TROUBLE falling asleep. My mind was spinning. I was so tired of talking about the Honor Code, the Honor System, and the investigations. Likely, Moon Dog and DaRold were having trouble sleeping, too. I grabbed my transistor radio on my desk and turned it on. Bob Dylan's voice came shooting through, playing "The Times They Are a Changin'." The song spoke to me like it never had before:

> Come senators, congressmen
> Please heed the call
> Don't stand in the doorway
> Don't block up the hall
> For he that gets hurt
> Will be he who has stalled
> The battle outside ragin'

It became so apparent what I must do next. In addition to newspaper interviews, I needed to talk to anyone who would listen.

Will soon shake your windows
And rattle your walls
For the times they are a-changin'

Times were certainly changing. As exhausted as I was from the whole controversy, I knew I had to see it through. Somebody must, and it looked like it was up to me. I was the only one here that wasn't accused of cheating on the EE304 assignment. I was here because of what I'd said to the under secretary of the Army. I was found guilty, without an Honor Board hearing, based on six affidavits from those present during that conversation. We had been encouraged to speak openly, so those affidavits should not have been admissible. It was all so FUBAR, *fucked up beyond all recognition.*

Having already told my regimental commander and company tactical officer that honor violations were widespread, I needed to be proactive about this situation whether it saved my own ass or my classmates. Captain Lincoln was arranging television interviews, and once they aired, I knew there was no turning back. The world would know that I, like Captain Lincoln, was airing the dirty laundry of the Academy which also happened to be the truth.

I would also make calls to the local newspapers and magazines: *The New York Times, The Times Herald Record, Middletown News,* and *Newsweek.* With my future at West Point already on the line, I walked the line—just like Johnny Cash, which made me smile, and my eyelids finally became heavy.

The next morning, my comrades and I in Transient Barracks, forming our own company, marched like prisoners to breakfast together. Not only did we live together, but we also now dined together, cut off from the rest of the Corps. We were the lepers, the disease of the Academy, the cancer they hoped to cut out in order to save the rest of the Corps.

I arrived at morning Physics class with noticeable glances turning my way. I overheard my name, so I looked in that direction, to my right, making it known that I had heard them. My eyes landed on one cadet a few chairs from me, and we held stares until the professor walked in. Clearly some of my classmates were eyeing me with disdain, others with worry and trepidation, as if interacting with me would automatically get them in trouble.

Cadet Brian Fraser was correct. Our classmates were getting paranoid, but who could blame them? Cadets were afraid of having fingers pointed in their direction. It was obvious the Honor System was not working to support us but was working against us. The fear of being written up for a violation of the Honor Code was heavy in the air. The worry of getting kicked out threatened every cadet's well-being.

Those that had not been charged with a violation were likely not willing to stick out their necks for those that had been charged; it would be too risky for them. Thus, it was up to us in Transient Barracks to continue to work together and act. We would have to fight the good fight with or without the support of the rest of the Corps of Cadets.

After morning classes, I went down to the payphones in the basement and placed a call to *The New York Times*. I reported to them that cheating was rampant throughout the Academy. Instead of going to lunch, I rewarded myself by going to the PX, our convenience store on the other end of campus, and bought a baseball. With my baseball in hand, I went over to the batting cages and played until some of my adrenaline-fueled raw energy got dispersed through the baseball bat. I had the illusionary feeling of control when I could hit the ball straight on. In my mind, I lined up the Honor Committee members, starting with

Cadet Adamson and then Cadet Irwin, whacking their heads right off their body with each stroke of the bat. Whack. There goes Adamson's head. Whack. And Irwin's. Whack.

I wasn't going to allow myself to spiral out of control. I was focused. Whack. I was calm, and I was still in control of my reactions. I was going to attack these false accusations head on. I was going to do my best and make progress every day. Whack.

"Good afternoon, Cadet Ringgold, what may I do for you?" Captain Lincoln said, looking up from his pile of papers on his desk.

"Is there a date yet for my Board of Officers hearing?" I asked.

"Not yet, but hopefully soon."

"My classmates and I in Transient Barracks are on board. We're all willing to go public and speak to the media."

"Good, good. That should help." Lincoln said, clearing his throat. "I am sure you have been reading the newspapers, Cadet. I have been reporting that we have uncovered misconduct within the Honor System. One Cadet, in particular, is being investigated for bribing Honor Committee Members."

"I did hear something of the sort, sir."

"This is just another example, in addition to your own experience, where the Honor System has failed to follow its own rules and regulations. Hopefully all this media coverage will lead to an outside investigation. Since we're not getting the help we need here inside the Academy, we need help from outside the Academy. We need an outsider to investigate West Point. I can't see any other way around it."

I nodded in agreement.

"I just don't know how much longer I'm going to be here," he said with a strained look.

"What do you mean, sir?" I asked.

"I got a call from the Pentagon asking where I'd like to be reassigned." He swallowed. "That's their way of politely telling me that they want me out of here, and this is after they granted my request two months ago, for a one-year extension," he said.

"That's a shame, sir."

"Yes, it is. I'm a West Point grad myself, class of sixty-six, and I would do anything to protect West Point, but what they're doing here is wrong. They don't like me pointing fingers at them. The Army's reputation has already been damaged by Vietnam, and here the administration is hellbent on protecting West Point's good name. I, too, would like to save West Point's name, but we have to be willing to look in the mirror."

"Yes, sir, I agree with you."

"I'm not surprised they want me gone though. I suspect this transfer has more to do with my representing Verr than it does representing the accused cheaters. I am one of twenty-two Law professors here, and I'm the only one being transferred. It's Verr's case that caused me to go public. The treatment he's received by the Corps of Cadets has been outrageous, and the administration hasn't stepped in to stop it. So," he sighed. "I've rocked the boat, and it looks like they're moving me to keep me quiet."

"That means we don't have a lot of time," I concluded. "I'll continue to make calls, tell my story, and encourage my classmates to do as well. I'll start spreading the message that we need an outside investigation."

"Okay, good. We're not the only ones asking. Nine other Law professors and I recently wrote to the secretary of the Army, Martin Hoffmann, requesting an investigation. The superintendent is not very happy with us for going over the chain of command. He feels the Honor Committee is competent enough to handle whatever is thrown its way," Captain Lincoln said, his face stern with disgust. "But we didn't have a choice."

"I think you did what you needed to, and all of us in Transient

Barracks are grateful. We don't feel like we have a lot to lose. The rest of the school looks at us like we're criminals. It certainly isn't innocent until proven guilty. Just being moved to Transient Barracks has branded us as dishonorable."

"I hear you, and that's exactly how the Honor System is not working properly. The Honor Code is necessary, but it's frequently pursued without due process. It may be doing more to undermine honor than to uphold it. The Honor Code is meant to protect you. It's meant to hold an ideal standard, but it has gone beyond its usefulness with its corrupt implementation. We Law professors see it clearly. We're fighting to protect you within a system that is broken."

"Well, I really appreciate all you're doing, sir, to help us. Our cadet careers are on the line, and I expect you, too, are putting your career on the line. I'm grateful, sir. Thank you."

"You are very welcome, Mr. Ringgold. I'm sorry that it has to come to this. We'll do what needs to be done. As soon as I receive the date of your Board of Officers, I'll let you know," he said in a tone that indicated the conversation was coming to a close.

"Thank you, sir." I saluted him, left and went straight back to my room in Transient Barracks to catch up on homework.

CHAPTER 13
ABC EVENING NEWS WITH HARRY REASONER

LIVING IN TRANSIENT BARRACKS HAS the natural effect of making us feel deflated and lower our sense of self-worth. My comrades in arms were starting to look like a disgraceful lot. The Academy treated us like prisoners, and we were starting to look and act like prisoners too.

"I read in the *Army Times* that a West Point spokesman said that we were going to classes and doing everything as normal, that our cadet lives have been unchanged as a result of the Honor Boards," I said to DaRold.

"What bullshit! We're separated from the rest of the Corps. We form our own company. We eat at a separate time from the rest of the Corps. We're banned from extracurricular activities, and we're accompanied by guards wherever we go outside of Transient Barracks. Do they not want the media to know?" DaRold asked.

"Of course not. They're portraying *business as usual*. We're not even allowed to wear our class rings," I said.

"I know. I've also heard that we've been removed from athletic teams because we're not worthy of representing the Academy," DaRold said.

"Which is why some of the guys have stopped attending parades, shaving, or shining their shoes," I said.

DaRold nodded in agreement.

"I also read that the superintendent had sent a letter to each parent of the accused, so if you haven't told your folks, they know now," I pointed out matter-of-factly.

"Yeah, it took me a few days, but I called home after moving into Transient Barracks."

"Same here. I talked with my mom a few days ago. She's glued to the TV. She also keeps cutting out any news articles she sees," I said, sighing. "I wished she didn't worry so much. She wants me to put blinders on, to pretend I don't see anything, to say or do whatever I can to in order to stay."

We sat in silence for a few minutes.

"DaRold, I'm glad you decided to shave and shine your shoes. The last thing I want is for you to look like a criminal."

"I think it's important to keep up with our appearances, especially for the camera," he said.

"I completely agree. I wish some of the other guys felt that way," I said.

"Well, yeah. It feels like we're in prison, so it's not surprising that they are starting to act like prisoners."

"Maybe we should plant the seed with some of the guys here to keep up appearances. We don't want them looking like Berkeley students in West Point uniforms," I said, smiling.

"So true!" he said, chuckling. "I'm not trading in my low quarters for sandals anytime soon. We also have to find a way to lift our spirits too. You can feel the fear in the air with what we're doing. We're David fighting Goliath. I don't know, man. I wished we felt like we were making some headway, that we were seeing some charges being dropped or overturned or something."

"We have to keep reporting. Keep up the cause. We're in the trenches right now. Until they agree to our request for an outside investigation, I don't see it getting any easier," I said.

"I know, man. You're so right. Well, I'm going to look the part of an outstanding cadet at the very least. You, on the other hand, might need to shave again. Your five o'clock shadow is showing," DaRold said, smirking.

"Once a day, DaRold. I shave once a day; that's it," I said, taking out my polishing rag and sitting down with shoes in hand.

"Are you going to polish that butt chin of yours too?" he asked.

"Maybe I will. My chin makes me look very distinguished," I said, rubbing it with my bare hand. "Oh, by the way, have you invited anyone up for June week?" I asked, changing the subject. Firsties were graduating on Wednesday, June 2, and there would be celebrations all week. It was the perfect time to invite someone and show off the campus and socialize.

"I don't know," he shrugged. "I haven't thought that far ahead. Everything feels up in the air right now. I know you're going to appeal to the Board of Officers, and that could take some time, but do any of us know how long we're really going to be here?"

"Dude, June week is just a few weeks away. Maybe you should call your sister? She might take pity on you," I said, winking at him.

"Thanks a lot, jackass. I was really planning on calling your mother," he said.

"Ha! I'll put in a good word for you. I'll tell her how you want to be a doctor. I, on the other hand, have an amazing girl I'm asking. I wouldn't want you feeling butt-hurt once you see her."

"You're that confident she'll come, huh?"

"Well, maybe I'm a little overconfident that she will. I should probably ask her first," I said, shrugging.

"How did you meet her? Did she write to you after seeing your name in the newspaper, hot shot?"

"No, she was my date for the Ring Dance. I'm not sure if she knows what is really happening here now."

"Oh, the pretty brunette. Didn't you originally meet her at the prep school?" DaRold asked.

"Yeah, she was dating my roommate at the time. Do you remember when she came up plebe year before Christmas break?"

DaRold nodded.

"Well, we've kept in touch. She seemed to have fun at the Ring Dance, so I feel like I have a chance. I don't remember if I told you, but she has a little girl with my old roommate. I'm okay with it. Single moms are upfront and don't play any games because they don't have the time. Heck, we don't have the time either."

"True. Do you think she could bring a friend for me?" His voice raised in hopefulness.

"Yeah, no. None of her friends are that desperate," I said, laughing.

The next day, Thursday, May 13, I got a notice on my desk that I had an interview that afternoon with James Walker for ABC Evening News with Harry Reasoner. As I started unpacking my bag to study, my name was called over the speakers to report to Colonel Rhyne's office. I sighed, knowing my homework would have to wait.

I knocked loudly, partly due to my agitation over the homework needing my attention, on Colonel Rhyne's door.

"Enter," his voice commanded.

I walked in, saluted, and stood at attention with a controlled look on my face.

He didn't say anything for a few minutes. "We've been going over your case. Do you have anything to say in your own defense?"

Remaining at attention, looking straight at the wall behind his desk, I kept control of my facial features, suppressing my annoyance and answered him. "Yes, sir. I had a private conversation with the under secretary of the Army. I stand by what I said. The Academy has found me guilty of an honor violation without any evidence and without the decency of giving me an Honor Board hearing." I paused, took a deep breath and continued. "And the past few days, while I have been locked up in Transient Barracks, my classmates and I've been talking freely about what's going on. I have *firsthand knowledge*," I emphasized, "of cheating. Fellow cadets have confided in me about their honor violations on the EE304 assignment as well as other assignments. And sir, I reported this both to my regimental commander and company tactical officer. Sir, you have a much bigger problem on your hands than you thought."

Colonel Rhyne sat silently. He had been a cadet during the 1951 cheating scandal. Some time passed, and I continued to remain at attention. I could feel his eyes on me as he decided just how exactly he was going to deal with me.

"Cadet Ringgold, upon careful review of your case and due to new evidence, the commandant, General Ulmer, finds that there is insufficient evidence to sustain the allegations against you. Therefore, the charges are dismissed. You are returned to the Corps of Cadets in good standing."

I let out my breath, only then realizing I had been holding it. *I'm not getting kicked out. Thank god.* Then it dawned on me. *Why?* I couldn't stop myself.

"Colonel Rhyne, I just told you that I have firsthand knowledge of honor violations." I knew I was poking the bear.

"Cadet Ringgold, I think now would be a good time for you to leave.

After a short pause, I saluted, did an about-face and started to go, knowing I had done my part to spread the message of widespread cheating.

"But before you go," Colonel Rhyne continued, "I'd like to give you some good fatherly advice. Use that phone right there and notify ABC News you are canceling your interview tonight."

Now, I understood his motivation for dismissing the charges against me. "With all due respect, sir, I intend to do the interview." I left right away before Colonel Rhyne could say another word to me.

While sitting at the hostess office between classes, I scanned the newspapers, specifically looking for information on the cheating scandal. Sometimes announcements were made at breakfast formation, and updates obviously passed through word of mouth, but I also felt it was important to see what was being portrayed in the media. Even if the media wasn't always accurate, it was our strongest way to advocate for an outside investigation. To our benefit, the cheating scandal was being reported on daily.

Captain Lincoln was really putting himself out there, in defense of Cadet Steven Verr and the need for changes to be made within the Honor System. Captain Lincoln had served in West Germany as a company commander and in Vietnam, as deputy staff judge advocate for the Military Region II, and as a member of the Four Party Joint Military Commission to implement the Paris Peace Accords at the end of the hostilities in Vietnam. He had to have whit and guts to be an active member of the joint military commission negotiating with the Republic of Vietnam (North Vietnam), the Democratic Republic of Vietnam (South Vietnam), and the Provisional Revolutionary Government of the Republic of Vietnam (Viet Cong). I knew he was a 1966 graduate from West Point.

In reference to transferring Captain Lincoln, the Army spokesman said to the *Stars and Stripes* newspaper dated May 14 that, "There was no punitive intent involved. There was never intent to remove him until he had completed his defense of the cadets accused of cheating." I wasn't convinced that was accurate, and it is not what Captain Lincoln believed. He likely was being transferred as a consequence of going public.

I scanned through *The New York Times*. One article, dated May 12, 1976, made me laugh out loud.

> Capt. Arthur Lincoln is clearly guilty of two violations of West Point's code of the gentlemanly cover-up. As a military lawyer, he committed the sin of defending a cadet who had been subjected to barbarous physical and psychological abuse under the guise of enforcement of the Honor Code. As a West Pointer, he breached the understanding that an officer does not "go public" with any criticism of the United States Military Academy. For those offenses, Captain Lincoln has been asked to leave West Point.

Exactly. I sat there nodding in agreement. *The New York Times* got it right.

> Captain Lincoln apparently understands the dangers of a military establishment that clings to two mistaken traditions: the notion that the soldier can only emerge after the destruction of the man; and the belief that the pure image of the Corps' honor justifies any strategy that prevents public exposure of military wrongdoing. The authorities at West Point and in the Pentagon apparently need to be reminded that a democracy cannot condone totalitarian brutality in the name of military conditioning. The greatest threat to honor at West Point is a cover-up of dishonorable policies.

My eyes widened in surprise. Even though the journalist was writing the same thing we were thinking and had been advocating, somehow seeing it in black and white carried more weight. Goosebumps went up my arms, and I suddenly felt exposed, as if I had told an ugly truth to a therapist about my own past. This was big. I could feel the intensity of the situation building. As with any storm that rages, destruction is left in the wake. I wondered what the outcome would be and whose careers would be destroyed. Clearly, it wasn't only the cadets' fates at stake here.

A few days later, I received a response from Senator Barry Goldwater.

United States Senate
Committee on Armed Services
Washington, DC 20510

May 12, 1976

Cadet Timothy D. Ringgold
Company E-2, U.S.C.C.
West Point, N.Y. 10977

Dear Cadet Ringgold:

This is in response to your letter of 7 May. I am taking the matter up with Secretary Augustine and I will write again when I have further information. I thank you for bringing this matter to my attention.

Sincerely,
Barry Goldwater

Upon waiting for a follow-up letter from Senator Goldwater, I decided to write to him again.

Company E-2
United States Corps of Cadets
West Point, New York 10997
18 May 1976

The Honorable Barry Goldwater
United States Senate
Washington, DC 20510

Dear Senator Goldwater:

Much has happened since my last letter, but your help is still requested to resolve the current situation.

Last Monday, 10 May 1976, I was found guilty of violating the cadet Honor Code and immediately moved to Transient Barracks. It was recommended that I be separated from the Military Academy for my statement to the under secretary of the Army, Mr. Norman Augustine, that cheating is very widespread.

Tuesday, 11 May 1976, I was asked to resign by the deputy commandant, Colonel Hal B. Rhyne. I declined to do so and requested that my case be appealed to a Board of Officers. Colonel Rhyne said he would review my case and make his recommendation to the commandant.

That same day, I had a telephone interview with Mr. Jim Feron of *The New York Times* and a video interview with Mr. Jim Walker of ABC News. Wednesday I was interviewed by Mr. Eric Gillman of *Newsweek* Magazine and Mr. Bob Monroe of Associated Press, and Mr. Gary Shepard of CBS News. At each of the interviews, I stressed the fact that cheating is widespread and the request for an investigation.

That evening I was visited by 2nd Regimental Commander Colonel Arvid West. At that meeting, I informed Colonel West that there was widespread cheating within the Corps of Cadets. Later that evening, I was visited by my company tactical officer, Major Aloysius Greenhouse, and I informed him of the widespread cheating within the Corps of Cadets.

Thursday, 13 May 1976, I requested an appointment with Colonel Rhyne and was told to report immediately. At this conference, I made it known to Colonel Rhyne that I was aware of widespread cheating and corruption within the honor committee itself as well as within the Corps of Cadets. Colonel Rhyne seemed most interested and wished to pursue the matter further.

At this meeting, I was told that the commandant, Brigadier General Walter F. Ulmer, has reviewed additional evidence and concluded that there was insufficient evidence to refer my case to a Board of Officers. Therefore, the charges were dropped and I was returned to the Corps of Cadets in good standing.

Just what this "additional evidence" was still remains unknown to me. In light of what I had previously told my company tactical officer, my regimental commander, the deputy commandant, as well as the news media, I feel the charges were dropped against me simply to keep me quiet. Returning me to the Corps of Cadets in good standing made me once again subject to the Honor Code and anything I now say can again be used against me in honor board proceedings. This is simply another stage in the Military Academy's attempt to cover-up and white-wash what is happening here. I have repeatedly made known the extent of the corruption and no one will listen.

The Military Academy is trying to protect a code that is not being followed, and at the cost of purging over fifty of my classmates. This can not be allowed to happen. I freely admitted to my company tactical officer, my regimental commander, and the deputy commandant of having violated the code myself by toleration, but they have decided I'll cause them too much trouble. Do they not have a conscience?

Sir, once again I request your support for a full investigation with immunity for those cadets willing to speak. For only with such immunity will it be possible for a cadet to speak truthfully without fear of being subjected to the same treatment I have received for the last month.

Sir, I know you have long been a friend of West Point, the Army, and all the armed services. You once told me that you had often wished you had gone to West Point and taken a commission in the Air Corps. It is time for all the friends of West Point to come to the aid before the monster of the cover-up is allowed to eat its own tail.

Sincerely,
Timothy D. Ringgold
Cadet Cpl, Co. E-2, 1977

The evening of May 19, I caught the evening news in Grant Hall. Seeing the West Point Crest on the television screen, the large room became instantly quiet as our attention focused on the news reporter, Harry Reasoner.

"A group of military lawyers representing West Point cadets accused of cheating have asked the secretary of the Army to appoint an outside investigator to dig into the scandal. Today the secretary said 'no.' Jim Walker has details."

The news cut to the reporter, Jim Walker. "The military lawyers felt that only an outsider could conduct an impartial investigation of alleged cheating more widespread than indicated by last month's scandal involving forty-nine cadets, but Army Secretary Hoffmann disagrees, telling them to stay within the chain of command. The lawyers call the decision a whitewash. ABC News has learned that some cadets have signed affidavits charging that three hundred to as many as five hundred cadets have violated the Honor Code, which says a cadet will not lie, cheat, steal, or tolerate anyone who does. Conviction means expulsion. Cadet Tim Ringgold of Phoenix, Arizona was first found guilty then cleared of tolerating cheating after he told the under secretary of the Army recently that many cadets cheat at West Point."

Those were not my words to the under secretary, but certainly *my* understanding of what was really going on. A few heads, aware of my presence, snapped my way. I didn't break my stare at the television, though, but I could feel the heat rushing up my face.

Jim Walker and I sat on a bench at Trophy Point as I talked about cadet cheating. "It is as widespread as the cheating and corruption is in the Honor System. West Point is just producing efficient liars, not producing honorable people. And there are no degrees to an honor violation around here. If you say you shined your shoes and didn't, you get thrown out as assuredly as if you rip off someone's car or cheat on an electrical engineering exam."

The camera turned to Jim Walker.

"West Point officials have repeatedly denied there is widespread cheating here and the Army secretary's decision rejecting a special investigation in effect supports them, but the cadets and the military lawyers involved in the scandal vow to keep up the pressure until, as they put it, 'somebody uncovers the Army's coverup.' Jim Walker, ABC News, West Point."

Knowing that my mom would likely see this interview, I took note that I should probably call home.

US Senator Barry Goldwater and 16 year old SMA Cadet Timothy Ringgold meet in Arizona, 1970. Senator Goldwater nominated Tim for West Point.

While at the USMA Prep School at Fort Belvior, Tim Ringgold was selected as the "How to Wear the Uniform" model for the Cadet Regulations.

*Tim Ringgold named the outstanding new cadet by
SMA Commandant COL John Cleveland, 1970.*

*The "unknown companion" during Tim Ringgold's first
visit to West Point, January 1971.*

Tim Ringgold spent a record amount of time walking punishment tours. Here he is being inspected by the Sergeant of the Guard.

Clowning Around. No recollection of who was wrapped in my reserve parachute, but the culprits are Cadets Steve Hunt, Bob Stewart, Peter DaRold, and Tim Ringgold.

Plebe Steve Hunt with his father, Colonel Hunt, West Point Class of 1950.

Typical academic class, Plebe year, 1973. Tim Ringgold half asleep in the middle.

Plebe year roommates Peter DaRold and Tim Ringgold. Fall 1973.

Company E-2, Fall 1974. Second and Third from the right, back row, is Peter DaRold and Steve Hunt. Tim Ringgold is second row middle.

CHAPTER 14
MR. NORMAN AUGUSTINE'S RESPONSE TO SENATOR BARRY GOLDWATER

A FEW MINUTES AFTER MY interview with Jim Walker had finished, a firstie walked by. Mr. Walker had turned to ask him a question, but the firstie took off running.

I heard him shout back to us, "I'm this close to graduation. You want to get me kicked out?"

After my interview aired, I was known as a whistleblower. If I had cheated, I would not have any credibility. The fact that I had not cheated, that I earned my mediocre grade all on my own, meant I had a credible voice. So, I was following Captain Lincoln's lead and going public. Being on ABC, a national broadcast, meant the entire country knew about the cheating scandal, and good or bad, my name was quickly becoming public knowledge.

I was being interviewed and quoted in practically every newspaper and magazine out there from the East to West Coast: *The New York Times, Newburgh Evening News, The Times Herald-Record, Army Times, Stars and Stripes, Time* magazine, *Intelligencer Journal, The Arizona Republic* and *The Los Angeles Times. The New York Times*'s journalist, James Feron, most heavily followed and wrote about the cheating scandal and about me almost daily.

In *The Bergen Record*, a New Jersey paper, I was quoted:

> Ringgold calls the high expectation and the strict penalties of the honor system "inhuman. A cadet, like everyone else in the world, makes mistakes," he says. "And," he adds, "a cadet, like everyone else in the world feels his greatest loyalty to his friends—not to an institution which says he must report his friends to the authorities."

Due to my publicity, I was a thorn in the side of the Academy, trying to force them to face the facts. The firsties, the class of 1976, were weeks shy from graduation and wanted nothing to do with the scandal. The same sentiment was true among most of my classmates, who feared getting involved. They didn't mind if fifty or so cadets, *the bad apples*, were thrown out as long as it wasn't them.

However, the scandal was growing. Cadets, mainly the ones who had been accused and thus had nothing to lose, were turning in lists of names of cadets they claimed had collaborated with or who had firsthand knowledge of their own cheating. In the same article, in *The Bergen Record*, Captain Lincoln was referenced as having "a list of well over 400 upperclassmen accused of honor violations."

In the mail, I was pleased to receive a xerox copy of Under Secretary Augustine's letter to my Arizona senator, Barry Goldwater. I was appreciative that Senator Goldwater had followed up with Mr. Augustine via my request, and that he was keeping me informed of the results.

Department of the ARMY
Office of the Under Secretary
Washington, DC 20310

19 May 1976

Honorable Barry Goldwater
United States Senate
Washington, DC 20510

Dear Senator Goldwater:

I appreciate very much your offering me an opportunity to comment on the matter raised by Cadet Timothy Ringgold of the United States Military Academy, particularly so because the impression left by a portion of the press coverage is incorrect as well as rather damaging to the Academy, Cadet Ringgold, and myself. As you may already know, an investigation has now been completed and all charges against Cadet Ringgold have been dropped.

Several allegations have been made, one of which is that I reported Cadet Ringgold to the Honor Committee because of confidential statements he made to me during my visit to West Point on 14 April 1976. This is not correct. The facts are that I reported Cadet Ringgold to no one and furthermore had not even discussed our meeting with anyone from the time of that conversation until May 16 after he had been reinstated. Presumably, some of the fifteen or twenty cadets also participating in the session felt there may have been an honor violation indicated by Cadet Ringgold's remarks either during or after the session and they thus raised the matter with the Honor Committee in accordance with the provisions of the Honor System.

A second allegation is that I had somehow granted "immunity" during the discussions in question. The nature of the discussion was a brief session with what I understand to be a randomly selected group of about twenty cadets during a routine visit I made to West Point to teach a series of classes. Although I left the subject matter of the discussion entirely open, I did not grant any form of immunity and, in fact, asked when the subject of the Honor System was discussed, that we not address any of the specific cases then pending. On the other hand, I did emphasize the informality of the session and the cadets were, I believe, most candid in expressing their views on a variety of subjects of interest to me and to them with regard to the Military Academy's programs. The faculty member who escorted me to meet the cadets indicated that he had not planned to stay in the session as he felt his presence might inhibit the discussions, and hence, did not remain in the room. Thus, although one of my military assistants was present, the atmosphere was clearly one of openness and candor.

Finally, as I attempt to recollect our conversations of that day on a whole gamut of subjects, I personally do not recall anything being said which would point to someone having knowledge of specific honor violations (which, under the Honor System, would have required the cadet having such knowledge to submit a report to the Honor Committee). A variety of diverse viewpoints were expressed on virtually every topic that came up. One cadet, who I assume was Cadet Ringgold, seemed very eager to talk and raised his hand to be called on a number of times throughout the visit. As best I can recall, he expressed the view that the Honor System was so all-encompassing as to be unworkable and that because of its coverage of large numbers of detailed day-to-day activities, virtually everyone, in his opinion, would at some time or another be forced to violate the Honor System.

With regard to the possibility of an overall review of the Honor System, as raised in your letter, both the secretary of the Army and the superintendent of the Academy are actively pursuing this question and we will keep you informed of their actions. I believe that this is the best approach to follow.

I hope that the above views will be helpful to you and I am most appreciative for the opportunity to provide my recollections. I appreciate your support of, and interest in, the Military Academy. In spite of our current series of problems, I believe that we may take great pride in the people and the institution represented by the United States Military Academy.

Sincerely,

Norman R. Augustine
Under Secretary of the Army

It had only been ten cadets present during the meeting with the under secretary. I had not raised my hand nor been eager to speak. I could have easily kept quiet and chosen convenience over speaking my mind. I'd have been perfectly happy if our meeting had ended thirty seconds earlier, before he asked my opinion. At least Mr. Augustine's letter validated that he had not turned me in to the Honor Committee and that "the atmosphere was clearly one of openness and candor." It was crazy to think how *that* conversation was the catalyst that brought forth my Honor Code conviction. That was the moment that I was pulled into the cheating scandal. I was not personally involved in it but felt called to stand up for justice.

CHAPTER 15
CONVERSATION WITH FRED KASS

"HELLO?" A SWEET FEMALE VOICE answered.

"Hi, is Gina home?"

"She is not. Who may I say is calling?" she asked.

"Okay. Yes, ma'am. This is Tim, Tim Ringgold. She won't be able to reach me directly. She'll have to call the Guard Post and leave a message. Make sure she tells when a good time would be to call her back."

"Tim, I remember you. You are calling from West Point, right?"

"Yes, ma'am. You must be Gina's sister?" I said, smiling. It didn't hurt to be gracious.

"No, this is her mother. You roomed with Don at the prep school. Is that correct?" she asked.

"Yes, ma'am."

"Well, you know Don is not in the picture anymore?"

"Yes, ma'am, I'm very aware," I said.

"But Tim, you know she has a little girl by him, don't you?"

"Yes, I know about Christine. Would it be possible for Gina to come up for June week? That's why I'm calling. I know with her being a single parent and finishing school that it might prove to be difficult, but I would very much like her to come."

"Okay, I'll let her know. If she's interested, I can help with Christine. I'll let her work out the details with you. I'll tell her you called."

"Thank you, ma'am. I appreciate it." I said and hung up.

Having my conviction overturned by the commandant meant I was forced to move out of Transient Barracks. For whatever reason, I was assigned to another company, E-1 instead of my original E-2, where I had spent three years. I spoke with my tactical officer, Major Aloysius Greenhouse, about staying in Company E-2, but he wasn't allowed to approve it. At least I could walk freely around barracks again without a guard.

My desire to publicize the cheating scandal and fight for an outside investigation didn't abate. My classmates in Transient Barracks were counting on me, and I knew I had to finish what I had been on the path to do.

That afternoon, Sunday, May 23, the Corps of Cadets was called into Thayer Hall. The superintendent, Lieutenant General Berry, took the podium. I sat with Cadet DaRold and Moon Dog.

"Good afternoon, Corps of Cadets. Upon light of new evidence, an internal review panel of officers is going to be formed to help investigate the recent honor cases. This panel is necessary because much of the Honor Committee is going to be depleted by graduation. The panel will be headed by Colonel Gilbert W. Kirby, the head of the Department of Earth, Space, and Graphic Sciences. This panel will replace the all-cadet Honor Boards. I understand that taking authority away from the cadets, might be upsetting, and I don't do this lightly. The four cadet Honor Boards within the Honor Committee, have been nobly working day and night to stay on top of all the honor charges. With recent events, having ten percent of the class of '77 being charged with Honor Code violations, it has come to my attention that cheating is widespread."

I looked to DaRold on my right, my jaw hanging open in surprise. Maybe this was finally the forward movement we needed.

"Thus, I felt it was imperative that we step in. The Internal Review Panel of officers will be working alongside the current Honor Committee members. I hope you welcome the panel with a sigh of relief that help has finally arrived. Needless to say, the secretary of the Army, Martin Hoffmann, and I will have the final say on all cases.

"Currently, the Electrical Engineering professors are conducting comparisons of the EE304 assignment between members of the same athletic team, as well as the same extracurricular activity.

"As leader of this new panel, Colonel Hal B. Rhyne, who has served as the deputy commandant the past two years, is now appointed special assistant to the commandant for honor matters. He was scheduled to leave West Point this summer to command an armor brigade at Fort Hood, Texas, but agreed to delay command until business is finished here. A major command is the dream of any officer. As such, this is a most *selfless* act. It demonstrates his dedication to the Academy, and his relationships with the Corps. With his leadership, I am confident we will flush out the guilty parties quickly, so we can return to business as usual as soon as possible." General Berry turned the microphone over to General Ulmer.

The commandant spoke of the honor and integrity of West Point. He ended his short talk by saying, "Obviously something has gone awry when so many cadets are being charged with cheating. However, the West Point Honor Code is alive and well. There are some flaws and points of illness, but it is alive. If the Honor Code ever died, the Academy would die with it."

I couldn't help but grunt.

General Berry took the microphone again. "We are confident that within the walls of West Point, we can address all the problems that arise and fix them efficiently. I ask for everyone's continued cooperation and patience as we work through these difficult matters. From a personal standpoint, I am saddened for those accused. From a professional standpoint, the Academy will get along. Thank you for your time. Please return to your scheduled activities."

As General Berry exited the platform, the cadets started filing out of Thayer Hall.

"How do you feel about that speech, Ringgold?" DaRold asked me.

I shook my head and shrugged. "I think it's all smoke and mirrors. I don't think keeping it within the family is going to work. The Academy is not going to change until it is forced to change, and that has to come from an outsider who understands the Academy but is not pressured into protecting its image."

"An outside investigation like what you, Captain Lincoln, and the other Law professors are advocating," DaRold said.

"Exactly," I said.

I turned to Moon Dog to see his response. He was nodding in agreement.

The next day, Congressman Tom Downey was visiting the school. The Long Island congressman was the youngest member of Congress, at age twenty-six, and the first congressman to make a personal visit to the Academy to study the ongoing cheating scandal. When I was coming from an interview with CBS, I met Fred Kass, the legislative assistant for Congressman Downey, who asked if we could get together and talk. We met up during lunchtime.

"So Cadet Ringgold, thank you for taking the time to meet

with me," Fred Kass said, starting the conversation.

"Not a problem, sir. I'm happy we can talk."

He smiled and looked at his notes. "It is my understanding that your charges have been dropped."

"Actually sir, my conviction by the Honor Committee was overturned by the commandant," I said, nodding and waiting for him to continue. I wanted to see what he knew before I jumped in.

"And now you're here to spread the message that violations of the Honor Code are more widespread than reported, and you're advocating for an outside investigation?"

"The way honor is defined, that is precisely it, sir," I said, continuing to nod.

"And did you make a deal in order for your conviction to be overturned?" Kass asked.

I had been ready for that question. There was a rumor going around that I had made a deal with Colonel Rhyne in order to drop my charges and be returned to the Corps of Cadets.

"Absolutely not, but I am very aware that the commandant overturned my conviction in hopes to keep me quiet. For the Academy to prosecute me, they would have to investigate my allegations of widespread cheating," I said, laying the truth right on the table. "I know Congressman Downey is also a member of the House Armed Services Committee, and I think he could help us." I looked Kass straight in the eye to show him how serious I was about receiving help.

"We're here to help you and your classmates as best as we can. Congressman Downey and I met in college at Cornell University. I know how important these years of your life are and the bonds that are formed, as well as the potential for cadets' careers to be ruined if they got kicked out. Congressman Downey has been investigating the situation for the past week."

"Good, I'm glad."

Fred Kass continued to talk about himself, sharing that he'd graduated from the New York University School of Law to show he understood the legal process. He was a very friendly, likable guy. I also think he told me as much as he did about himself in order to make me feel at ease with him and get me to tell him as much as I could.

I told him about my meeting with Under Secretary Augustine, the Honor Committee's findings, the statements to the press, my meetings with Colonel Rhyne, and the fact that I had never been charged with cheating. I explained that there were no charges of any kind pending.

"I have told Major Greenhouse, my company's tactical officer, and Colonel Rhyne, the deputy commandant, that I have personal knowledge of widespread cheating," I said, reiterating the message. "However, I don't think Colonel Rhyne is taking my comments seriously or he just plans on ignoring them. They want to keep me quiet. I was told by one reporter that he'd been told by the public affairs office, that I didn't wish to give any more interviews, which you know is bogus. I also was told that reporters were given the wrong company that I was in."

"Well, West Point officials don't have to abide by the Honor Code." He laughed. "Have you had the opportunity to speak with the superintendent?"

"No, but I did write him a letter requesting that he investigate my allegations of Cadet Adamson and Cadet Irwin."

"Interesting and what do you hope to get out of all of this?"

"Well, sir, as you know my honor conviction has been overturned, but I am very much aware that we have a bigger problem on our hands. I could walk away, wash my hands of this situation, and just simply graduate next year. That's what my mom wants me to do. However, my conscience won't let me remain quiet when I feel my classmates facing charges are simply sacrificial lambs being slaughtered for the Academy's pride. In truth, the minute I went public there was no turning back. I've been personally threatened by people, some who used to be my friends. The Academy has given me the official cold shoulder. However, since I went out on a limb by myself last month, other cadets have come forward to support me. They are providing lists of fifty, seventy-five, one hundred, and maybe even more names of other cadets who they cheated with. Cadets have also started going to the Law Department with names."

"Do you think the cadets accused did not cheat? I am really curious about your answer. Three of the forty-nine cadets found guilty are from Long Island, so Congressman Downey has a special interest in finding out the truth." Mr. Kass asked.

"It's a bit more complicated than that," I said. "Let me ask you this: what do you think when someone is accused of cheating?" Not waiting for an answer, I said, "You think of someone in a classroom looking at another student's paper or sneaking unauthorized notes into an exam. That's cheating at West Point and everywhere else, but that's not what happened here. In this one course, we were previously given two take-home assignments, problems to solve, and we were encouraged to work with our classmates. The third homework assignment we were told should be done independently, and it was worth maybe five percent of our grade. Not understanding the problem, a large number of my classmates sought help from other students. Under the Honor System, helping a classmate is a violation. Seeking help from a classmate is a violation. Being in the same room and observing the giving or receiving of assistance is a violation. And there is only one penalty for an honor violation, which is to be kicked out unless you resign first."

I waited for Kass to process what I had said and then continued. "We love and respect the Honor Code. It's an ideal we strive for, but the Honor System has become a *disciplinary* system. The Honor System went from being a method of teaching integrity to being used to enforce rules and regulations. The judge and jury are our fellow cadets, often younger than the accused. Where is the adult supervision? I'll tell you: they have abdicated their responsibility to teach, train, and supervise the cadets and are relying on the Honor System to do it for them." I paused and then went on.

"When you have cadets being kicked out for minor discrepancies like saying they did twenty pushups when they only did eighteen or for asking your roommate a question about a homework assignment that was supposed to be completed independently, we have a problem. The high expectation and the strict penalties of the Honor System are inhumane. What happened to James Pelosi and Steven Verr is not teaching us to lead in combat, it's teaching us to be cruel and unforgiving. A cadet, like everyone else in the world, makes mistakes. And, a cadet, like everyone else in the world, feels his greatest loyalty to his friends—not to an institution that says he must report his friends to the authorities," I said, taking a deep breath. "How do you build a bond of friendship when you're required to spy on each other?"

"So it's about who you know?" Fred Kass asked, his right eyebrow raised.

"It is absolutely *who* you know. Cadets have been finding out who was sitting on their boards and making deals to make sure they'd get off. Honor Committee members use their personal power to resolve personal vendettas. Sometimes, it's not a question of being guilty or not, but rather who you know. One negative vote on the twelve-member board ensures acquittal. You don't have to convince everyone, just one vote."

"I see," Fred Kass said, taking it all in. "You're describing a much larger problem than the superintendent reported to us."

"Likely so, sir. The supe and commandant are more worried about the reputation of the school than looking at the truth. Who would know it better than us cadets?"

Fred Kass shook his head in acknowledgment.

"So, to answer your question, the long-term goal is to change the Honor System by making it honorable again. The only way to do that is to have someone, an outsider, look at the whole system objectively."

"And what are your short-term goals?"

"In the short-term, I'm hoping to take steps to save my classmates from expulsion. All the cadets who testify in these Officers Boards need immunity so they can come forward without the fear of putting their careers at risk. But better yet, we'd like to stop the boards from starting."

"How do you plan to do that?" he asked, sounding curious.

"A group of us have requested a restraining order to stop the Officers Boards, and to declare the Honor System unconstitutional because of the violation of due process. You would think, with all the evidence of widespread cheating, that the administration would quash the charges before the boards began."

Mr. Kass shrugged his shoulders in understanding and then asked, "Are you in support of the Honor Code?"

"Absolutely. Let me be clear: I am not in any way opposed to the Honor Code, but only the manner in which it is implemented. The Honor System is broken. Changing the system is the only way to clean up the current mess and to prevent similar occurrences in the future."

"Wow. I'm glad we had the opportunity to speak. Cadet Ringgold, you've painted a much broader picture of the current situation," he said, sounding grateful. "If you know of any other cadets that'd be willing to share their experiences, please send them my way. They could come in without name tags too. Will you help me?" Mr. Kass asked, looking at me straight on.

"Will you help us?" I responded, holding his gaze.

"I speak for both Congressman Downey and myself when I say that we will do our best to help."

CHAPTER 16
COMMANDANT BRIGADIER GENERAL WALTER F. ULMER, JR.

THE NEXT DAY ON TUESDAY, May 25, *The New York Times* carried an article by Mr. Jim Feron:

> The commandant of Cadets, Brig. Gen. Walter Ulmer, indicated during a news conference by saying that although Cadet Timothy Ringgold had been "convicted" by an honor board—he was cleared soon after—he would have the opportunity to "prove his nonguilt" later at an officer hearing.

What the hell did that mean? I wondered why anyone would have to prove their non-guilt, especially since there were no charges against me. Ulmer himself had overturned my honor conviction and returned me to the Corps in good standing.

Likely, General Ulmer was lumping me in with the accused. I could picture the administration going through my EE304 assignment with determined precision, comparing it with my classmates line by line in hopes of finding a shred of evidence so they could charge me again—this time with cheating. Too bad going over my assignment with a fine-tooth comb was not going to result in any proof of my having cheated because I hadn't. Feeling frustrated over my own uncertain future, I asked to speak with the commandant.

"Come on in, Cadet Ringgold. Please close the door behind you," General Ulmer said, clearly wanting our conversation off the record.

As I closed the door, I realized he was likely expecting to see me at some point. I saluted him and stood at attention, with eyes forward focused on the wall behind his desk.

"At ease, Cadet Ringgold. What may I do for you?" General Ulmer said, looking right at me. I shifted to parade rest, my feet shoulder-width apart and my hands linked behind my back. I could feel the intensity of his gaze.

"Sir, I'd like to understand your remarks to the media about my case," I said directly.

"Cadet, I speak to the media quite often. In fact, General Berry and I are hounded constantly by the media, so what remarks are you specifically referring to?"

I cleared my throat and answered. "That I would have my own chance to prove my non-guilt at a board of officers." I paused. "Sir, there are no charges against me, so I'm not sure what you meant by that comment."

"Ringgold, I don't remember speaking about your case at all."

I went on. "Colonel Rhyne had informed me that charges against me had been dropped due to new evidence. What was that new evidence, sir?"

"Cut the crap, Ringgold," he said, standing up and walking toward me. He was a tall and trim man, disciplined with firm muscles probably until the day he died. I could feel him trying to intimidate me. He was, after all, the 56th commandant of cadets, a brigadier general in charge of the disciplinary measures for the

Corps of Cadets, and I was just a cadet. He held the power in his hands over my stay at West Point and my future career in the Army. "What is your goal here, Ringgold? Have you witnessed any honor violations that you have not reported?"

"Sir, I continue to report that there is widespread cheating."

General Ulmer sighed. I could tell he did not know what to do with me. "What are you trying to accomplish?" He paused, then asked. "What do you want?"

The last few words rasped in my ears. It was evident General Ulmer was pissed, and the source of his anger was me. He did not appreciate the negative spotlight on West Point or my questioning authority. Cadets are supposed to obey, not question an officer, much less a general officer.

"Sir?" I asked, not quite sure how to respond. He clearly thought I had a hidden agenda or something.

General Ulmer walked over closer, and in an air of feigned casualness as if confiding in a friend asked, "Ringgold, *what do you want?*" He seemed eager for a response, like I could tell him something privately that would be different than what I'd been saying publicly.

I wanted an outside investigation of the Honor System because I wanted West Point to have integrity again. I wanted this cheating scandal to disappear. I wanted my classmates' charges to be dismissed and for West Point to fix the system, but clearly those tasks were unrealistic, too noble a desire, a fantasy. I knew I was too far into my mission to retreat now, even if I was waist deep in shit. It was only a second until I responded with the only answer that seemed relevant.

"I just want the truth, sir," I replied with a strong conviction.

Done with our conversation, General Ulmer buzzed the door and said, "I find it necessary to reopen your case, Ringgold. You may leave now."

Apparently, I hadn't given him the answer he wanted.

Wanting the truth was not enough. Stunned and at a loss for words, I walked out.

I headed over to the Law Department, the only place that I felt a reassurance of the role I was playing in this whole mess. The corridor outside Captain Lincoln's office, as well as that of the other Army lawyers, looked like the waiting room of a busy hospital. The Officers Boards were starting on Friday, so the attorneys were working around the clock to prepare defense strategies and witnesses for their cadets' cases.

I knocked firmly on Captain Lincoln's door, not sure if I would find him free.

"Enter," Captain Lincoln shouted, surrounded by mountains of paperwork stuffed in various folders.

"Captain Lincoln, I'm sorry to bother you. It had been a while since we talked. I thought I should inform you that the commandant is reopening my case," I said, matter-of-factly.

"It's not a problem, Mr. Ringgold. Come on in." He signaled me in. Captain Lincoln had a glazed expression on his face, having been deep in thought. "One second and I'll give you my undivided attention."

"Thank you, sir," I said and sat down on the chair in front of his desk. I watched as Captain Lincoln scribbled something quickly, paused, and then finished his thought on paper. He nodded, put his pencil down, and looked at me.

"So, Ringgold, did you just say your case was reopened?" He spoke as if just processing what I had said.

"Yes, sir. I came straight from a meeting with the commandant. I went to General Ulmer to discuss his recent remarks about me in the paper. I had no charges against me, so I inquired what he meant when he told the press that I'd have an opportunity to prove my 'nonguilt' at an officer board."

"I see and that led to him reopening your case?"

"Yes, sir, because I continued my stance that cheating is widespread. My ultimate goal, of course, is getting that outside investigation. What it boils down to is that he'll put me back in the Corps if I keep my mouth shut. When I wouldn't shut up or back down, he had no alternative but to reopen my case. I have no other plans at this time but to fight this with the last ounce of energy I have."

"I understand. The whole Law Department is completely overwhelmed. We're literally up to our eyeballs in paperwork. We likely have more than we can handle, but we are pushing through," Captain Lincoln said.

"What's the likelihood of getting that outside investigation?" I asked, just to hear his opinion.

"Well, as you probably know, on May nineteenth the secretary of the Army turned down our request for an outside investigation," he sighed and leaned back in his chair.

"I'd heard that," I said, frowning. "That was disappointing."

"It's hypocritical. How can they expect us to send our allegations through the same system we want investigated? The other Law professors and I were shocked and appalled by that decision. We can't understand why the secretary of the Army is not hearing us, not doing what we recommend. We are the ones here at West Point, seeing the Honor System with our own eyes. Well, you know," he said, brushing his hand through the air. "Despite that disappointment, though, the Law professors and I are staying the course. We'll put on the best defense we can."

"I'm happy to find you still here at the Academy," I said, just then realizing that the last time we'd spoken, he'd told me about his scheduled transfer.

"Yes, well, I got another call from the Pentagon. My transfer has been called off, for now, or at least until I see the Officers Boards through." He shrugged. "I'm where I need to be, where I want to be."

"I'm glad the Pentagon saw the error of their ways," I said, joking.

"Yeah, I wouldn't take it that far. The Army is not quick to admit any failings. They explained to me that my transfer had been a *promotion*," he said, hinting at the sarcasm of that word. "So my promotion has been delayed."

"Well that's excellent, sir. Here we are a little over a week from graduation for the class of 1976, do you think we have any hope of saving my classmates?"

"To be honest, Cadet Ringgold, I have no idea. My clients, your classmates," he said, directly, "have been coming forward with lists and lists of the names of others that have cheated or who they have cheated with, as well as evidence about jury tampering. All of these facts will be coming out in court."

I nodded, understanding the gravity of the situation.

"Also, an additional seventy to ninety cases were referred to the board of officers by the Internal Review Panel. The scandal keeps mushrooming. No one knows how many more cases will be referred by the time this is all said and done."

"Sounds like there will be hearings all summer," I said.

"Likely so, and right now I'm most concerned about Cadet Verr. Last Saturday, he had been assigned a twenty-four hour guard for protection because of the multiple death threats he'd received."

"That's a shame, sir. Do you know who specifically was threatening his life?" I asked, curiously.

"Apparently the threats were coming from the Honor Committee chairman himself as well as from other Honor Committee members. Cadet Verr's father had been contacted by an employee here who had overheard the threats. Then, Cadet Verr's father notified Secretary Hoffmann."

"Honor Committee members or not, no cadet should be allowed to get away with making death threats. The superintendent himself overturned Verr's honor conviction; that should be the end of it. You would think circumstances like this would encourage Secretary Hoffmann to approve an outside investigation," I said.

"You'd think. If the Honor System was functioning well, and you and I know it is not, then things like this wouldn't happen. We wouldn't have to worry about protecting cadets from one another. Why do we have silencing and threats from other cadets after a cadet has been judged innocent?" Lincoln asked, rhetorically. "It's very sad."

"I agree, that sounds awful," I said, sympathetically.

"Ringgold, do you remember in February when Cadet Wayne Adamson sent that memorandum to the Corps of Cadets about a second-chance clause?"

"For the Honor Code? Yes, I voted for it. It was about whether there should be other forms of punishment for an Honor Code violation other than expulsion?" I asked.

"Exactly. The clause would have taken into account other circumstances that led to the offense, like the cadet's previous record and the amount of thought that went into the violation. A cadet could be put on probation or suspension before the finale of getting kicked out. Well, fifty-five percent of the Corps of Cadets were in favor of it, but it didn't pass because it needed a two-thirds majority." He sighed again. Captain Lincoln was looking the worse for wear. "If that second-chance clause had passed, we likely wouldn't be in this situation."

"That may be true, sir, but there have been discrepancies in the Honor System my entire time here. Our plebe year when Ronald Schmidt, the Honor Captain, was allowed to graduate after being found guilty of an honor violation by his own Honor Committee, that was the first of a series of events that I did not understand. And James Conner got kicked out for lying because he did eighteen push-ups, but he reported he had done twenty. And Cadet Verr. And now ten percent or more of my class. Where does it end?" I asked.

Captain Lincoln nodded. "And what has come out recently is a letter that the current superintendent, General Berry, had received from his predecessor, General Knowlton. There had been major concerns about how the Honor System was being run then, in 1974, when General Berry took over. It was General Berry who ordered the study of the Honor System in October of that year. Colonel Harry Buckley, head of the Psychology and Leadership Department and General Berry's classmate, headed the study, made up of thirty Army officers and cadets, and the findings were reported last year. Have you read it?"

"I've read what has been publicized in the newspapers. Colonel Buckley's son, my classmate, was one of the original hundred and seventeen charged," I said.

"That's correct, but he was cleared," Lincoln continued. "Now, the study's findings simply showed that the Honor Code is idealistic and unrealistic. I am using the details of the study for my defense arguments. About eighty percent of the cadets believed that the honor violations were punished more severely at West Point than in the Army. The study also showed that sixty-two percent of the Corps believed some honor violations should be considered minor, and seventy percent agreed the code was not consistently enforced," Captain Lincoln read. "The study foreshadowed the situation we are in. It is most certainly time for change."

"That it is, sir, and it appears my future at West Point is once again in a precarious situation," I said matter-of-factly.

"When I asked you if you were sticking your toe in the water or if you were all in, you said you were all in. Now, we're all swimming with the sharks. It's not surprising to hear you've gotten bitten again. I will contact you as soon as anything comes across my desk about your reopened case," Captain Lincoln said, reassuringly.

"Thank you, sir," I said, stood up, saluted him and left.

CHAPTER 17
CBS EVENING NEWS
WITH WALTER CRONKITE

ON WEDNESDAY, THE COMMANDANT CALLED a meeting of our class after dinner to inform us that no one was to go on leave after the firsties graduated next week. We were to remain on campus for seven to ten days following graduation. Half of our class was supposed to stay for the new cadet training program anyway in preparation of the incoming plebes. The other half of our class was supposed to go on summer assignment for Army training. However, summer assignments had yet to be announced for our class. We were to remain because the Internal Review Panel was still deciding who was charged, and the Law professors were deciding who was needed as witnesses.

On Thursday, May 27, I sat in the back of the hostess office with Cadets Brian Fraser and Peter DaRold. We were waiting for the evening news when one of our classmates, Cadet Tom Lagarenne, a husky kid, came up to me.

"Hey, Ringgold, are you the one responsible for all these lists? You want to be noble? You should just resign," he said, hissing at me. "Or better yet, come by my room sometime and see what happens. I'll bust your face in."

"Anytime, jerkface, you ready right now, Lagarenne?" I said, not intimidated in the least. I was easily three years older than he was. Besides, I didn't think he would really do anything. He was upset but not really spoiling for a fight, as was evident when he walked away.

"Knock it off, Lagarenne," DaRold snapped.

I turned to Fraser and DaRold. "I've clearly pissed off a few people. I'm just telling it like it is, and these bastards can't see that."

"You don't have to explain to us, Ringgold. We know. Lagarenne's upset because he just got called before the IRP and they're going to charge him. He doesn't know what to do," Fraser said.

"Oh, wow, I didn't know," I said. "I always thought him a decent fellow."

"After the news airs tonight, those same guys will be just as pissed at me," DaRold said. "You've been sticking your neck out. It's time for me to do the same. Besides, I don't think I'm going to be here much longer."

"But you were found not guilty by your Honor Board," I said, not understanding.

"I know, but likely I'm going to get kicked out anyway because I just failed my Economics final," DaRold said, causally. "So I'm going to resign."

"Why?" I asked DaRold, looking stunned.

"I've been giving it a lot of thought. I'm going to transfer to another college and hopefully go to medical school. You know that my whole goal was to be a doctor. I think it's best if I switch gears and head in that direction."

I patted him on the shoulder, nodding. "Makes sense, Pete. Makes sense."

"But I'll do what I can while I'm here," DaRold said, smirking.

"By the way, did you hear that the panel has grown? Instead of one panel of five with three officers and two cadets, there will now be five panels of two officers and one cadet," he said, changing the subject. "I hope the panels are successful enough in changing the Honor System in order to save the rest of you guys because we're running out of time," DaRold said, discouraged.

"Yeah, I heard. I hope things get moving pretty soon, too, otherwise anybody's chance of coming through this is slim," Fraser said.

A few minutes later the news came on. Walter Cronkite reported, "The West Point cheating scandal may be much more widespread than was originally thought. Steve Young reports on the latest developments."

"The military academy still insists the cheating scandal is limited in scope, but it now told the entire junior class they will have to stay on post seven to ten days after graduation pending further investigation. This as several cadets submitted long lists of fellow cadets allegedly involved in cheating or toleration of cheating. One list alone reportedly runs to six hundred names, another to five hundred and one names, according to a third cadet, who submitted a list of his own."

I knew Steve Young reacted favorably to the things I told him, but they were so extraordinary that he had trouble believing them. He had asked me to find him somebody who could confirm my story. Young said that the other cadets wouldn't have to be filmed but would give him more of a feel for the situation I was in and up against. This is why DaRold was interviewed. I had suggested to Pete that he keep a low profile, since I knew firsthand the consequences of being in the public eye while still being a cadet, but he didn't listen. I hadn't known he was going to resign, but I could see that he felt he didn't have anything to lose, so he was going to try and help our classmates if he could.

On the screen, Steve Young turned to DaRold. "You submitted

a list of one hundred and eighty-five names. How many incidences do you have personal knowledge of?"

"I would say about, between seventy and eighty people is firsthand knowledge. The effect of this, to just add fuel to the fire, is to make it aware to the officials of the Academy that a change is necessary in the present Honor Code because obviously it is not working," DaRold said.

Steve Young continued, "DaRold admits he has cheated and now he could be expelled. The investigation was triggered by charges brought by Cadet Timothy Ringgold, who this week became the only cadet charged with toleration of cheating."

The camera turned to me. "Could it be that you or others have gotten together and said, 'look we'll just put forward so many names they can't possibly prosecute them all?'" Young asked.

"That's exactly what we're doing," I said on the screen. "We're trying, if we can, to show them what really goes on here. Either they're going to have to dismiss the great majority of my class or hopefully keep everyone. That's all we're after is to keep everyone."

"Officially the Army still insists that less than one hundred and fifty cadets are being investigated. If the cheating scandal has cascaded to anything approaching six hundred than the entire junior class may have to stay much longer than ten days after graduation day. Steve Young. CBS News. West Point."

DaRold and I looked at each other and grinned. We had just aired on national television. We were partners in crime now.

"I guess I better start carrying around a baseball bat for protection like you, Tim," DaRold said.

"Might not be a bad idea," I agreed.

As Friday, May 28, arrived, so began the first Officers Boards, despite our efforts to have them delayed. The first boards scheduled were for Cadets Kruse, Schnepf, Hardnett, and Porter.

Since DaRold and I had completed our exams, we decided to go to Captain Thomas W. Burt, the prosecutor, in our last attempt to spread our message.

"Sir, the last thing that we want to do is get anyone thrown out, but we had to make the Academy aware of the problem," DaRold said, taking the lead.

"I'm planning on going to the superintendent, so anything that you tell me will not be used to prosecute anyone. Would you mind if I record our conversation? It will just help give the superintendent the feel for the magnitude of the problem," Captain Burt said, encouraging us to speak.

I shrugged my shoulders, looked at DaRold and he nodded in agreement. "I have one hundred eighty-five names on my list of cadets who have violated the Honor Code," said DaRold.

"That's very good," Captain Burt replied. "I have long lists of names, collected from multiple cadets. If properly investigated, it could mean an additional three to six hundred cases of Officers Boards."

My eyes went big. This was exactly what we had been hoping for, blowing up the cheating scandal so much that the school had no choice but to look at the Honor System and hopefully keep everyone.

After DaRold spoke about his list of cadets, I stayed and made my own tape recording with Captain Burt of the violations that I had firsthand knowledge of. I repeated my allegations, but this time I included specifics as to the nature of the allegations, the approximate date of their occurrence, and witnesses that may have been present.

Later that day, Captain Gonzales saw me at the hearing and asked me to testify against Cadet Henry Schnepf based on my tape with Captain Burt.

I replied, "That tape was made with the understanding that it would not be used to testify against anyone."

"Well, I'm sorry, Cadet Ringgold, but I have a job to do, and I'm going to do it the best way I know how," Captain Gonzales retorted.

A few minutes later, I was called in as a witness against Cadet Schnepf. I hated every minute of it.

When I was asked to point out Cadet Schnepf, he winked at me to make me feel relaxed. He knew that I wasn't trying to screw anybody. Once they started questioning me about the EE304 homework assignment, I pleaded the Fifth, refusing to answer on the grounds that I may incriminate myself. I had no intention of testifying against any of my classmates.

Since they couldn't get a word out of me, they called Captain Burt to the stand. Captain Burt told them what I had told him in confidence, which was messed up because his testimony should have been considered hearsay. I was so angry that Captain Burt did not keep his word, especially since there was very little I could do about it. Cadet Schnepf had a good chance of being acquitted until Captain Burt testified. Now, I was left feeling hopeless because he was likely going to get kicked out.

Where was the honor in Captain Burt's actions? He could lie to us with impunity while at the same time prosecuting my classmates for collaborating on a take-home assignment? Was that what *honor* meant to Army officers? My classmates would get thrown out, and Captain Burt would probably get a promotion.

Cadet Porter took the stand in his own defense and got off. Cadet's Kruse's case got delayed, and in the end both Cadet Hardnett and Cadet Schnepf were found guilty.

CHAPTER 18
NEWSWEEK FAME

THE NEXT DAY, GINA WAS arriving by bus for an overnight visit. I was grateful for the distraction and seriously needed to do something fun away from the Academy.

I waited eagerly at the bus stop with a dozen other cows waiting for family and friends. I'd seen Gina a few months ago when she came up for our Ring Dance as my date, but it felt like years ago with how much had happened. It had been a fun weekend but had also been the first time Gina and I had seen each other since my plebe year when she'd come up in December for our formal winter dance. We'd kept in touch by writing letters the past few years. When she came up for our Ring Dance, we were not necessarily strangers, but hadn't officially started dating yet either. We hadn't kissed or even held hands that weekend. I was hoping this weekend would change that.

The bus pulled up just a few minutes behind schedule. As passengers exited the bus, I saw Gina and approached. I wasn't in uniform but wore jeans, a black T-shirt and Adidas sneakers. That morning, I had gotten my weekly haircut and hoped I still looked put together outside of a uniform.

"Hi, Gina," I said, reaching for her bag.

"Tim!" She smiled, leaned in, and hugged me. She had long, dark, wavy hair parted in the middle. She was wearing a flowery spring dress, skin-colored stockings, and black baby doll shoes. It didn't look like she used makeup except lip gloss. She wore a simple diamond stud necklace and no other jewelry. Her brown eyes were adorned with long eyelashes. She was naturally beautiful and didn't need all those accoutrements.

"We have a bit of a walk to the hotel if that is okay with you. There are buses that can take us, but I thought you would enjoy the walk," I said, smiling. It was nice to be in the company of someone not connected to the school.

"You're right, I'd like the walk, especially after sitting so long," she replied.

"How was your bus ride?" I asked, reaching for her bag.

"Totally fine, no problems. It's fun to take another trip up here. I don't leave West Chester often, as you know. School, teaching, and Christine keep me on a tight schedule."

"I bet. Doesn't Christine have a birthday coming up?"

"Yes. In August she will be two," she said.

"Did you bring any pictures?"

"I have a few in my wallet I can show you."

"And how is school going? Are you almost done?" Gina was a violinist and pianist, majoring in music education.

"Yes, almost. I can walk at graduation next month, but I still have a few courses to complete over the summer from the semester I took off for maternity leave," she said, smiling at me.

"That's fantastic. You should feel very proud to finish on time," I said, admiring her.

"I'm very proud of graduating on time and have no intention of returning to school, ever. I look forward to college being over. It's very demanding. I like private teaching, and I'm good at it, so I'm happy."

"I'm sure you are. Have you heard from Don lately?" I asked, curiously.

"Not much. I sent him some photos a few months ago. I feel it's my duty to keep him informed, but he's not involved."

"I see," I said, nodding.

"It's better that way. He and I were never the right fit," she said, matter-of-factly.

"I noticed that right from the beginning. When he'd spoken of his girlfriend, when we were at the prep school together, he described you very differently," I said.

"We didn't always see eye-to-eye. Christine looks a lot like his family, though, and not at all like me," she emphasized. "She's blonde!"

"You're kidding?"

"No. She doesn't look like she came from me." She laughed, clearly in love with being a mom despite the challenges.

"I don't know how you juggle going to school and being a single mom," I said. She was clearly a tough cookie.

"My mother is helping me raise her. They have a special bond. I couldn't do it without my mom."

We started to climb the hill to the historic Thayer Hotel, the hotel where alumni and visitors stayed. The hotel, with a mixture of stone layered on the bottom half and brick exterior on the top, resembled a castle with distinguished stone-covered twin entrances, adorned with the United States and Army flags.

"This is a very pretty hotel," she commented, as we walked into the expansive foyer with high ceilings, a candlelit chandelier, vast seating, and a gigantic fireplace.

"That it is and the only hotel on campus, so I'm glad you like it."

"After dropping my things off, do I get to see the inside of barracks this time?" she asked. "I always wanted to walk around and get a real feel for what it's like to be a cadet at such a prestigious academy."

"Sure, if you want. I'm not with my original company anymore, though," I said.

"Yes, I remember. You'll have to update me on the whole scandal. I haven't kept up with the news," she said.

"I'll tell you everything over dinner. There isn't much in Highland Falls, so I thought we would take a trip to the city, if that's okay with you."

It was a beautiful evening and the sun was still high in the sky. It often rained at West Point, but this particular day was sunny. It almost made me cheerful. As we walked toward the cadet area, I pointed out the academic buildings, the library, and Washington Hall where the Ring Dance had been held. Construction was always happening on campus to accommodate our expanding school. I pointed out Eisenhower Hall, which had been built during our plebe year.

As the name implies, Central Barracks was in the middle of the cadet area and surrounded by other barracks and academic buildings. We went through a sally port in Pershing Barracks to reach Central Area, where I spent many hours walking off penalty tours in previous years. It was quieter than normal because many cadets were on leave. As soon as exams were completed, a cadet could go on leave. Each regiment had different academic schedules and military responsibilities, but the whole Corps had to be back no later than Tuesday evening by Taps at 2200. Graduation was scheduled for Wednesday, June 2, and the graduation parade included the entire Corps of Cadets.

I opened the door to my room to find it unoccupied.

"That's my bunk, my wall locker, and my desk," I said, pointing.

"It is very spartan in here. Wooden desks, wooden chairs, and wooden bed frames. It's very simplistic," Gina observed.

"This school is anything but simple," I said.

"And why do you have a metronome on your desk?" she asked, eyeing me with suspicion.

"I like how they look."

"Are you a closet musician?" She still looked confused.

"Nope, but I do like to listen to classical music on my transistor radio while I study."

"But why would you need a metronome?"

"It helps me think," I said, shrugging.

"Okay," she said, walking around the room. "It must be nice to wear a uniform and not have to pick out your outfit every day," she said, looking at my wall locker. "I find it a chore to pick out outfits. Often if I find an outfit I like, I will buy it in three different colors," she said, completely serious.

"Yeah, well I have been living in uniforms for over seven years now. I'm accustomed to it," I said.

"Your bed does not look very comfortable."

"Well, it's better than sleeping in the woods, as I did as an infantry soldier. That seems like a lifetime ago," I said. "The bed works fine. We're too exhausted to think about it. Besides, sleep is just a privilege, not a right, or so we've been told. If you're ready, shall we head to the city? It will be nice to get away for a few hours and take my mind off all this West Point stuff."

"Sure, I'm ready."

As we approached the parking lot, I heard my name called. When I turned around, I saw Fraser approaching.

"Ringgold!" he said again, beaming. "My charges got dropped! I'm going to be okay!"

"Fraser, that's fantastic! That's great news, man," I said, giving him a hug and patting him on the back. Fraser had been saved, thank goodness. "Gina, this is one of my friends, Brian." Turning to Fraser, I introduced Gina.

"Nice to meet you, Gina," he said, holding out his hand for her to shake.

"I'm so happy for you, man. This is awesome," I said, feeling completely relieved. "Hey, we're heading into the city for dinner.

Can I catch you later?"

"Yeah, I need to call home anyway. I'll look for you tomorrow, okay?"

"Okay, great. We'll talk more then."

"Have a good night, you two!" he said and ran off, beaming with joy.

I was so grateful for the good news and felt a sense of relief while driving away from campus.

I took Gina to a nice Italian bistro, not too fancy or too casual. I knew she liked Italian food. We spent the evening talking. It was always easy to talk to her. I updated her on the whole scandal. Her eyes went wide when I told her about my television interviews and my confrontation with General Ulmer.

"I really had no idea how serious this scandal was. I barely watch TV, much less the news. You're really putting your career on the line, aren't you?" Gina asked in puzzlement.

"A lot of our careers are on the line, but it's really the Law professors, like Captain Lincoln and Captain Sharphorn, who are risking their careers. They wrote the secretary of the Army requesting an outside investigation. The superintendent wasn't too happy about the Law Department going outside the chain of command, but they didn't feel like they had a choice; the administration was not listening."

Gina listened intently, captivated by my storytelling.

"But don't get me wrong. I have a lot of respect for Colonel Rhyne, General Ulmer, and General Berry, even though we are on opposing sides. The problem is bigger than us. If we are to make West Point have integrity again, some serious changes need to be made."

As we left the restaurant, I turned to Gina and grabbed her hand.

"You don't mind if I hold your hand, do you?" I asked and looked at her.

"No, I don't mind," she said.

I wasn't eager to return to West Point and could use a breath of fresh air. As we walked, we passed shops and street vendors. Earlier in the week, I had seen the *Newsweek* article that included side-by-side pictures of Cadet Steven Verr, Captain Lincoln, and myself.

As we passed one street vendor, I scanned the magazines and grabbed the *Newsweek*. I flipped through the magazine, finding what I was looking for, and turned the article towards Gina. "Did they get a shot of my good side?" I said, teasing.

"Oh my goodness, Tim! That's you!" Her eyes went wide in surprise, and she grabbed the magazine from my hands.

"I told you I've been widely publicized," I said, grinning.

"Tim, I heard what you were saying, but to see your picture in *Newsweek*! Oh my goodness. I had no idea I was dating someone famous!" She said, aghast. Her jaw remained open as she scanned the article. Then she read it out loud. "At West Point, one cadet accused of cheating maintained that the Academy had purposely not expanded the investigation because it would just about collapse if it faced the summer and fall with half the seniors missing. Academy officials denied there had been a cover-up."

"Yep, that's the gist of it," I said.

There had to be some benefit to this publicity, even if it was simply to impress a girl, so I seized the moment. Putting my arm around her waist, I pulled her in for our first kiss.

CHAPTER 19
SHADES OF GRAY

THE MORNING OF MONDAY, MAY 31st, I was jerked suddenly awake by what I thought was gunfire. Panicked, I reached for the lamp on my desk and knocked it over with a crash on the concrete floor.

Disoriented, I rubbed my eyes and then suddenly jumped up as the feeling of cold soaked my shirt. "What the hell?" I exclaimed.

The lights flipped on, and hysterical laughter reverberated through the room, revealing Mamer holding an empty bucket. DaRold, Hunt, and Flanagan were in bathrobes with firecrackers in their hands and pockets.

"Happy birthday, jackass!" DaRold yelled as Hunt threw snapdragons on the floor, the cause of the loud popping.

I grabbed my pillow and swung it. Mamer quickly sidestepped it. It was grabbed by DaRold, who propelled it back at me.

"Happy twenty-third birthday, Ringgold!" DaRold said. "I wasn't going to miss my last opportunity to mess with you on your big day."

"Me neither," Mamer said. "This is our year together to remember."

"You're an old man now!" Flanagan said, laughing.

"Oh yeah?" I lunged for Flanagan and had him in a headlock in seconds. "You want to tell me again that I'm old?" The other guys were laughing.

"You guys aren't going to help me?" Flanagan said, his head bent to one side, still in my grip.

"Nah, I'm going to let Ringgold deal with you," Mamer said, with the brush of his hand.

"So lunch today, twelve hundred, at our normal table," DaRold said to everyone. Likely it had been him who had brought everyone together.

"Yeah, I'll be there," Mamer said.

"Me too," Hunt said.

"Yep, I'll be there too," Flanagan said as I let go of him.

As my friends left, my roommate, who I had known less than two weeks, eyed me suspiciously. I pulled my wet shirt off over my head and grabbed my bathrobe.

I was fully aware everything was changing: DaRold was resigning; Mamer was likely getting kicked out; but Flanagan and Hunt were fine, as far as I knew. Our pack was dispersing. In fact, I'd barely seen Hunt or Flanagan the past month or two since I had been originally charged. It was unbelievable to think how much had happened in such a short time.

Lunch was normally our time for the five of us to see each other, but I had recently missed so many lunches. Lunch was the one meal we were not required to attend. For breakfast and dinner, we had to form up with our individual companies and march to the Mess Hall. I had been using the lunch break to speak to reporters or call home.

★ ★ ★

"So, guys, I handed in my resignation letter today," DaRold said, starting off the conversation.

I shook my head. I knew that was what DaRold wanted to do, and I supported him, but I was also sad at his decision.

"That's crazy, man. I refuse to resign. If they want to kick me out, then they're going to have to escort my ass off campus," Mamer said.

"They haven't come up with a verdict yet?" I asked.

"No, the Board of Officers are weighing the evidence. Then the superintendent and the secretary of the Army have to review my case. I may find out today what the result is. The whole thing is just crazy. I'm still in shock over this bullshit. I would never have expected to get kicked out for an honor violation. Even as I sat there in my own Officers Board, part of me couldn't believe it was really happening," Mamer said, shaking his head.

"I'm so sorry, Moon Dog," I said.

"That's unreal, man. I'm so sorry," Hunt said, sincerely. "This scandal doesn't really make sense to me, but there is a process for this and it should end up in the right place, right?"

DaRold and I exchanged glances. "You think so, huh?" I asked.

"Well, yeah. We have a strong Honor System in place. I don't understand how so many cadets could be so wrong, though." Hunt continued.

"It's because the system is broken," DaRold said.

"I don't know, guys. I'm not sure if I believe that. West Point has been around for a hundred and seventy-four years. It's based on years of tradition. I've been dumbfounded by this whole scandal. We've been trained to understand that no collaboration means that *no* discussion of the assignment with other cadets is allowed," Hunt said.

"Well I didn't think we were cheating, Hunt," Mamer said. "I was used to working together."

"I'm just grateful I haven't been pulled into this mess, no offense, Mamer. Maybe the assignment was presented in an unclear manner to some? There must have been some confusion on that point; it couldn't have been a blatant disregard for the *no collaboration rule*. Not on such a broad scale. Do you think it's happening because it's so competitive here? I mean, our class standing is everything—choice of branch and first assignment. An engineer in Germany or a grunt at Benning." Hunt pointed out.

"Intense competition can bring out the best or worst in people," DaRold reflected.

"I think it would have been easier if, after the problem was discovered, that the dean or the superintendent came up with an alternative solution, like submitting another assignment," I said.

"What would that say to the cadets? We're soft on cheating?" Hunt asked.

"Do you think I am a cheater, Hunt?" Mamer asked, astounded.

"No, I didn't say you were. I really don't know who is and who isn't. The reality is only known by the individuals themselves. Something obviously went very wrong," Hunt said.

"If I do get kicked out, I still have to serve as an enlisted man. It will be starting my career over," Mamer said, defeated.

"That's why we're fighting for an outside investigation. Our classmates' careers are being ruined because of one take-home assignment. It is unjust. Our classmates are good people, good cadets. Who goes to a school like West Point?" I asked, rhetorically. "It is the high school valedictorians, class presidents, accomplished athletes, honor students, or Eagle Scouts like you, Hunt. We are the cream of the crop. Because of that, we should expect exceptional behavior, but we shouldn't expect perfection. The public also thinks we're supermen. We're not. We're really no different from anyone else."

I didn't mean to lecture, but I didn't know if Hunt got it. I could feel the tension between my friends, reflective of the tension throughout the Corps of Cadets. We were bonded because of the past three years, our demanding experiences as cadets together, but the scandal was testing all the relationships. I wondered if Hunt thought the Academy was going to fix itself or if the Honor System was fine the way it was?

"Do you think the electrical engineering faculty is at fault somehow?" Hunt said. "It was a challenging assignment. I barely passed it. Maybe the coursework will be taught better in the future," he suggested.

"The faculty were at fault because they changed the rules abruptly. We had been collaborating for a semester and a half. Most of us had become dependent on each other to help each other understand electrical engineering," Mamer said.

"I've tried to avoid the whole mess. I just want to work hard in my classes and keep a low profile," Hunt repeated. He was not alone in feeling that way; a lot of the guys did not want to touch the *third rail* at West Point because it posed a risk to them as well.

"Well, I am grateful you and Flanagan have not been charged," DaRold said, genuinely. "I'm also glad I haven't had to report you for an Honor Code violation," he said, winking at Hunt.

"Me too. It would've sucked to turn in a friend," I said, teasing. The toleration part of the clause, which was personally affecting me, was also the least followed. Cadets did not want to turn in their friends. The toleration clause made us feel like we are spying on our classmates. In truth, I was grateful Hunt and Flanagan were safe—for now at least. "But you do see how easily any of us could be pulled into the scandal? How your words could be turned around to prosecute you, if you were called to testify for one of our classmates? Captain Lincoln told me that the panel has reported seventy to ninety new cases."

Flanagan looked up at me when I said that. He looked startled but didn't say anything. I could see on his face, though, that it was filled with worry. On one level, every classmate was worried about being pulled into the scandal, so the common goal was to keep a low profile and get through the year without being charged. It seemed like Flanagan's fear was genuine.

"Did you hear about that cadet who showed up to court, thinking he was there as a witness, but was actually present for his own Officers Board? They didn't even give him time to prepare. They just put him on the spot, right then and there, in his own Officers Board!" Mamer shared.

"That's insane," DaRold said, shaking his head.

"I sure hope I don't get called in as a witness," Hunt said. "It's huge that the cadets in the Honor Committee have the power to determine another cadet's future. That would be hard to handle. Thankfully, the Internal Review Panel is overseeing the Officers Boards now."

I nodded in agreement, but I wasn't as optimistic as Hunt.

After lunch, I walked over to the library to read the newspaper. I was pleased with one report, in *The Times Herald-Record*, dated May 27.

> James Malcolm, class of 1977 president, said he believes there is a "good chance" the honor system will undergo major changes next year because his classmates were beginning to consider the system "from more of a legal aspect. They seem to feel that maybe honor isn't such a black and white thing; maybe there are shades of gray."

I agreed; there were shades of gray. Hopefully, at the very least, some changes would be made next year in the Honor System, but it sounded like it would be too late to save my classmates, including Moon Dog.

Malcolm continued, "I think it (the code) should be dealt with as a learning tool. You can't expect people to come in here snow white, but you can expect a certain level of integrity after four years here and in class."

The News of the Highlands, dated May 27, stated: "The implication of cheating at the USMA, Ulmer said, is mainly that the selection, indoctrination, and education processes at the Academy are imperfect."

I appreciated that statement by the commandant. It was less of a statement about who were the good guys versus the bad guys. The whole scandal was more complex than that. Let's not save the reputation of the Academy by labeling the accused cheaters as the disease, the tumor that needs to be cut out in order to save the rest of the body. Instead, let's acknowledge there is a reason the disease showed up in the first place.

In a few different articles, it reported about Congressman Downey being the first congressman to investigate the scandal. Downey had confirmed that "at least a quarter of the junior class cheated," reported in the *Baton Rouge Advocate*, May 28, article. A quarter was over two hundred cadets. One cadet was quoted as saying: "the Academy has been trying to cover up the extent of cheating for fear of the devastating psychological and practical consequences of mass expulsion."

I was pleased how well publicized the scandal was and the fact more cadets were coming forward. West Point was certainly under a bright spotlight of critique. One article, "West Point's Honor Code Isn't Working," in *Newsday*, on May 28 stated:

A thorough public discussion of the training methods employed at the military academies couldn't possibly hurt cadet morale any more than selective and cruel enforcement of the Honor Code. Military conditioning is one thing; promoting coverups and brutality is something entirely different. Surely a way can be found to have one without the other.

"Selective and cruel enforcement of the Honor Code," I repeated to myself. I was feeling more hopeful that all this publicity would lead to an outside investigation. Until the investigation was a guarantee, though, I would play my part.

JUNE 1976

CHAPTER 20
JUNE WEEK

THE MORNING OF TUESDAY, JUNE 1, I was called into Colonel Rhyne's office.

"Cadet Ringgold, I have completed the investigation of your allegation against Cadet Adamson."

I stood there slightly surprised. I was under the assumption that the Honor Committee had dismissed my allegation against Cadet Adamson, chairman of the Honor Committee, and Cadet Irwin, vice chairman of the Honor Committee. I remained silent, interested in what the deputy commandant had to say, but was suspicious that anything would actually happen to Cadet Adamson; he was graduating tomorrow.

"The facts have been concluded that indeed Cadet Adamson had made the statement that you were not under investigation," Col. Rhyne stated.

I sighed deeply.

"However, he had not committed an honor violation. Rather, I believe it had been a poor choice of words," Colonel Rhyne explained.

I resisted rolling my eyes. It seemed to me that any lie would be a *poor choice of words*.

"Let me clarify the discrepancy. The cadet who had originally reported you to the Honor Committee following the meeting with the under secretary, had not in fact reported you for an honor violation, but thought you might need some counseling concerning your statements."

"Counseling, sir? What does that mean?" I asked, knowing full well this conversation was going nowhere, but was happy to let Colonel Rhyne dig his hole deeper.

Colonel Rhyne picked up a piece of paper from his desk and read. "The fact sheet prepared by the United States Military Academy and released by the Department of the Army to Senator Jacob Javits, the Military Academy unequivocally maintains that one of Cadet Ringgold's classmates who attended the conference, interpreted Cadet Ringgold's comments that he personally had knowledge of specific cadets who had cheated on the EE304 home study problem but had not reported them to the Cadet Honor Committee," he said, pausing before continuing. "As such, the classmate reported to his company honor representative the statement made during the meeting. Then, on April 20, 1976, that company honor representative in turn reported the possible violation to the chairman of the Cadet Honor Committee." He paused, putting the paper down. "As such, the Academy now maintains that your original allegation is fact."

I tried to process what he had just said. First, my classmate hadn't reported me for an honor violation, thus Cadet Adamson just used "a poor choice of words." Then the fact sheet stated that my classmate reported me to his company's honor representative, contradicting that my classmate hadn't reported me for an honor violation. "And who was this classmate that originally reported or didn't report me for an honor violation?" I asked, trying not to sound sarcastic.

Colonel Rhyne cleared his throat and straightened his glasses. "Well, that of course, is confidential."

"Of course, sir," I nodded, not understanding the point of this meeting whatsoever. What was the point of arguing, though? The truth was I had a lot of respect for Colonel Rhyne. I felt he was getting the short end of the stick, with having to delay his command of an armor brigade to oversee what was quickly becoming an honor debacle. In order for a colonel in the Army to be promoted to a general, he has to command a brigade. By postponing his opportunity to command, being ordered to stay at West Point to serve as the special assistant to the commandant for honor matters, he was likely jeopardizing his career. I couldn't help but feel sympathy for the man. I just wished he would see the big picture: that West Point's cheating scandal was a reflection that the Academy had failed the cadets, not that the cadets had failed the Academy.

There was really nothing else for me to say. "Colonel Rhyne, thank you for completing the investigation and letting me know of its findings, sir," I said.

"Cadet Ringgold, earlier I tried to give you some advice, and you didn't hear me," Colonel Rhyne said. I remained at attention. "The Honor Code is the arch stone of the Academy. It is all pervasive. It is not a code for four years within these granite walls, but for the rest of your career. I suggest you adopt this code as a way of life."

"Yes, sir. Thank you, I understand, sir," I said, saluted him, did an about-face and walked out. Twice he'd offered advice and both times the message was *Shut up, or else*....

June week was a time of reunion as the Academy grounds were swarming with alumni visiting and reliving their past glories as a cadet. The cheating scandal was a storm cloud that hovered over the Academy. Despite the cloud, the alumni spoke positively about the Honor Code and System, showing support of their beloved school.

My whole class was still present on post for at least the next week or so. DaRold chose to stay until our class was dismissed for summer assignments. Mamer received a verdict of guilty. This verdict was not completely unexpected, but was a shock to him, nevertheless. He felt, like others that were accused, that he was being prosecuted for violations that were commonly overlooked.

I certainly felt sad for him, but this was why Captain Lincoln, DaRold, and I had gone public. Fortunately, parents and friends of those found guilty started to come forward and speak to the media about the Academy covering up the real extent of the cheating. Convicting and expelling 5 or 10 percent while ignoring the 40, 50, or 100 percent was not reassuring to parents who had sent their sons to West Point.

The results of the scandal were being felt widespread across America; taxpayers were feeling like the Academy was throwing out men who had been a huge financial investment. It was reported by the US Government General Accounting Office that each cadet had been over an $80,000 investment, with each graduate having cost $100,000. Saying that, if fifty cadets were kicked out, that totaled a four-million-dollar loss.

I was once again faced with the idealism presented when I read the *Sports Television Magazine* article, "The Long Grey Line: Is Its Honor Tarnished?"

> Ulmer defended the need for a strict Honor Code against lying, cheating, and stealing, saying, "If a cadet can withstand the pressures of the moment and resist lying at all cost, it indicates he is a solid individual who will be a reliable leader.

The question we are trying to answer of each cadet is, is he worthy of trust even when many lives are at stake?"

His argument was strong, but not realistic. We shared his vision but knew all too well that his West Point and our West Point were completely different places. We wanted his place but were given something entirely different and unworkable.

In *The Times Herald Record*, the article "Pre-trial Publicity Hangs up First of Cheating Trials:

> Brig. Gen. Walter F. Ulmer was quoted by the *New York Daily News* in its Friday afternoon edition saying that unless "extra" circumstances came out during the boards, the 48 would be expelled. One defense attorney said he "felt the statement was 'proof' that the board members could be prejudiced against his client."

Graduation week brings nostalgic alumni, extra parades, twenty-one-gun salutes, a graduation ceremony and the commissioning ceremonies. I had heard nothing of my case in reference to the commandant reopening it. Since our entire class was required to stay seven to ten days after graduation, my classmates had yet to receive their summer assignments.

Many of the alumni visiting West Point were high-ranking officers, including General William C. Westmoreland, the guest speaker on Tuesday, June 1, the day before the graduation for the class of 1976. Westmoreland had been the long-time commander in Vietnam, 1964–1968, and former Army chief of staff, 1968–1972, as well as a former superintendent of West Point, 1960–1963. The retired general looked distinguished with his salt and pepper hair and tanned skin. He still fit into his uniform and stood straight and tall. We'd heard the story that President Johnson chose Westmoreland to command in Vietnam because he looked and sounded like a general. He certainly did.

"Good afternoon, cadets, administration, alumni, guests and members of the graduating class of 1976. It is a gorgeous day here at Trophy Point overlooking the Hudson River. I revere this place. Hearing the "Song of the Sandre Meuse," I felt such pride marching across the Plain with my class of 1936. It honestly does not feel like forty years have passed since I was a cadet.

"One of the cornerstones of my beloved Academy is its Honor Code. We all know West Point has been under heavy cannon fire lately with the substantial amount of cadets accused of cheating. Fear not, the Academy will survive this crisis as it has past crises. These proceedings should be reassuring to the American people that there is a system and the system is working!

"The Code serves a purpose, to weed out the weak from the strong. The Honor Code, originally founded by Colonel Sylvanus Thayer, the superintendent from 1817 to 1833, was based on the *gentleman's code* of the Army officer. Originally, lying was the only transgression which led to dismissal. Over the years, stealing, cheating, and tolerating were added to the code. The Merchant Marines, the Coast Guard Academy and the Naval Academy do not have the toleration clause. The only other service academy to have the toleration clause is the Air Force.

"West Point's standards are high for a reason because we train men to lead others under the most extreme and dangerous conditions. The Army is for the strong!" he said, pumping his fist in the air.

"I am proud that West Point is weeding out the weak, and those accused of cheating will be separated from our beloved school," he said with finality. "The national interest demands that the officer corps be comprised of men who are honest in word and deed. The vehicle that has been successfully used over the years has been the West Point Honor Code, administered by the cadets' honor system. The code is immutable; the system has required some modification from time to time. Let's have a little idealism. That's the side I'm on.

"Tomorrow the class of 1976 graduates. As part of the West Point alumni, they are part of the strong. They have not only survived the high demands of West Point but have thrived under pressure. Their service is welcome. I would feel confident to serve alongside each and every one of them.

"The nation needs West Point leadership. As always, may we honor what West Point has taught us. May we live by what West Point stands by: Duty, Honor, Country."

At the conclusion of his speech, the glee club sang "The Long Gray Line of Us Stretches Through the Years of a Century Told."

After the ceremony, DaRold, Mamer, and I left campus and went out to dinner at the local pub in Highland Falls.

"I don't want this to feel like my last supper," Mamer said, attempting a joke.

I reached over and clasped his shoulder. "You may have lost the battle, but you haven't lost the war," I said, encouragingly.

"But I'm getting kicked out, so I *have* lost the war," Mamer said, hopelessly.

"I know, Mamer, but don't let it defeat your self-worth. You're strong and healthy. Your life is by no means over, just your time at West Point. You're going to have to find another dream is all," I said.

"Yeah, after my two years of enlistment," Mamer said, looking deflated. "With just one year left before we graduated. It is unreal."

"Well, I'm going to take some time off and figure out where I want to go next," DaRold said. "My family hasn't spoken to me since I went public, so I need to figure out things on my own, like how I'm going to pay for medical school," he said, shrugging his shoulders.

"You'll figure it out, man. I'm happy for you, DaRold. You know who you want to be, and you're going to make it happen. But I'm going to miss you both," I said sincerely. "West Point is not going to be the same without you."

"You, Hunt, and Flanagan will just have to march in step without us. I expect there will be some changes in the Honor System next year. You'll have to keep us posted on what happens," DaRold said.

"Well, so far, I did read about one possible change. When a cadet is accused, he will have a lawyer when he goes in front of his Honor Board instead of standing alone," I shared.

"Excellent. I don't know why that hadn't been done before," DaRold said, aghast. "You can't have a true due process without representation. It's ridiculous."

"Exactly. I'm disgusted with the whole matter too," I said.

"So what did you think about good ol' Westy's speech?" DaRold asked.

"I'm not a fan," I said, shaking my head.

"Oh yeah, why not, Ringgold? You didn't like the *there is a system and the system is working* part?"

"Correct. Did not like that. William Childs Westmoreland is a hypocrite. He described the scandal as weeding out the weak. Here we have a large percentage of our classmates getting kicked out for collaborating on a *homework assignment*. The general spent four years commanding American troops in Vietnam, from '64 to '68, and he continued to lie to the extent of blatant cover-ups by inflating our success in Vietnam. He called for more and more troops, which led to a couple million men being sent to Vietnam, including my two older brothers. His use of power was corrupt and cost us as a nation. He painted the picture that we were winning the war, which you know was false, just because we had less casualties. So, *he* can lie to the American public to the detriment of thousands of American lives, but fuck the cadets who collaborated on a homework assignment? That's bullshit."

"How do you know all that, Ringgold?" Mamer asked.

"I read a lot. You'll see, one day, good ol' Westy will be viewed as the main cause for why we lost the war in Vietnam."

"That's interesting, Ringgold. Westmoreland has so many admirers. I didn't appreciate his speech, though, either. All the while Officers Boards were taking place next door. *We just need to cut out the disease to save the Academy* . . . bullshit."

"Yup," I said. "Exactly. So what are we drinking boys?"

CHAPTER 21
GRADUATION DAY

WEDNESDAY, JUNE 2, WAS THE class of 1976's graduation day. Firsties were always eager to graduate, but this year the eagerness was multiplied. With details about the scandal being printed daily in the newspapers, the class of 1976 was eager to get out and away from all the publicity. They did not want to be associated with the scandal or the breakdown of the Honor System. They were also disappointed by the honor controversy which had taken the spotlight off of them during what should have been their week of celebrations and praise.

Furthermore, it was the last year for an all-male academy. One hundred and nineteen women were scheduled to enter West Point as plebes next month for summer initiation and training called Beast Barracks.

The firsties sat in the center of Michie Stadium under gray skies as the secretary of the Army, the Honorable Martin R. Hoffmann was called to the podium as the keynote speaker to address the 835 graduates. Hoffmann had a kind smile and a full head of dark hair. He wore a light gray suit with a red tie and looked very comfortable addressing the crowd. Over 10,000 spectators, proud parents, and friends stood, getting drenched, while a rainstorm passed overhead.

On behalf of the US Army, I am both gratified and privileged to welcome you, the members of this bicentennial class of 1976, to your leadership roles in our proud institution, and indeed to the Armed Forces of the United States. It is a joyous day and I congratulate you heartily on your completion of the basic qualifications for one of the nation's most honorable professions.

It is a happy day for the Army as well. This yearly celebration of renewal of the Army by the graduates of this cornerstone institution is real. We count on the infusion of youth, enthusiasm, high standards, imagination, and humor which you represent, and which you bring to the Army.

You have a right to feel exhilarated by today's events. You have a right to anticipate keenly the beginning of a career to which you have made a most solemn commitment and for which you have worked so hard in preparation. To lead the nation's youth, to command its soldiers, and to deserve the respect it takes to do so is at once among your greatest challenges and the highest honors the nation can bestow.

You have already won your commissions; your diplomas are close at hand. Your education, of course, is far from over. As you face the challenges of adventure, duty, danger, and leadership, the examinations will continue. Some will test all your faculties; all will test your values and your perceptions.

The choices that present themselves will never seem clear-cut; answers will never be easy. You are leaving an institution marked by rules and regulations, by a certain sternness, simplicity, and dedication to traditional values. You are about to enter a world of complexity, contradiction, and uncertainty.

We tend to reflect on our beginnings, and indeed much of our past, as simpler times when choices and objectives were clearer than in the present. The concentrating perspective of hindsight; the ability to review past situations and decisions in the light of events and consequences that followed ... all tend to argue that earlier times were less complex.

The corrosive events of recent years provide some warrant for skepticism, for a lapse of confidence in our system of government, and even for a questioning of the basic strengths of our society. It is understandable if many among us should wonder how to proceed from here.

It is remarkable how often in the past, when faced with comparable trials and doubts, the nation has found in the Army the ideals, inspiration, and leadership it seeks. It is equally remarkable how often it has found them, not only in such commanding figures as Washington, Marshall, and Eisenhower, but also in the dedication and integrity of many thousands of soldiers—citizen and professional—who have compiled an enviable record of the nation's trust upheld.

This trust is neither surprising nor suspect. It has survived well because the Army has been a symbol of the nation at its best. Despite the desperate winter of 1777, the Army held itself intact at Valley Forge. Despite the tragedy of civil war, the Army fought with bravery and dedication that transcended the deep divisions in the nation and its people. Despite the controversies and recriminations of the past decade, the Army stood its ground and did its duty in Vietnam. Whatever the surrounding circumstances, this old institution has faithfully performed its mission.

The nation may be at peace and yet we of the defense establishment must gird ourselves in readiness for the contingency of war. The bugles may be silent, but day in, day out, the Army must be ready, on call. Wherever its far-flung units are found, the Army must be prepared to deploy, and, if necessary, fight, with little or no warning.

The United States has not been too proud to sacrifice and even to fight in the past. Now, as in the past, its safety depends on the dedication and confidence of the individual soldiers and their leaders, and the measure and depth in which they embody the basic trust implied by those three words: duty—honor—country.

There has been an erosion of trust—in our institutions, in our ability to hold to basic values, and even in our sense of purpose as a nation. The Army can provide—it must provide—an example of discipline, openness, and honor to which the public can repair. That it can do so is in no small measure due to the steadfast example and teaching of West Point.

Recent events have combined to pose questions relating to the foundations of this institution, which has been the conscience of the Army. I have no need to come before you and defend the Code of Honor—it is timeless. Indeed, I dare say the present public debate, in its critical appearances and often biting commentary, is born of the sincere hope that these principles will endure in a troubled time.

Those who founded the Military Academy one hundred and seventy-four years ago were not striving to create some small and separate elite. They were seeking to institutionalize the conscience of the Army—an Army tested in the crucible of the War of Revolution. They sought an enduring source of professionalism, of lasting standards of leadership. Those needs are no less now than they were in 1802. This institution, however small, must continue in these troublesome times to keep the flame of conscience alive. If West Point does not do it, where else will it be done?

It would be out of place to explore with you here the merits of the Honor System as it is presently constituted. Its immediate proceedings are in mid-passage and the process is one of which I myself may ultimately be a part. It is essentially your system, men of the Corps, finding its roots and substance in the Corps. It is a living system that adapts to the need for change as wisdom, experience, and judgment so dictate.

But as you leave the reinforcing routine of West Point and as the supporting immediateness of the Corps fades behind you, do not overlook the practicality and individuality of what you have done, and learned, and grown to be here. The practical test of leadership is to have the courage, the discipline, the wit and the faith to inspire in others and in the Army those basic ideals of duty, honor, country. Do not mistake it: those ideals to which you have aspired while here are the ideals to which the Army has aspired over the years, and to which it aspires today.

I ask that you bring your highest expectations and retain them intact, bringing with them strength and patience to fuse them with the standards you find there. In thus elevating our common vision for the Army and the nation, we can together assure fulfillment of this historic, honorable and most sacred trust.

At the conclusion of Hoffmann's speech, each member of the class of 1976, distinguishably dressed in swallow-tail gray tops and starched white cotton trousers, filed up. They all had their swords strapped to their waists with white chest bands connected at mid-point with a large gold buckle. They were lined up in order of their academic class standing. As their names were individually called, each firstie saluted Lieutenant General Sidney Berry and received his diploma scrolled up and tied with a bow.

When Cadet Wayne Adamson walked across the stage, there was a momentary silence until the parents of the graduating class and many of his classmates stood to honor him. While Adamson received a standing ovation, many cadets from the under classes booed and hissed.

The *class goat* was the last cadet who graduated and was met with a loud cheer from the crowd. Cadet Jesse F. Owen received his paper bag full of money, a tradition where the last graduating senior received a dollar from each of the cadets who graduated above him.

At the conclusion of the ceremony, with the firsties back in their seats, at the command of "class of 1976, *dismissed,*" they jumped up and threw their dress white hats into the air with loud cheers of joy. *We made it!* was the common thought throughout the graduating class. Following the ceremony, a group of children ran onto the field to retrieve the hats to take home as souvenirs.

That evening when I returned to the barracks, it was eerily quiet. There was a radio playing off in the distance and chatter throughout the stone building, but the contrast of life from when school was in session was startling. The firsties had graduated, packed up, and left with undue speed. The yearlings and the plebes had also left for their summer assignments. It was our class, the class of 1977, that was required to stay for the continued Officers Boards. I felt the depressive feelings of staying.

When I arrived at my room, there was a note for me from Mr. Sidney Siller.

> Cadet Ringgold-
> Judge Richard Owen has denied your request for a temporary restraining order to stop the Officers Boards. He has set a hearing for next Wednesday, June 9.
> —Sidney Siller

CHAPTER 22
FATHER THOMAS CURLEY

THE NEXT DAY, THURSDAY, I read in *The New York Times* that Secretary Hoffmann was considering a review of the Honor System, but he wanted to keep it "within the military establishment." Hoffmann was suggesting that the outside investigation would be completed by the Pentagon's Civilian Committee on Excellence in Education, "a three-year-old committee of two high-ranking Defense Department officials and the secretaries of the three military services." It was essentially a civilian committee associated with the Defense Department. This sounded hopeful until I read that "the review would not begin before the completion of the current cases."

I sighed. The secretary of the Army wanted to wait until my classmates were kicked out before reviewing the Honor System, which wasn't good enough.

On Friday, June 4, thirty-six more names were sent to the superintendent by the Internal Review Panel. The second Officers Boards failed to reach a verdict on six cadets brought before them.

In the *Times Herald-Record* on the same day, an article

titled "Rep Demands West Point Academic Probe" discussed two reports that Congressman Thomas J. Downey released, the first being his observations and the second detailing his recommendations, which was scheduled to be released on June 14. It had only been a week and a half since I spoke to Fred Kass, Downey's assistant, and much had transpired. I had felt, though, that Fred Kass had been interested in the truth, and it appeared now that Congressman Downey was being a pioneer in Congress, advocating a congressional review of West Point's Honor System.

> The New York lawmaker was sharply critical of Army Secretary Martin Hoffmann's suggesting Wednesday that the West Point honor system be reviewed by the Pentagon's committee on excellence in education. He said that a committee . . . is too restricted in its membership and could not supply fresh ideas or outside perceptions of the problem. A thorough, objective group, such as the Congress, is the only way to resolve the structural problems of the Academy.

I was in agreement with Congressman Downey and very much desired to meet him face to face.

On Saturday, I was called in to testify against six cadets from Company E-1, my new company, who were on trial at an Officers Board. I was being called to testify because of my conversation with Captain Burt. I refused to answer any questions on the grounds that it may incriminate me, as before, to avoid giving testimony about my classmates. The system was broken; they needed to see that I wasn't going to help them convict my classmates. During the hearing, I was ordered to testify in violation of my rights under the Fifth Amendment of the Federal Constitution and Article 31 of the Uniform Code of Military Justice. I was instructed that if I refused to testify, I would be criminally charged under Article

92 of the UCMJ for disobedience of an order which could mean up to two years imprisonment and a bad conduct discharge. The president of the board ordered me to testify. This was probably the single most disgusting thing that I had ever had to do. I was so angry they made me testify because of what I had told Captain Burt "in confidence."

★ ★ ★

Not knowing what to do with my anger and feeling heavily discouraged, I walked up the hill to the Catholic chapel.

Gratefully, I found Reverend Thomas Curley in his office.

I knocked gently. "Father, may I have a word?"

"Absolutely, come on in, Cadet Ringgold."

"Father, I am just . . . I don't know . . ." I said, slumping into the seat in front of his desk.

"I continue to see your name in the paper. You, Verr, and Captain Lincoln have generated a lot of publicity."

"That we have, sir, but our efforts to get an outside investigation of the Honor System seem to fall on deaf ears."

"You're not alone in your mission. I, too, have complained to General Berry about the failure of Academy brass to protect the confidential nature of my chaplain's office. Without sharing the names of the cadets who have spoken to me in confidence, I can tell you that there are many others that share your views but are too scared to speak out. It most certainly seems that the system is broken."

I looked at him, realizing that he did in fact understand the complexity of the situation.

"I'm feeling hopeless that our efforts will be in vain," I said.

"It's understandable to feel that way. This institution has almost two hundred years of tradition. Your efforts are heroic, and I commend you for speaking the truth and going public."

I cringed at the description of being heroic. I certainly didn't feel like a hero. "Thank you, Father. I'm playing a role that I feel I must play. I see the injustice and couldn't remain silent but speaking truthfully has gotten me into this mess. I'm so far in the trenches now that there is no way to retreat, so I must see this mission through."

"You're certainly in a vulnerable position, one that is jeopardizing your own future at West Point," he said.

I nodded. "General Ulmer has announced plans to reopen my case, and I'm apparently being retried for the same crime twice. I wonder if I'll be invited to the hearing this time?" I said, sarcastically.

"Double jeopardy," Father Curley said and nodded. "That does seem to happen here a lot, one of the unjust parts of the Honor System."

"Are you aware that three other cadets and I are suing the United States government on behalf of our class?"

"I did hear something of the sort. Has the hearing taken place yet?"

"Well, our original request for a temporary restraining order to stop the Officers Boards has been denied, but the hearing is set for next Wednesday. We filed in district court in Manhattan with the firm Siller & Galian. Sidney Siller is our pro bono attorney. He is the president of the New York Criminal and Civil Court Bar Association. After the West Point Cheating scandal in '51, the same association recommended the reinstatement of the ninety cadets who'd been kicked out."

"I see, a little *déjà vu*, very smart," Father Curley said, listening intently. "And what do you hope to accomplish in court?"

"We're asking to ban the Honor Code and to stop all Officers Boards. We tried to delay them from starting, but now we're trying to stop them all together. The argument is that the Honor System is unconstitutional in its selective application. We really don't expect much from the court. It's just another way of applying pressure to the Academy in hope of getting an outside investigation."

"You are David fighting the giant Goliath, Cadet Ringgold." He smiled gently at me.

"It certainly feels that way." I sighed. "We're trying anything at this point. The Army doesn't want to play ball with us, so we're taking it out of their court. How naive are we, Father, to be doing this?"

"Well, Tim, what's your endgame?" he asked.

"To stop the Officers Boards," I repeated, "to reinstate all the cadets found guilty, and then ideally to change the Honor System."

He nodded. "Well," he sighed. "Your path is not a simple one, and your future is not clear. If you succeed, however, you'll not only be helping hundreds of your classmates, but thousands of future cadets. Because of that, I think it is very honorable and very risky to try."

"It does seem bigger than just my classmates, Father. West Point needs to have integrity again. Vietnam ruined the Army, and West Point trains the Army leaders. As the most powerful military force in the world, we need to make West Point honest again, so we can make the Army strong again."

"This scandal does seem to be an intense period of introspection for the cadets and the administration alike. I've been personally trying to understand why this scandal has happened. What's the spiritual meaning behind it all? It appears that self-reflection is needed by all of us. Maybe the wounding caused by the devastating losses in Vietnam triggered a need to protect the image of West Point to the detriment of its cadets," Father Curley said.

"I completely think so. My classmates are the scapegoats, representing what is shameful and bad about the institution in order to make the rest of the school look good. Right now, we're being directed to say that everything is fine, that recent investigations prove that the honor system is fair and that it is working, but we know that's not the case. West Point taught us to always tell the truth when I first came, but things are different now. You can't tell the truth anymore without consequences. If you speak truthfully, you get thrown out, so cadets have to lie in order to survive, and the biggest lie being told is that everything is perfect. It is not so. The way honor is defined and applied here insures nearly everyone is guilty of an honor violation at some point in their time as a cadet," I said.

He nodded in understanding. "I, too, son, have been speaking up. I could no longer remain silent and have suffered alongside you because of it. As you know, I frequently take meals with the accused cadets in the mess hall. Mr. Liguori, who's in charge there, has always welcomed me with warmth and respect; he knows what I'm about. Last week, though, he approached me shyly, saying he was very embarrassed, but that the major, his boss, told him I could not eat after today in the mess hall without a meal ticket. I was stunned. The major and I had always been cordial, and we both sat on the commandant's staff. Where did this come from? I told Mr. Liguori to relate to the major that General Ulmer was holding my meal tickets, and he should ask Ulmer for them."

"And you feel that General Ulmer supports your interaction with the accused?" I asked.

"Absolutely. In my heart, I know Ulmer would never direct me not to be with your classmates—never! This is where he wants his chaplain. That's how we operate together. He understands what I'm about and has never uttered a word of criticism to me."

"I'm so glad to hear that, Father," I said.

"But just so you understand, because of choosing to speak up, there has been a split within the Catholic community here. Some parishioners are angry with me, similar to the anger you have faced within your class for speaking up. They don't like the good name of West Point to be tarnished, none of us do, but there are those who see the bigger picture," he said, smiling in encouragement. Father Curley was a young priest, thirty-two years old. I appreciated his support and willingness to speak out against the injustices.

We sat in silence for a few moments.

"Tim, don't lose heart. I think that's the most important lesson you're being faced with right now. Remember why you love West Point. Remember why you wanted to be a cadet, an Army officer. Remember the good in people, all people, even those defending the illusion of perfection here. They are being faced with their own demons. And let's have faith, that if we continue to listen to what's in our hearts, we will be guided on how to act. Have faith that the truth will be revealed. It's only a matter of time."

"Will you pray for us?" I asked, sincerely.

"Let's pray together, right now."

I nodded, closed my eyes, bent my head and went inward as Father Curley spoke.

"God in heaven, hear our prayers. May all the cadets affected by the current cheating scandal be protected. May those that are defending the cadets be guided to help serve their clients to the best of their abilities and may those in power make just decisions.

"In these uncertain times, as the turmoil at West Point escalates, may the truth be revealed. May those in power act with integrity and help this institution heal. Please give us the strength to act upon what we hear in our hearts. May everything fall into place in the highest and best for all involved. In Jesus' name we pray. Amen."

I sighed with relief. "Thank you, Father Curley, for your prayers."

"Stay strong. I have faith this will work out as it is meant to. Let me know how things progress, especially how court goes on Wednesday. I'm always an ear to listen when you need it."

"Thank you, Father." I shook his hand with sincerity and gratitude.

★ ★ ★

On Monday, June 7, thirty-four more names were referred to the Officers Boards, bringing the total to 164 plus the four who had resigned. It felt like a body count. The superintendent, Lieutenant General Berry, requested backup from the Pentagon, asking for additional Judge Advocate General Corps (JAGC) officers to help with the Officers Boards.

CHAPTER 23
JUNE 9 HEARING

I WOKE UP WITH A jittery stomach because of today's hearing. I felt both excited and terrified. My classmates, Mark A. English, Garrett P. Keane, Stephen S. Hutton, and I were suing the United States Government together, but I was leading the lawsuit so it was labelled as:

> Cadet Timothy D. Ringgold, Individually and on behalf of all other similarly situated cadets of the US Military Academy
> —against—
> The United States of America, Marin R. Hoffmann, as secretary of the Dept. of the Army, Lt. Gen. Sidney B. Berry, as the supt. of the U.S.M.A., Brig. Gen. Walter F. Ulmer, commandant of cadets, U.S.M.A., Cadet Wayne Adamson, as outgoing chairman of the U.S.M.A. Honor Code Board Committee, and Cadet Mark Irwin, as incoming chairman of the U.S.M.A. Honor Code Board Committee.

Cadet English and Cadet Keane had been charged with

cheating. Cadet Hutton had originally been charged with jury tampering but was actually found guilty of lying because he answered evasively. All of us provided signed affidavits supporting the suit. The four of us rode to Sidney Siller's office together, and then rode over to the courthouse together. We were united in our mission, but at the same time nervous about taking this stand.

ABC News was waiting for us as we walked up to the courthouse. It was all very impressive and intimidating. I finally got to meet James Feron from *The New York Times* in person who had quoted me in numerous articles. My friends and I were feeling cautiously optimistic that something positive was going to come out of this hearing.

Walking into the courtroom, we could see the secretary of the Army, the superintendent and the commandant sitting at the defense table on the left. Lieutenant General Berry and Brigadier General Ulmer were in uniform while Army Secretary Martin Hoffmann wore a suit and tie. Lieutenant General Berry was a tough veteran of two wars. He sat with his back straight, the tallest of the men, and had a full head of silver hair. He looked very distinguished, with dark intense eyes, and wore small spectacles for reading that he took on and off. Secretary Hoffmann had dark brown hair and sat in the middle of the superintendent and the commandant. Brigadier General Ulmer's continual stern face reflected the threatening look of a drill sergeant at boot camp that would eat a cadet for breakfast.

I had never been in the same room with all three of them, and I would be lying if I said that it didn't feel a bit unnerving. I was grateful for having a well-known attorney to argue our case for us. The four of us sat at the table on the right. There were many people present in the audience. Newly commissioned Second Lieutenant Wayne Adamson and our classmate Mark Irwin were sitting in the audience behind the superintendent's table. Wayne Adamson looked right at me. It was obvious he was trying to intimidate me, and I looked back with equal determination. Cadet Irwin ignored me.

"All rise," the bailiff by the door commanded as the judge walked in. "The Honorable Richard Owen presiding."

"Good morning, gentlemen," Judge Owen addressed the defense table first and then our table. "There is a lot before us today, so let's get started." He directed his attention and nodded at Sidney Siller to begin.

"Good morning, Your Honor." Mr. Siller stood up and straightened his suit jacket. "I am here on behalf of Cadet Timothy Ringgold, a second classman of the United States Military Academy, and his classmates affected by the recent cheating scandal. It is our request for a preliminary injunction and stay prohibiting the commencement and continuance of Officer Board hearings and other disciplinary measures pursuant to and in furtherance of the implementation of the Cadet Honor Code.

"The Honor Code states a cadet will not lie, cheat, steal nor tolerate those who do, a noble ideal. The only punishment for an Honor Code violation at West Point is expulsion. We challenge the constitutionality of the system used to implement the Code. We have evidence that the Honor System is detrimental to and impedes the fulfillment of the mission of West Point in that it is subjectively invoked, unequally implemented and enforced, and creates a divisiveness and discontent among the cadets, who are expressly required thereunder to spy and inform upon their peers.

"Cadet Ringgold, who has not been accused of cheating, but has been accused of tolerating, continues to spread the message that cheating, as defined by the Honor System, is widespread at West Point. His charges were originally dropped by the commandant, Brigadier General Ulmer, who recently reopened Cadet Ringgold's case a second time for the same charge," Siller said.

I could feel myself begin to sweat. My mind was clear and I felt focused, but my nerves were betraying me. I tried to quietly take a few deep breaths and let them out slowly.

"Cadet Ringgold has a list upwards of three hundred names, all members of the class of 1977, who have violated the Honor Code, and yet the Cadet Honor Committee exercises favoritism in who they select to be charged with Honor Code violations. This clearly constitutes a deprivation of due process and equal protection guaranteed by the US Constitution.

"In fact, Cadet Ringgold also has evidence that the outgoing honor captain, Wayne Adamson, now a second lieutenant in the Army, has violated the code himself in pursuing and prosecuting investigations. The Academy allowed him to graduate even though there were allegations against him still pending.

"The other cadets here today, Cadet Mark Anthony English and Cadet Garrett Paul Keane, have been charged with cheating while Cadet Stephen Scott Hutton has been charged with lying. All have witnessed varying degrees of prejudice during their Officers Boards, where defense rights appeared to differ drastically from prosecution rights."

I glanced at Mark to my right. He, too, was feeling the heat of the room and the situation.

"Currently, there are almost two hundred cadets being charged with Honor Code violations. The number changes daily as accused cadets implicate others. Cadets have submitted laundry lists of names of classmates they report have cheated. It is also likely there are many cadets who have information about cheating but may not have said anything yet because of the hazard of being charged with having known of the cheating and not coming forth earlier.

"We believe that the current cheating scandal is a deliberate cover up of the true extent of the Cadet Honor Code violations so as to perpetuate the illegal, illusory, and unworkable standard for cadet behaviors. Cheating, as defined by the corrupt Honor System, is in fact widespread throughout West Point and those accused should not be the scapegoats to a much larger problem.

"As such, we seek to reinstate all the cadets previously judged guilty of all Honor Code violations. We ask to reinstate them to their prior rank, position, and class, as well as the removal from cadet records of all references to such violations. We also ask for the rejection of all resignations.

"The integrity of the entire class of 1977 and the Corps of Cadets, has been tarnished and will not be vindicated until such time as the so-called Honor System, with its unjust implementation, has been fixed. Thank you," Sidney Siller said and sat down.

Judge Owen looked thoughtful, processing what had just been argued. I thought Mr. Siller's argument well described our situation and our intentions. I heard a few murmurings throughout the courtroom, but mainly everyone was eager to hear what was going to be said next. I subtly scanned the room. Only a few cadets were present beyond the four of us at the plaintiffs table. The audience was mainly made up of reporters and journalists.

The defense attorney stood up. "Your Honor, the Honor Code is the foundation of the United States Military Academy. Over thirty thousand cadets have lived under the uncompromising code for over one hundred and seventy-four years. The Honor Code states that a cadet must not lie, cheat, or steal. These are noble qualities that we Americans should expect from our future leaders. I ask you, is it really so burdensome for strong young men to pledge not to cheat and mean it? It is a privilege for every cadet who attends West Point to be there, and it is completely reasonable that we expect honor in return. Why should we lower our standards just because some cadets, who have been found guilty nevertheless, seek to save their own careers? This suit is simply based on pure self-interest and not the best interest of the Academy. It is true many cadets have come forward with lists of names, but those lists are also without evidence or facts.

"Last year, a similar suit was brought before the US Court of

Appeals by eight cadets who had been expelled for Honor Code violations in '73. That case was thrown out, and I see no reason why this case shouldn't have the same fate.

"West Point's Honor Committee has acted nobly in addressing the massive amount of charges. The superintendent, Lieutenant General Sidney Berry," he said, nodding towards the superintendent sitting to his left, "created an Internal Review Panel, since the number of cases grew past the Honor Committee's capabilities. As such, the school has made swift decisions to cater to the needs of upholding honor at West Point.

"As such, we defend the Honor Code to remain as it is, as it has for generations of men, for it is geared to build character, integrity, and discipline. We defend to allow the Academy to move forward with utmost speed to resolve the current charges. Thank you." He finished and sat down. His defense was short and sweet. He also made no mention of the Honor System. We on both sides respected the Code, but the Code was not the problem; it was the implementation of the Honor System that was the problem.

Judge Owen nodded and sat for a moment. "Lieutenant General Berry, is there anything you would like to add?"

General Berry cleared his throat and took off his glasses. "Your Honor, I've never been in more of a combat situation that I am now. There are things that make me heartsick in the whole situation—so many young men may have violated the Honor Code, but, by God, I've been heartsick in battle and done what I had to do. Rest assured, the three of us, with the support of many other great men stationed at West Point, are handling this crisis to the best of our ability."

Judge Owen nodded and then addressed us. "Gentlemen, the line must be drawn in the sand. The high standards of West Point should remain."

Mr. Siller jumped in. "Your Honor, we are not arguing the high standards of West Point, but when it is forbidden for a cadet to even ask a roommate how to spell a word while writing a paper, the Honor Code is being applied impractically."

"I have heard your argument, Mr. Siller. If the cadets are guilty of breaking the Honor Code, they should admit their guilt and resign rather than ruining the reputation of this great institution."

Mr. Siller was taken aback by the judge's statement, so his partner, Mr. Edward Galian, quickly stepped in. "Your Honor, it is impossible for a cadet to go through years of schooling without making a mistake. Education is supposed to be an environment of learning and that includes making mistakes. Some of the best lessons in life come from the mistakes we have made, and cadets should not be severely punished for making those same mistakes. The punishment must fit the crime!"

Judge Owen shook his head. "Mr. Galian, many great men have graduated from the United States Military Academy. Many graduates have gone before this class of 1977, and many cadets will graduate after. The plaintiff is asking for me, in effect, to stop the Academy in its tracks. I will not do so. This case does not appear to be a constitutional one, and I see no reason why the legal system should intervene when there is a sound system already in place. As such, I rule to dismiss. The Army has latitude in administering its own system of justice. I leave the issues with the United States Military Academy to clean up its own mess. I suggest to you, cadets," he said, directly to us, "that you exhaust the legal remedies available to you at West Point first."

I looked at English to my right. Our eyes met with mutual understanding of the narrow-mindedness of the judge. We knew this hearing had been lost. English leaned in and whispered in my ear. "Duty, Country...two out of three isn't bad." I lowered my head and shook it in total disgust.

In leaving the courthouse, the police were there to escort us through the crowds outside. At the base of the courthouse, Jim Walker from ABC News interviewed Mr. Siller and me.

CHAPTER 24
PRESIDENT FORD DEFENDS CODE

THE NEXT DAY, I WENT to the hospital on post to visit DaRold. He had had an emergency appendectomy the Sunday before and was still living in the intensive care ward of the hospital.

"Hey, Ringgold, how was court?" DaRold asked the second I walked in. Father Curley was sitting beside him.

"Good, I'm glad you're here," I said to Father Curley. "I can tell you both at the same time. We did not succeed in our mission. All in all, it was terrible. Judge Owen approached us with the same narrow-minded mentality that we've been dealing with here."

"Oh no," Father Curley said, disappointed.

"Likely, his mind was made up before we even came to court," I said, resolved. "He was convinced that since we were fighting the Honor System, then obviously we must be supporting lying, cheating, and stealing. We were portrayed as wanting to tear down West Point's high standards. He didn't get it. We want West Point to have high standards that are realistic and fairly enforced, not corrupt and arbitrary."

"I wish I'd been there," DaRold said.

"I know you would've. You could have been interviewed by Jim Walker," I said, smiling. "So, brother, how are you? All patched up yet?"

DaRold adjusted his position in bed, sitting up a little straighter. "All better. Should be out of here in no time. I swear my appendix acted up just to keep me here longer."

"Maybe you need to learn how to be a patient first before you can become a doctor," I said, winking at him. I pulled up a chair, opposite to Father Curley, next to the hospital bed and sat down.

"Tell him the good news, Father," DaRold encouraged.

"Good news? Yes, Father. I could use a bit of uplifting news," I said, encouragingly.

"Well, I just spoke with Steven Verr who had just talked to Jim Feron of *The New York Times*. Feron told Verr that the Senate has announced they plan to conduct a hearing on the honor incident at West Point!" Father Curley explained.

"Really?" I asked, sort of stunned.

"Yes! I was hoping this news would bring you joy since this was exactly what you've been working for all along," Father Curley said.

"Wow. Yes. I'm confident that once the Senate hears the true story about our classmates, they'll be in a very good position to support a sanction less than expulsion," I said, processing this wonderful news.

"So we're finally getting what we have worked so hard for, Ringgold?" DaRold said, encouraging. "Now, I can leave West Point knowing everything will be okay," he said with a half smile.

"You'll be missed, nevertheless. With you and Moon Dog gone, it won't ever be the same here, I assure you. We should get a drink and celebrate the good news! Should I sneak something in?" I asked with a grin.

DaRold shrugged. "Won't mix with my meds too well, but rain check, man, for sure."

"You got it," I said.

"So, Ringgold, we were just discussing two cadets before you walked in. It might help your case to know about them. Have you heard about Cadet Fred Barnum or Cadet Robert Farish?"

"I haven't," I said. "Who are they?"

"Cadet Barnum and Farish are both currently in Transient Barracks."

"In our class?" I asked, not recognizing their names.

"No, they are both plebes. Cadet Barnum looked a bit like a hippie when he arrived in July with his long hair. He was singled out quite a bit at the beginning because it was obvious that he was going through a culture shock during Beast Barracks. He'd been subjected to *clothing formation*," Father Curley said, laughing.

"So, he was forced to show up at formation dressed in everything he owns?" I asked, laughing. "I haven't witnessed it, but I've heard that used as a form of punishment, or should I say *motivational training*? Seems harmless enough."

"Well, it didn't take long for Cadet Barnum to get his act together. After a few months here, he was listed first among his squad in leadership and made the dean's list. He even worked at the cadet radio station, WKDT. Anyhow, he's recently been found guilty both by the Honor Board *and* the Board of Officers of an Honor Code violation for lying about something insignificant," Father Curley shook his head in disgust. "He'd been asked about his transistor radio, if he had been listening to it, and he'd said no. Cadet Barnum thought the upperclassman was referring to that day, but he was written up because he had in fact listened to the radio the night before. Seems like someone is determined to run him out of the school."

"Oh my. He should be taken out back and shot," I said, sarcastically. "That's just plain stupid."

"Well, the story doesn't end there," Father Curley continued. "Barnum's friend, Cadet Farish, has just resigned after having been found guilty of lying, as well, over a pair of socks!" Father

Curley said heatedly.

"What?" I asked. "Are you serious?"

"Absolutely serious. Apparently, Cadet Farish lied about borrowing a pair of socks from a friend. What I don't understand is why Farish won't fight this," Father Curley said. "I have encouraged him to do so."

"Amazing. I am stunned . . . I have nothing to say to that," I said, throwing my hands into the air.

"So, Ringgold, where are you going for your summer assignment?" DaRold asked.

"I haven't been given one," I said. "But, I have been considering going down to Washington, DC to talk to anyone who'll listen about the need for an external investigation. Now that it's happening with the Senate, I definitely want to be down there to give them a true picture of what's been happening here."

"I think that's a great idea. I saw President Ford defending the code on the news. He believes it should be continued as is because it has produced a distinguished corps of graduates," DaRold said, smirking.

"Well, he should be surprised, too, once the Senate investigates," I said, hopefully. "It is just a matter of time for the truth to be revealed."

"Indeed," DaRold said, laying back on the pillow.

"I'll let you get some rest," I said. "Glad you're okay."

"Do keep us informed of your adventures in DC," Father Curley said.

"You'll both be the first to know everything," I said.

CHAPTER 25
TRIP TO WASHINGTON, DC

THE NEXT DAY, FRIDAY, JUNE 11, I inquired to my tactical officer whether I could go on leave. Since General Ulmer never actually preferred new charges, I was informed that I could leave and be gone until August 8. That was some six weeks, so I was grateful. Before I left, though, I was questioned by Captain Rivest about three classmates: Cadet Kruse, Cadet O'Lughlin, and Cadet Robbins. I didn't know anything about them, so the captain let me go. Our class was given permission to go on leave. We were told to keep in touch in case we were needed as witnesses for hearings by the Officers Boards that were expected to last throughout the summer.

I planned to go to Washington, DC long before the Senate decided to hold hearings, but once they did, I knew it was essential that I be there. My only point of contact was Fred Kass, Congressman Tom Downey's assistant. Monday morning, June 14, I went immediately to Congressman Downey's office and waited for Mr. Kass to arrive.

"Cadet Ringgold! I'm so very glad to see you. What can I help you with?" Mr. Kass asked genuinely.

"I'm here to help. I know that the Senate is going to hold a hearing over the honor scandal. I, more than anything, want to testify," I said.

"Yes, come into my office. Let's talk," he said. "The hearings are scheduled to start next week on June twenty-first, but there is much to be done. Are you aware of Mr. Downey's two reports?"

I nodded. "Just from what has been reported in the newspaper."

"Okay, good. We've received good publicity on the reports. His first report essentially states that the problems of the Honor System lie within the Academy and not with the country's social climate or in a lack of integrity among the cadets," Kass said.

"I'm glad to hear it," I said.

"Mr. Downey is fully aware that there is a bigger problem here. He knows that honor violations have become a way of life for cadets. He knows that "cheating" is much more pervasive than Academy officials believe or are willing to admit. His second report is scheduled to be released today with his recommendations. He has been the catalyst for the congressional review of West Point's Honor System."

"I'm very grateful." I said, sincerely.

"Most importantly, Mr. Downey wants to intervene in the current cases. He has recommended that the cases be placed in limbo until a full probe of the Honor System is completed and get this congressional review before more cadets are found guilty."

"Fantastic. Three other cadets and I tried to halt the Officers Boards with a lawsuit, but the judge didn't rule in our favor," I said, updating him.

"I see. That was a valiant effort, nevertheless, tilting at windmills. Hopefully, we'll get the results here that you are looking for. Mr. Downey does have some support, including Rep. Lucien Nedzi, the chairman of the House subcommittee on military personnel. They are both in agreement that an outside group, such as Congress, is the only way to resolve the structural problems of the Academy."

"I am hopeful, sir," I said. "So what can I do to help?"

"Well, let's get you introduced around here. Give me a few hours, and we'll set up a place for you to work from. You're going to need a desk and a phone. Umm, let's start with sending you to Senator Sam Nunn's office. Senator Nunn is the chairman of the Subcommittee on Manpower and Personnel."

"Sounds great. I'm ready."

I ended up being first introduced to Jeff Records, Senator Nunn's assistant for military affairs. Senator Nunn was a Democrat from Georgia.

"My boss is alarmed by the growing cheating scandal at West Point," Records said. "He believes the Honor System needs to be thoroughly looked at and its deficiencies corrected."

Records seemed well aware of the situation.

"Cadet Ringgold, do you wish for the Honor Code to be rewritten?" He asked me. "Because the subcommittee on Manpower and Personnel has legislative authority to do so."

"Not exactly," I answered. "I completely support the aspiration of the Honor Code, but not its implementation. The Honor System has ruined many careers over trivial offenses. If we can keep the Honor Code, but change the Honor System, I think we'll be okay," I said, simply.

"That was my understanding as well," Records agreed. "Senator Nunn's aim is to determine if the code can be made more compatible with reality. I want you to know, though, that Senator Nunn does not want to get involved in the current cases of any individual cadets. His probe into the Honor System would be much broader than just the current cheating scandal."

I was not completely happy with that comment, but once again this situation was much bigger than just my classmates. Overall, I was very impressed with Mr. Records' knowledge of the situation and felt confident that the subcommittee would do something to help.

After our meeting, I went to Senator Barry Goldwater's office. After writing to him, Senator Goldwater had followed up with Norman Augustine, the under secretary of the Army, about the April 14 cadet meeting that had led to my initial charge of toleration. I wondered if that meeting had never taken place if I would still have ended up playing the role I was now playing.

"Good afternoon," I addressed the assistant in Goldwater's office. "I'm Cadet Timothy Ringgold, Senator Goldwater's 1973 nominee for West Point. May I speak with him?"

"Oh, I know who you are," she smiled at me. "I'm sorry to say, but Senator Goldwater is in Arizona recovering from a hip operation. Is there anything I can do to assist you?"

"Well, I had initially heard from Senator Goldwater when I had written to him in April, but my last letter has gone unanswered. I'd very much like to speak to him about the West Point cheating scandal."

"Yes, I understand. Senator Goldwater is well aware of what's been happening, as am I, and I'm sure he'll make time to speak to you. Can you come by our office tomorrow? I'll try to set up a time for you two to talk."

"Absolutely, ma'am, I plan to be here all week. The Senate hearing is scheduled next Monday about the scandal. Do you know if Senator Goldwater will be back in DC for the hearing?"

"It is not determined yet."

"Okay, ma'am. Thank you for passing on the message to him. I hope he heals quickly. I'll be back tomorrow."

I was given free accommodations—a couch—for the week from one of Congressman Downey's assistants. That night, I got a call from Major Long, the adjutant at West Point. I have no idea how they tracked me down. To my utter displeasure, Major Long informed me that my leave had been cancelled and that I had four hours to return to West Point or that I would be considered AWOL (absent without official leave), and they'd send the military police after me. I was furious. I had not been on leave for more than two days, after being granted six weeks, and the Academy was calling me back. I knew I wasn't needed back, but rather they were playing games with me. I left, though, and drove back to West Point, just to be safe.

The next morning, I went to speak with Captain Lincoln for some legal counsel. He wrote a letter requesting that I be given leave because I wasn't needed on post.

I returned to Washington, DC early the next morning. I spent the rest of the week essentially going door to door of congressional offices speaking to anyone who would listen. Since there were a lot of people listening, I sent word back to West Point that I could use some help in Washington. Our base of operations was the desk and phone Fred Kass set up for me in Congressman Downey's office in the Longworth House office building across the street from the US Capitol.

On Friday, June 18, *The New York Times* reported that

> the chairman of the House Armed Services Committee, Representative Melvin Price, called on the Defense Department yesterday to establish a blue ribbon panel of civilian and military experts to investigate the honor systems. As the cheating-scandal investigation at West Point entered its third month, Mr. Price, an Illinois Democrat, asked the Defense Secretary, Donald H. Rumsfeld, to act "without delay." More than 160 cadets face expulsion and 250 other cases are being examined.

In the *Times Herald-Record*, New York Congressman Benjamin Gilman was quoted as saying,

> I'm not happy with the Senate's decision to hold hearings on West Point. The blue ribbon panel would be composed of educational experts and professional people to conduct an independent review of the Honor Codes at the service academies. It would evaluate the entire curriculum and the manner in which it is presented to the cadets, as well as the Honor System. It could offer constructive proposals for strengthening and improving the quality of education at service academies.

I supported Rep. Gilman's push for a fresh set of eyes from people outside of the military system. Their advocacy for a blue ribbon panel seemed much broader than the congressional review of the current scandal.

However, I again read that none of the reviews could offer any hope for the cadets whose trials had been concluded or were in progress. I hoped that after a review of the Honor System that one major revision would be to remove expulsion for relatively minor first time offenses. Then, just maybe, my classmates that had been found guilty could get reinstated.

That night, I read *The New York Times* and found an article I thought was well written, "Out of Step at the Point" by Frederick C. Thayer, dated June 16, 1976. It spoke of the benefits of students working together, of collaborating and learning from each other.

> If large numbers of cadets are assigned the same problem, what is more natural than intensive discussion of it? Out of such discussion comes a higher level of learning for those involved, and even the occasional discovery of

better solutions than the one "approved" by the faculty. The system, in other words, is based upon educational assumptions that are increasingly discredited.

One is that individual students cannot, do not, and should not, learn anything from each other. A second is that instructors never learn anything from students, because the instructors "know" what is "right." The likelihood is that a number of cadets involved in the scandal learned more about the engineering problem from talking with their colleagues than they otherwise would have learned. It is a peculiar system that defines learning as cheating. Even worse, the system is totally at odds with the lives cadets lead after graduation.

Whether in the Army or in civilian life, West Point graduates will spend their working lives in organizational situations. Even in times of crisis, battlefield or office, decisions will be made only after as much interaction and discussion as time will allow.

It is absurd to teach students that the way to "pass the test" is to shut oneself completely off from colleagues, make an isolated and solitary decision, then present it for "grading." The task at hand is always to discover the best solution to the problem . . . .

The honor system is educationally and operationally insane, a relic of the assembly-line approach to education that has outlived whatever usefulness it might once have had. A system (at West Point or anywhere else) that punishes students for learning from each other is hardly worth retaining.

The irony of the author's last name, Thayer, was not lost on me, whether related or not. Sylvanus Thayer, a former Superintendent, 1817–1833, is known as *the Father of West*

Point. For most of its history, West Point had taught its courses by what was known as the Thayer method of instruction. The philosophy of the Thayer method is that cadets are responsible for their own instruction. Indirectly, the younger Thayer was arguing that my classmates probably learned more by collaborating on the homework assignment than from the instruction in class which was exactly what the elder Thayer had advocated.

The next day, two classmates responded to my call back to West Point for reinforcements. Cadets Craig Howard and Chris Tomsen had just been adjudged not guilty at their Officers Board the week before. However, their consciences were bothering them. They admitted that they had collaborated, but rather than disappearing, they travelled to Washington and asked what they could do to help. Their courage impressed me. They had escaped but chose to run back into the burning building to help others. As soon as they arrived, an opportunity presented itself unique to their recent experiences.

Ike Pappas, from the CBS Evening News with Walter Cronkite, contacted me through Congressman Downey's office and asked for a meeting. We agreed to meet for a late dinner at a low-cost pizza shop near Capitol Hill. Pappas was famous as the reporter interviewing Lee Harvey Oswald thirteen years earlier while Oswald was in police custody after being charged with the assassination of President John F. Kennedy. As Pappas asked Oswald "Do you have anything to say in your defense...?" Jack Ruby brushed Pappas aside and shot and killed Oswald.

When we met that evening, I jokingly told Pappas, "I was reluctant to meet with you."

Pappas looked at me puzzled.

"I'm aware that while you were interviewing Lee Harvey Oswald, he was shot and later, when you were covering student protests at Kent State University in Ohio, National Guardsmen shot four students. It appears that people you interview have a habit of getting shot."

We both laughed.

Pappas said, "I have a unique request. I'm aware of how widespread cheating is from other reports that have aired on the Evening News. I specifically want to interview cadets who'd not been charged but who would admit on camera that they were guilty of cheating. Do you know anyone that would be willing? They wouldn't have to be identified by name and the camera could just show the backs of their head."

"Of course you know what you're asking these cadets to do?" I asked.

"Yes, well, it would be a powerful way to promote both the integrity of the cadets and the disfunction of the system, wouldn't you agree?" Pappas asked.

"I do have someone I can ask."

Craig Howard and Chris Tomsen both could have walked away, but instead agreed to be interviewed and told the world that even though they had been found not guilty, they in fact had collaborated and were guilty of violating the Honor Code. Even though they could not be identified by name and their faces were not shown, there was no doubt in anyone's mind that everyone at West Point knew exactly who they were and that they'd likely face honor charges again.

CHAPTER 26

THE SENATE
HEARINGS BEGIN

ON MONDAY, JULY 21, THE Senate hearings began before the Subcommittee on Manpower and Personnel Committee on Armed Services. This hearing was not specific to the West Point crisis, but a generic look at honor codes of the service academies. The secretary of the Army, the Honorable Martin R. Hoffmann, was the first one to testify. The secretary of the Army has the authority for all the affairs of the Army under the command of the president of the United States, as the commander in chief, President Gerald R. Ford, and the secretary of defense, Donald Rumsfeld.

The hearing was open to the public. I wore my West Point uniform, ready to testify if called upon. The chairman, Senator Sam Nunn, a Democrat from Georgia, started the hearing and introduced the secretary of the Army, who sat in the middle of the large rectangular table facing the semicircle of committee members. Lieutenant General Berry and Brigadier General Ulmer were sitting to the left of Secretary Hoffmann. Secretary Hoffmann cleared his throat and began.

"Let me state at the outset that we are mindful of the concern of the committee that has resulted in this hearing. Anything affecting honor anywhere in the Army, especially at West Point, concerns the chief of staff of the Army, General Frederick Weyand, and myself.

"The United States Military Academy is a fundamental national institution whose purpose since its establishment in 1802 by act of Congress has been to educate and train officers for the Regular Army of the United States. The Military Academy is a link between American society and the land battlefield. Its function is to transform select young Americans from civilians into exemplary soldier-leaders. For four years, West Point builds upon the qualities cadets bring into the Military Academy and seeks to nourish, strengthen, and develop those qualities and attributes, attitudes, and ideals that prepare its graduates to deal effectively with the harsh, uncompromising constants of the battlefield. Such character development has been a major theme since the founding of the Military Academy."

Hoffmann went on to describe the history of the Honor Code in great detail. Simply, *lying* remained open to interpretation. Punishment for *cheating*, could be severe, but did not automatically include dismissal. *Stealing* was always considered a dishonorable act. Surprisingly, it was only six years ago, in 1970, that the non-toleration clause was officially written into the Honor Code.

"The history makes clear—as the present code and system are designed to make clear— that the foundation of the Honor System lies with those who agree to live within its bounds."

The Honor System began in the 1800s when cadets began forming grievance committees called *vigilance committees*. General MacArthur, when he was the superintendent, established the Honor Committee formally in 1922 after the vigilance committees, which specifically focused on honor convictions, in contrast with the Tactical Department which oversaw the disciplinary measures for the Corps of Cadets.

Hoffmann then described the step-by-step process followed when a cadet is charged with an Honor Code violation. "If the superintendent agrees with the findings of the Board of Officers that the respondent has violated the Honor Code, he forwards the case to Headquarters, Department of the Army.

"At the Department of the Army, the reviews are conducted by the Office of the Judge Advocate General and the Office of the Deputy Chief of Staff for Personnel. If there are no unusual or controversial aspects of the case, the deputy chief of staff for personnel makes the final determination. If the case presents unusual or controversial aspects, it is referred to the secretary of the Army personally for final decision."

Hoffmann then outlined the dates and facts of the current cheating scandal. He didn't share anything that wasn't already common knowledge at West Point.

Senator Sam Nunn spoke up. "Let me ask one question, just to get the numbers straight. What is the total number who have been implicated already, including some who have been dismissed and including those whose cases are still pending?"

"The total number in that category is one hundred and seventy-one," Secretary Hoffmann said.

"And that includes both the original numbers and the numbers that were reduced on recheck?" Senator Nunn asked.

"Yes, sir. In the original Honor Board action which reviewed one hundred and seventeen accused, forty-eight were found for violation and sixty-nine were adjudged to be not guilty of a violation," Secretary Hoffmann said.

I had been confused over the numbers that had been reported daily at the Academy.

"So there was some overlap in numbers, but the total is one hundred and seventy-one?" Senator Nunn concluded.

"Yes, sir." Secretary Hoffmann answered. "Identifying the causes of such apparent large-scale deviations from the well-known tenets of the code requires patient, sensitive effort by the Corps of Cadets, the West Point staff and faculty, the Army, and other outside agencies such as this subcommittee. The determination of causative factors is particularly complex within a dynamic educational institution such as the Military Academy.

"At an appropriate time, with relationship to cases presently in process, it will be a constructive step to request a group of distinguished citizens from various fields of endeavor to review the matter and make recommendations. We are presently making plans to do so and will keep the members of the subcommittee and the public informed as these plans develop."

Okay, good. The secretary of the Army was now open to forming an outside investigation, which he had denied only a month ago when the Law professors requested it. The question always remained: would it be in time to help any of my classmates?

"Mr. Chairman, Senator Nunn, and members of the subcommittee, let me conclude very briefly by underscoring the confidence that the Army has, and the confidence that the Academy has, that the basic notion of an honor system is realistic, it is possible, it has provided a source of strength for cadets, and for officers and for the Army over the years, and our belief is that, notwithstanding the present circumstance that we face, as yet unresolved, that we have in this system and in the code a national resource, and a resource for the Army that is worthy and that should continue. This concludes my statement. I welcome your questions."

To me, that seemed like a lot of pomp and circumstance, but it was only the first day of Senate hearings. Since the foundation had been laid with the history of the Honor Code and System, the facts of the current cheating scandal, and the desire to protect the tradition of the Academy, hopefully tomorrow some positive changes would be suggested.

Senator John C. Culver, a Democrat from Iowa, spoke up.

"Here you have what appears to be a relatively innocuous quiz, an examination worth about five percent of the final grade in that course, and probably no one would likely have their final grade altered by the outcome. Yet the investigation to date indicates that one hundred and seventy-one cadets were involved in alleged cheating on this particular quiz. These are third year people, juniors. If you have one hundred and seventy-one involved there, it also seems to suggest on the face of it that people were rather cavalier about risking cheating. It wasn't a question of passing a course or not. It was a quiz, and a quiz that wasn't all that important.

"As I understand it, it has been suggested that one of the reasons that many people were involved is not because of the fact that widespread cheating was discovered in this particular instance, but because of the method by which you went after the facts involved here. There was a more diligent inquiry."

Secretary Hoffmann responded, "Yes, this would be evidence of a more widespread condition than simply this test."

Senator Culver asked, "You will agree, then, that it is hard to imagine how a cadet who had never cheated in three years at West Point would suddenly cheat on a quiz which would not likely have any effect whatsoever on his final grade. I wouldn't want to generalize, but I think it is a perfectly reasonable assumption that others may have cheated before."

Senator Nunn spoke up, "Does the Army itself have any kind of Honor Code? With the relatively recent My Lai Massacre, the illegal bombing of Cambodia, and the reports of false body counts, you can see why this is a valid question. What happens to an Army officer who lies, cheats, or steals?"

What a great question, I thought. I was very much interested in the answer.

Secretary Hoffmann responded, "The Army does not have an explicit honor system because an officer's word is his bond."

Senator Dewey Bartlett, a Republican from Oklahoma, asked,

"If you have an indication of lying or cheating or stealing by an Army officer, would there be just one penalty, and would that be dismissal from service?"

Secretary Hoffmann answered, "The ideal should certainly be true. I am talking about the system of implementation where, of course, court martial rules apply."

Senator Nunn then asked, "In the Regular Army, if an officer observed another officer on some minor matter, not a great importance to national security, either cheating or lying, is it his duty to turn in his fellow officer?"

Secretary Hoffmann answered, "I would think there would be a duty to address the situation at least with that officer. There are some insignificant things or minor matters that would be regarded as personal."

Senator Nunn spoke, "So you are saying that there is a difference between personal and duty?"

"No. I guess it depends," Secretary Hoffmann answered.

Senator Nunn said, "Let me ask the commandant one question along that line. Let's suppose, hypothetically, that a cadet observes another cadet lying to his girlfriend, and he knows that it's a lie. It has nothing to do with his academic performance, and it has nothing to do with his Army duties or his cadet duties. What is the duty of a cadet who observes another cadet lying to his girlfriend? I assume that happens occasionally?"

General Ulmer replied, "I have heard several cadets tell their girlfriends that they were the most beautiful women in the world. And I'm not sure that that was true at the time. I think that, sir, is something that falls in the same category as when the hostess asks a cadet if he enjoyed his meal, and he says, "Ma'am, it was great," and actually he never has liked liver. Those situations I don't think upset cadets. I think they handle them properly and rightly, and I don't think they come under the responsibility of maintaining the Honor Code."

Senator Nunn continued, "I'm not saying a frivolous lie. I'm saying an intentionally misleading lie that was told to a person outside the cadet corps or outside the Army would not be a violation of the Honor Code?"

General Ulmer replied, "It would certainly not be outside of the Honor Code. Regardless of who the cadet is dealing with, the other cadet does have the responsibility of maintaining standards of honor, yes, sir."

Senator Nunn continued, "But I believe the secretary distinguished between something that was outside the Regular Army duties and something that was totally personal, is that correct? I understand, too, that was a distinction in the Army, but I understand now that that is not a distinction of the Corps?"

Secretary Hoffmann responded, "Again, I am talking more about frivolous verses not frivolous."

Senator Nunn said, "I'm not trying to be cute or funny or frivolous on this, but let's say an Army officer observes another Army officer lying to his wife about his relationship with a third party, another woman. Let's take that same example with a cadet, where a cadet observes another cadet lying to a girl about a certain matter, certainly serious to her, about his relationship with another girl. Those are two things along the same lines. Should they be treated alike?"

General Ulmer answered, "I am not certain that each member of the Army feels an obligation to expose social misbehavior when it is not directly attendant to the military tasks at hand."

Senator Nunn asked, "With the examples just given, would it be a violation of the Honor Code at West Point?"

"It certainly would, sir," General Ulmer replied.

Senator Nunn continued, "And a cadet who would not turn that other cadet in would have violated the toleration clause himself?"

"He certainly would. The Honor Code is all pervasive and does not stop at West Point," General Ulmer replied.

Senator Culver spoke up, "If we don't have some clarification and precision in this matter, what do the terms *lie, cheat, and steal* mean to a cadet? Is it cheating, for example, to ask a roommate how to spell a word?"

"Under certain circumstances, it could be," General Ulmer answered.

Senator Culver continued, "So if there were three students studying in a room and one of them is working on an English theme and he turns to another and says, "how would you spell—" whatever the word, and he gets that answer from one cadet, if another cadet overheard that and he didn't turn it in, would he be in violation of the Honor Code?"

"Absolutely," General Ulmer said with stern finality.

I watched the proceeding with intensity, my eyes ping-ponging back and forth between the speakers. The Honor Code did need such parameters, but General Ulmer's rigid way of interpreting it meant we were all screwed. What cadet, at one time, didn't violate the Honor Code by his standards or those of the current Honor System?

Senator Culver asked, "There would be no lesser remedy available to deal in mitigation with the seriousness of the offense in the violation of the Honor Code?"

"The question, sir, is whether or not he intended to deceive. You can't have an accidental honor violation," General Ulmer said.

General Berry clarified, "According to the Honor Code, in the definition of lying there are two elements. First, a misstatement of fact, and second, the intent to deceive, which has to deal with the cadet's state of mind."

"The Air Force system allows discretion in situations where the cadet is a plebe, that he was under stress at the time of the incident, or that he turned himself in, all of which goes to the state of mind General Berry is referring to," said Secretary Hoffmann.

Senator Barlett asked, "Would the code at West Point have

any chance of working if the cadets were not required to report violations, in your opinion?"

Secretary Hoffmann responded, "In my opinion, the non-toleration portion of the Honor Code puts duty above friendship. I'm not sure that a code would work effectively without that feature."

General Berry added, "I do agree with the secretary that the non-toleration clause is an essential part of the code, but I think some sanction for certain conditions less than separation from the academy would make the non-toleration clause more workable."

Likely, any changes to the non-toleration clause in the near future would not affect my case. Regardless, it could be a step in the right direction, I thought.

Senator Gary Hart, a Democrat from Colorado, interjected. "I want to thank you, Senator Nunn, for letting me sit in. I'm not a member of the subcommittee but am interested as a member of the Board of Visitors of the Air Force Academy. I support the concept of an honor code as most members of Congress do. One might strongly argue that it might be timely to have an honor code for members of Congress too."

"Ha!" I said out loud, accidentally, and immediately adjusted my face so as not to draw attention to myself.

Senator Hart continued, "But I feel very strongly that, as an individual, it is difficult to sit in judgment. We have some housekeeping to do ourselves. The difficulty, it appears, is that the code combines both legal and moral principles. It is illegal to steal, and it is immoral to lie or cheat. It is not illegal to lie unless one is under oath. We ought to consider what the burden is on the cadet for tolerating. What duty does he have to go out and investigate some rumor that he may have heard? General Berry, does a cadet have an obligation to report a rumor?"

"No, sir," General Berry replied.

"I think, sir, that in some instances, the cadet could go to his company Honor representative. The Honor representative then would go to the chairman of the Honor Committee. The chairman of the Honor Committee would then talk to the deputy commandant or myself," General Ulmer intervened.

Senator Nunn clarified, "So, the superintendent is saying, on the one hand, that there would be no violation of a toleration if the cadet that heard the rumor did nothing but go to his room and forget it. The commandant is saying, on the other hand, that the cadet could pass that rumor up the line, but if he doesn't pass it up the line, would both of you agree that he did not violate the toleration clause?"

"That is correct, sir, unless he has specific knowledge," General Ulmer answered.

Senator Hart interjected, "He has no positive duty to find out specific knowledge?"

"I think he has a moral obligation not to let it drop unless he thinks it is a wild rumor," General Ulmer answered.

"Okay, thank you, Mr. Secretary, Mr. Superintendent and Mr. Commandant, we appreciate very much your being here. I think that West Point and the other academies can be examples for the entire country. I think that we can all agree that we alike want to make sure that we have a system that is realistic. Tomorrow morning, Congressman Downey will be testifying on his report conducted last month at West Point. The superintendent of the Naval Academy will also be speaking. We plan to start at nine o'clock. Thank you all."

CHAPTER 27
CONGRESSMAN THOMAS DOWNEY TESTIFIES

IT WAS TUESDAY MORNING, JUNE 22, as I sat in the Senate Hearing room with a small group of reinforcement—classmates who came to Washington to help me out. Senator Nunn started by summarizing the objectives for that day's hearing. Congressman Downey was the first to testify, and I was eager to hear him speak. Congressman Downey stood confident, with a full head of dark, wavy hair parted on one side. In 1974, he was elected as the youngest member of Congress at age twenty-four. Because his birthday was on the twenty-eighth of January, he was too young to swear into office at the beginning of January when the ceremony was held. Constitutionally, a congressman has to be at least the ripe age of twenty-five, so he didn't officially take office until after his birthday. I knew he was only a few years older than I was, and I appreciated his willingness to stand up for our cause.

"Mr. Nunn, Mr. Chairman, I'd like to thank you and the members of your subcommittee for this opportunity to appear here this morning. On Sunday, May twenty-third, I began my personal investigation of the situation at the Academy, accompanied by my legislative assistant on my right, Fred Kass. I met Sunday evening for three hours with many of the prosecution and defense counsel who are involved in the present hearings. On Monday morning, May twenty-fourth, I met with the superintendent of the Academy, the commandant of cadets, the dean of students, and six members of the Cadet Honor Committee.

"Business forced me to return to Washington, DC Monday afternoon. However, Mr. Kass remained at the Academy until Wednesday afternoon to conduct additional interviews. We conducted nearly forty hours of interviews. We took great pains to ensure that our selection of cadets and officers enabled us to obtain a wide sampling of opinion.

"Mr. Chairman, I regret to say that my investigation led me to the conclusion that cheating and toleration of cheating occur at West Point far more frequently and pervasively than Academy officials have been willing to concede. Indeed, I believe that cheating has become commonplace."

I nodded along as Congressman Downey spoke.

"Although one hundred and seventy-one cadets have been formally charged with cheating on this exam, a substantial portion of those who collaborated on this exam and virtually all of those who tolerated such collaboration have not been, and probably will never be, charged with an Honor Violation.

"This is not to say that the Academy has not vigorously pursued those who collaborated. Indeed, Academy officials are to be congratulated for the extremely thorough and sophisticated methods which they have used to analyze the exam papers.

"Cheating at West Point can easily go undetected. These cadets cheated freely and openly, often copying the test papers of others verbatim. This kind of carefree cheating on such a vast scale can only tell us one thing: it is easy to cheat at West Point and get away with it.

"The scandal occurred because of the unusual intensity of

the search for cheating due to the one student who had written *I got help*, at the bottom of his paper. The Electrical Engineering instructors broke tradition and went hunting for honor violators, something that cadets clearly thought they would never do.

"I hesitate to speculate about what we would find if previous take-home exams were gone through with a fine-tooth comb. One thing, however, is clear. There was nothing unique about this exam. In fact, I believe that it defies logic to assert that those who cheated on this exam cheated for the first time. Those who admitted to us in confidence that they were aware of the cheating acknowledged that for many cadets it had become an accepted practice.

"It appears that cadets often have enormous difficulty applying the Honor Code to their daily experiences. This is especially true in cases where cadets observe violations of the code which they do not believe are indicative of a lack of integrity. The basic aspects of the Honor Code against lying, cheating, and stealing are as fundamental to human integrity as the Ten Commandments."

Senator Nunn interrupted. "You are referring to the Toleration Clause? Are you saying if there was variation in punishment and some degree of discretion in punishment, the chances of the Toleration Clause working as it is intended to work would be much higher?"

"I believe that is a most logical conclusion," Congressman Downey answered. "Take for example, there is a pizza stand near the middle of the campus at which plebes are not allowed to eat after eight o'clock in the evening. If a plebe is found in the area after hours, he has not committed an Honor Code violation, but has simply broken one of the regulations. As a result, he may be *slugged*; that is, he may be required to march around in full dress uniform for a certain amount of hours as punishment. However, if that same cadet was found at the pizza stand after hours dressed in a sweatsuit rather than in his regular uniform, he may be charged with an honor violation on the theory that he wore his sweatsuit in an effort to disguise his identity, and therefore is guilty of having the *intent to deceive*."

Senator Nunn spoke, "Do you conclude that there ought to be a clear delineation between the regulations and the Honor Code itself?"

"I would think there would have to be," Congressman Downey answered. "I don't believe, for instance, that a cadet is any less honorable if he has tolerated cheating and turns himself in. Should he be removed from the Academy for that? I think not. I would think that he has shown the highest precepts of manhood, not only the ability to recognize his own wrongdoings, but the courage to come forward and admit it.

"We talked with a great many cadets, but no two cadets seemed to have the same understanding of the requirements which the Honor Code imposed. Some cadets described themselves as *hard line*, frequently admitting that under their own standards most of their friends at one point or another had committed an Honor Code violation. Others felt that they were more *liberal*, believing that Honor Code violations should be reserved for conduct which was truly reflective of moral character.

"One thing is for sure, there is resentment among the Corps of Cadets which has significantly lessened the esteem in which many cadets hold the Honor System. Moreover, these problems are frequently exacerbated by the actions of officers at the Academy, who themselves appear to be guilty of making haphazard judgments about the type of conduct which constitutes an honor violation. For example, take the case of Cadet Timothy Ringgold."

I could feel the heat rise up my neck and cheeks. Other than my classmates who were working with me, few people present in the audience knew who I was; nevertheless I was there in uniform with my nametag. I tried to keep my face calm as I listened intently.

"One evening, he was asked by the chairman of the Cadet

Honor Committee, Cadet Adamson, to discuss a conversation that he had had with Army Under Secretary Norman Augustine during which he said that cheating was pervasive at the Academy. Cadet Ringgold was hesitant to talk about the conversation. As encouragement, Adamson assured him that he was not under investigation. Ringgold was not convinced and declined to talk. At eight o'clock the next morning, Ringgold was formally charged by Adamson with toleration of cheating. When Ringgold complained to the deputy commandant, Colonel Rhyne, that Adamson had committed an honor violation by lying to him when he said that Ringgold was not under investigation, the deputy commandant responded by saying that Adamson had used a *poor choice of words*.

"Ringgold, who has never been accused of cheating, now faces expulsion for trying to bring out the facts about the current cheating, while Adamson recently received his commission as a second lieutenant in the US Army.

"The Ringgold incident brings me to my final point. The Honor Code, as presently implemented, will only hinder the Academy's attempt to get the truth. The Academy can't ask for the truth and at the same time punish men for telling the truth. To expose cheating is to admit toleration of it. The penalty for telling the truth is expulsion from the Academy. The only people who know the full extent of cadet dishonesty are the cadets themselves. Unless cadets at West Point can tell their stories without fear of punishment, we shall never learn the truth.

"I believe that someday we are going to have to face the fact that whatever West Point does for an officer in the US Army, it *does not* make him more honest. The experience may strengthen his commitment to make the Army a career, but it does not bolster his integrity under battlefield conditions. Thank you."

Senator Nunn spoke, "Thank you very much, Congressman Downey. If you were placed in the position of the secretary of the

Army, what course of action would you recommend?"

"That's a tough question, but I've thought about this a great deal. There are two problems because I think there are two separate issues. The first is the short-term problem: what to do about the one hundred and seventy-one cadets. I would recognize the fact that the number, and possibly one hundred more, who have tolerated or who have not been caught, indicates a tear in the fabric of the Honor System more than it does in this individual class of '77. From what we could glean from the cadets, they've had an attitude of hear no evil, see no evil, with respect to the Honor Code, so I can't justify a hundred or so separated from the Academy for what might possibly be the sins of four hundred of them.

"I found the cadets at this Academy to be the frankest, most sincere group of individuals I've ever run across, and they'll tell you the truth because to that extent the Honor Code has worked. I mean, they want to tell the truth. You can see it welling within them, wanting to come forward. They want the system to be good.

"The second problem is the long-term goal of what to do with the Honor Code. Clearly, the code needs some flexibility. I think we should consider giving part of the responsibility of instilling honor to the tactical officer corps."

"Excellent. Thank you, Congressman Downey for your testimony. Our next witness is Rear Admiral McKee, superintendent of the United States Naval Academy."

I stayed and listened to Rear Admiral McKee testify.

Congressman Downey and Fred Kass were all over the news that evening. I couldn't have been more pleased with Congressman Downey's testimony. We had a little celebration in his office afterwards with champagne. Then I called my mother to check in.

"Tim! I'm so glad you called. Some captain, I wrote his name down somewhere, called and told me you were AWOL," she said sounding hysterical.

"No, Mom. That's not true. I'm fine. I was given permission to leave."

"Then why would I get a call like that if it weren't true?"

"Because they're messing with me, Mom. Everything's okay. I promise."

"Why would they be messing with you?"

I let out a big sigh. "Mom, you've been seeing all the reporting on the scandal?"

"I sure have. I have a folder here of newspaper clippings I've been collecting for you."

"Oh okay, thanks, Mom. You've been staying current," I said, smiling.

"Tim, tell me where you are and what you've been doing," she asked eagerly.

"I'm in DC, Mom. The Senate has been holding a hearing about the honor codes at the service academies. It all came about because of West Point's scandal, so I wanted to be here in case I could testify."

"Why would you testify?" she asked, sounding uneasy.

"Well, I know firsthand what's been happening at West Point."

"Is it safe for you to testify? Will there be any consequences if you do?" she asked nervously.

"Maybe, I don't know. Right now my career is on the line, though, Mom. I should be okay because they have no new evidence against me." I tried to reassure her.

"But I thought your charges were dropped?" she asked.

"That's true, but umm, General Ulmer also reopened my case."

"Oh no, Tim." I could picture her holding up the phone pressed to her ear with her eyes closed, in a maternal state of concern and worry.

"Mom, you have to understand, I'm in this deep. I see the

hypocrisy. I see my classmates getting kicked out for minor violations and that includes my friends, Pete DaRold and Mike Mamer. Things are a mess, and I have to do everything I can to help fix it."

"Tim, this was never your fight. You have one more, just one more year, to go and you graduate. You worked so hard to just get into West Point. The years you spent at Staunton, and then waiting to get nominated to enter West Point. Two years in the Army and then one year at the prep school. You're just one year away from graduating, son! You were supposed to keep your nose in your books and just get through the year."

"I know, I know, Mom, but this isn't just about me. I'm trying to prevent my classmates from getting thrown out with the trash!" I said, my voice escalating slightly. I took a deep breath to calm down. I didn't want to take out my frustration on my mom. "Just know my grades are fine. I got through finals," I said, trying to ease her discomfort.

"You were always strong academically."

"Yeah, thanks, Mom."

"So what happens next? Do you have a trial coming up?"

"Captain Lincoln says it'll likely be at the end of July. I wasn't given a summer assignment, so that's why I'm spending time in DC. I want to be on the front line, seeing this scandal resolved."

"What do you expect will happen, Tim?"

"The hope, minimally, is that the Honor System changes, but it's yet to be determined whether the changes will come in time to help my classmates."

"I see," she said.

I could hear her processing. "Tim, I'm just concerned. You're putting your whole career on the line. You think opportunities like attending West Point come often?"

"Mom, this thing is so much bigger than just me. In fact, when I heard the Superintendent from the Naval Academy testify today, I got hopeful. Rear Admiral McKee spoke about the Naval Academy's Honor Concept which does not include the toleration clause. He said that when a midshipman suspects another of violating the Honor Concept, that he's allowed to discuss the matter with the individual. He may drop the matter if he feels certain that the individual took responsibility for his behavior. Admiral McKee described the Naval Academy's approach to honor as an academic subject, a subject that would have a few A's, a few B's and a few F's, but few obtaining a max grade. It really sounded like a humane system. He referred to their honor code as an *honor concept*."

"That sounds good. You think West Point's system will change and follow that?"

"That's my hope, Mom. In fact, at the Naval Academy, plebes are immune from being prosecuted, which I think is smart; that would've prevented Cadet Verr's situation."

"Right, it would've. Well, that sounds more reasonable," she said.

"Yes, it certainly does. Also, I believe self-reported cases should have some leeway because it shows moral character to admit you've made a mistake. Cadets make mistakes just like everyone else, and there should be some room to grow and mature. Isn't that the point of going to college—to learn?" I confirmed.

"Of course," she answered.

"At the Naval Academy, the cadets are encouraged to talk privately with a suspected cadet to learn his side of the incident. If he has a reasonable excuse, the matter can be dropped then and there. Even if the Honor Committee finds a cadet guilty, they can give a lesser punishment than dismissal."

"That sounds a lot more decent than getting kicked out."

"Did you know that cadets at West Point used to take daily quizzes facing individual blackboard squares where any turning of heads was assumed to be an honor violation?"

"I did not. That sounds rather ruthless, Tim. Do they still do that now?"

"No, not that I know of," I said.

"So, Tim, are you putting your own career at risk by attending these Senate hearings?" She asked again.

"Maybe, Mom. I don't know. I just know I need to be there."

"Okay, I know you must do what you feel is right. You've always had a strong moral backbone. I rarely had to discipline you as a child. Chris and Mike, on the other hand . . . they always liked to challenge me." She chuckled. "But you and John both have been good kids. Are we going to see you anytime soon? Do you plan to come home at all this summer?"

"I don't know yet, Mom. So much is yet to be determined. I know you've been keeping up with the news, but the media isn't always accurate. If you want the most up-to-date information concerning the scandal, there is a number you can call. I have the number right here in my wallet if you want it. Okay, you ready?"

"Yes, I have pen and paper," she said.

"Okay, the number is 914-938-4589."

"Got it, but be sure to call me after your own case gets resolved, okay? I can't help but worry about you."

"You wouldn't be my mom if you didn't."

"No I wouldn't be. I love you, son."

"I love you too. I'll be in touch."

"Okay. Stay safe. Bye."

On Thursday, June 24, Captain Bruce Sweeny, a professor from the Electrical Engineering Department, testified before an Officers Board that, in his opinion, as many as 400 of the 823 who took the EE304 take-home assignment may have collaborated, not including those who tolerated. He testified as the government's expert witness and has personally reviewed at least 800 of the exams. His estimate was based solely on the exams without any contributing evidence. In other words, simply by comparing assignments, it appeared that half of the class of 1977 cheated. While there was no valid way to estimate the number of cadets who knew of this and did nothing, it appeared two-thirds or more of the class was guilty of an honor violation on this one assignment.

On Monday, June 28, the Academy brought in forty-two new attorneys, snatched suddenly from duty assignments around the world, to help process the Officers Boards. That meant about eighty lawyers to prosecute and to defend cadets in the cheating cases. School officials said they want the hearings to be finished by summer's end.

On Tuesday, June 29, there were more cadets present at the Senate hearing, some in uniform, like myself, including Steven Verr. There were also some in civilian clothes who had recently been kicked out. I had a chance to speak with Steven Verr during the recess for lunch. I couldn't help but like the guy. We both had, in fact, been in the spotlight along with Captain Lincoln. We'd been pioneers together, shining light on the same system.

"I knew they'd get me one way or another," Verr said. "I'd done well in most of my courses. I was in the top of my Russian class, little good that has done me now," he said, shaking his head. "I've officially been kicked out for failing *math*," he said as if the word tasted poorly.

"I'm sorry, Verr. You fought long and hard," I said.

"I knew they'd get me one way or another," Verr repeated. "In truth, I'm hoping to get reinstated just so I can resign!" Verr said with a sense of conviction.

"To save face or so it's your decision, not theirs?" I asked.

"Something like that," he said, smirking at me.

"We're fighting against a system that doesn't want to change. If it makes you feel any better, my own future is on the line," I said.

"Well, you've been at West Point a lot longer than I have. I hope you're able to push through to graduation."

"Thank you. I hope, too, you're able to move on from all this. At least this puts an end to the Academy's ability to harass and punish you. No cadet should have to endure what you were put through. You've had it a lot harder than I have."

He nodded. "I'll survive. I've received scholarships for my running. Running is therapeutic for me, and I'll always keep running. I'll keep competing until I drop. I was accepted by other colleges before deciding to attend West Point. I'll figure out my next path soon enough. I'll be ready to put all this behind me and have a normal college experience."

I smiled at that. Both of our experiences at West Point had been far from the typical college experience and far from what either of us wanted. "Good luck to you, Verr."

"To you as well, Ringgold."

The faculty members and cadets who took part in the 1974 review of the Honor System were present to testify before the Senate subcommittee later that day.

Lieutenant William Reid, the chairman of the class of 1975 Honor Committee, said that several cadets charged with honor violations in 1975 were intentionally found innocent because expulsion was considered too severe a punishment. Lieutenant Reid said his examples point out the need for the Academy to change the system to allow for punishment to fit the crime.

Colonel Harry A. Buckley, chairman and author of the 1974 internal study, recommended an end to the two years of active service as enlisted men for those found guilty of honor violations.

Colonel Buckley suggested that discretion might make the system more "humane."

On Wednesday, June 30, Senator Sam Nunn assured West Point that he would not legislate a new Honor Code from Washington, DC, which didn't surprise me. Even though the toleration clause could be debated, our argument was with the implementation of the Honor Code, not the code itself. He didn't say it, but Senator Nunn knew changes to the Code or System would have to originate at West Point. If the Academy did not embrace the change, the changes would not take root and would be rejected or circumvented. That is why an outside investigation led by someone close to West Point, but not part of West Point, was becoming so necessary. Strictly an outsider, like Senator Nunn, would have no credibility with cadets, administration or alumni. It had to be someone that all these groups would listen to or it was doomed to fail before it began.

JULY 1976

CHAPTER 28
A RESURGENCE OF HOPE

ON JULY 1, CADET KENNETH Harms of Emerson, New Jersey, filed a suit in federal court after being accused a second time for the same charge that he had been acquitted from in March with a twelve to zero vote. Double jeopardy was a common story among my classmates. With the formation of the Internal Review Panel, the EE304 assignment was put through the computers to find similarities. If the computer produced cadet names, regardless of any new evidence, some of the cadets were charged again.

I left Washington, DC early that week, there being little I could do with the Fourth of July congressional recess coming up and the next week being the Democratic National Convention. The Senate hearings were put on hold for a few weeks and scheduled to reconvene Monday, July 19.

I asked Jeff Records, Senator Nunn's assistant, if I'd be allowed to testify, but I did not receive any assurance. I pointed out the injustice that would be done if the hearings were to end after only the administration was allowed to testify. Mr. Records assured me that a full hearing would be conducted.

Being back at West Point, my first stop was Captain Lincoln's office. He told me my name appeared on the Department of Law's schedule for an Officers Board scheduled July 30. Up to that point, though, I had not been officially charged with a violation. My only knowledge was through word-of-mouth from the commandant. Before a Board of Officers, I must be served notice at least fourteen days in advance. Captain Lincoln, of course, agreed to accept service for me in the event I was charged. Captain Lincoln was scheduled to go on leave and return home to Maine for a few weeks. There wasn't any new evidence against me, so Captain Lincoln was already prepared to represent me when the time came.

During the time that I was gone from the Academy working in Washington, Cadet Raymond Betler, one of my accused classmates, had organized a cadet defense fund and had hired civilian attorney Michael T. Rose, Esquire, to represent part of the class. Cadet Betler asked everybody, not just the cadets involved in the scandal, to contribute to the fund including the new plebes. Father Curley gave the first donation, for one hundred dollars. The cadets were individually asked to give twenty-five. The response from uninvolved cadets was generally poor because they didn't want to get involved.

The reason the cadets wanted to hire Michael Rose, instead of using one of the military lawyers at no cost, was because Mr. Rose was widely considered the legal expert on service academy honor codes. Mr. Rose was a civilian attorney who had served in the Air Force after graduating from the Air Force Academy, class of 1969. While still in law school and as an editor of the *New York University Law Review*, Mr. Rose wrote *A Prayer for Relief: The Constitutional Infirmities of the Military Academies' Conduct, Honor and Ethics Systems*, a study which cost him $18,600 and took two and a half years to complete.

All of us were navigating in the dark, but I was really proud that Ray Betler organized the accused cadets. I was spending my time in Washington and receiving good support from the class, but completely lost track of the happenings at West Point. I believed any salvation we might receive would eventually come from Washington, but this was not a war being fought on a single front. I welcomed the work of Mr. Rose and was very happy to see other cadets finally fighting back in their own defense.

★ ★ ★

July 7 was a big day for the Academy because the first class of women arrived at Michie Stadium with their plebe class of 1980. This event was well publicized and would have taken the spotlight but was overshadowed by the current cheating scandal. To date, 173 cadets had been accused, with five who chose to resign voluntarily, twenty found guilty, and four acquitted, leaving 144 cadets waiting to face their Officers Boards. It seemed unlikely the Officers Boards would be completed by September.

In *The New York Times* the article "Prosecutors Say West Point Limited Code Cases," Captain Daniel Sharphorn, one of the military attorneys, was quoted saying, "The reason they are afraid to proceed with a full investigation is that 173 guilty cases can be explained in terms of dishonest cadets, but with half the class involved you have to question the system itself." In the same article, it said: "The lawyers point out, however, that the Academy's intention to limit expansion of the investigation became apparent to some in mid-June when General Berry reversed a decision to grant testimonial immunity to cadets who had been found guilty."

I couldn't figure out why General Berry would reverse the decision to grant testimonial immunity, unless he was trying to keep the cadets quiet. If cadets were forced to testify, though, their words could be used against them. It didn't make sense to me. Captain Sharphorn was additionally quoted saying, "There seems to be a clear intention to limit prosecution to that number. They just don't want to think that the cheating was more widespread."

Boy, the administration was in denial of the truth. Didn't they know Captain Sweeny, the EE professor and government witness, had testified two weeks ago that 400 or so collaborated and unknown numbers would have tolerated? Why limit it to 173? Denial had become their coping mechanism. Denial had become their lens.

On Tuesday, July 13, thirty-seven of my classmates involved in the scandal asked the US Military Court of Appeals to stop the Officers Boards. The judges, Albert B. Fletcher, Matthew Perry, and William Cook, were in debate about whether they had jurisdiction. The cadets' point of argument was over the formation of the Internal Review Panels, in that it had taken the Honor System away from the Corps of Cadets. They argued that because the whole class of 1977 was ordered to remain after graduation, rather than attend summer assignments, that there were enough cadets present to fulfill the obligations of the Honor Committee. Thus, the Honor System should have remained in the cadets' hands.

After my own effort to sue West Point was dismissed by Judge Richard Owen on June 9, I doubted the cadets would get the relief they were seeking. However, I thought their effort was commendable and contributed to the larger picture regardless of outcome. Perhaps a military court would be more willing to engage than a civilian court.

Shortly after I left West Point to return to Washington, DC for the Senate hearings to reconvene, attorney Michael T. Rose flew into New York from Denver, Colorado. I didn't stick around to meet him. I figured he couldn't do anything that New York attorney Sidney Siller and the others couldn't do.

★ ★ ★

Monday morning, July 19, I went back to the desk I had used in Congressman Downey's office. At least ten classmates were working on Capitol Hill, under my direction, advocating for an outside investigation. There was a message waiting for me to call Captain Lincoln. He pretty much told me Mr. Rose's game plan and asked me to provide an affidavit for the records. I agreed. Later that morning, Mr. Rose called me himself. He had been well briefed as to what was going on in Washington, DC, and to the extent of our limited success thus far. He wanted to see what he could do to contribute. Specifically, he asked me to set him up with as many appointments as possible for his upcoming visit next week. He wanted to meet with as many members of the House and Senate as I could arrange.

Early that afternoon, I went to Senator Nunn's office to see Jeff Records.

"Good afternoon. What's going on? I thought there were going to be hearings this morning?" I asked.

"Yeah, about that . . ." Jeff Records trailed off. "It's undecided when or *if* the hearings are going to be continued. Well, actually, they have considered stopping the hearings."

"What? Why?" I asked, devastated.

"Frankly, one of the members of the subcommittee has been getting a lot of pressure from the Army to stop the hearings. The Army has really been hauling out the heavy artillery," Records said.

"So, Senator Nunn is the only member of the subcommittee that you can honestly speak for and he is the chairman of the subcommittee and the only one who has the power to stop the hearings?" I asked, rhetorically.

"Well, yeah," Mr. Records said, looking down, obviously avoiding my eyes.

"So it appears that they're not going to hear our side of the story after all," I said, shaking my head in disbelief. "Is there any way I could testify?" I asked, hopefully.

Weeks prior, Mr. Records had been eager for me to testify, but now he seemed reluctant to even hear me.

"I don't think so, Tim," he said.

I couldn't believe that they would stop after hearing only one side of the story. With so many good men standing to lose so much, they were closing their eyes to the injustice. I had placed so much hope in the Senate's handling of this, and now they were betraying that trust. I was instantly disheartened and reminded about how much I had to learn.

I went ahead and made contact with Senator Culver's and Senator Goldwater's offices in order to set Michael Rose up when he arrived here next week. I was able to secure arrangements for Mr. Rose to meet with Senator Culver, Senator Goldwater, Senator Javits, Senator Nunn, Congressman Gilman, and of course, Congressman Downey. My small army of classmates were asking their members of Congress to meet Mr. Rose as well; he was going to have a busy week on Capitol Hill.

Completely bewildered about what to do next, I sought out solitude in reading. It did not take much effort to find articles on the scandal. In fact, James Feron of *The New York Times* had been reporting on West Point almost daily. I picked up a *Christian Science Monitor* magazine in hopes of finding inspiration, only to discover another article on West Point. The name of the author caught my eye, Robert H. Moore. I knew Professor Moore and liked him. He had taught English at West Point before I'd entered in 1973, but I had met Professor Moore during his many visits back at West Point when he was doing research for the book he co-authored, *School for Soldiers: West Point and the Profession of Arms*. Professor Moore was currently teaching at The University of Maryland at College Park. Living so close to Washington, DC,

I had gone to visit him a week before and kept him updated on the progress we were making in Washington.

The article, titled "West Point's Provincialism," dated July 13, 1976, pointed out the fact that most of the faculty at West Point were not permanent career educators, but Army officers who rotated in and out every three years on military assignments. Thinking back, Captain Lincoln had received approval of his extension to remain at the Academy an additional year, which had been revoked and then reinstated, so he could finish representing his clients. Army officers have a lot of military training which includes leading and training their subordinates. Most of the professors, there on assignment for three years, did not have a teaching background, which didn't seem relevant to point out since the culture within the military is of constant training and leadership. What was interesting about the article was the point Professor Moore was stressing about the identity of West Pointers in relation to the Honor Code.

> It should be noted there is probably less cheating, lying, and stealing at West Point than there is at most civilian schools. However, West Pointers seem obsessed with claiming much more for their code and their own individual honor than observable facts justify. This obsessive overreaching is one of the more intriguing mysteries about West Pointer behavior.
>
> One is compelled to question what West Pointers' excessive rhetoric may conceal. Could it be that the Academy is experiencing a more profound crisis of identity and purpose than it can acknowledge?

I nodded in agreement with Professor Moore's assessment.

The Academy's traditional provincialism is its own worst enemy. For what the Academy most needs is to know itself, not as the stuff of legends and past glories, but as a functioning contemporary institution. And given the inbred nature of the faculty and staff, it will take skillful outside intervention by civilian investigators if West Point is to come to terms with itself.

I sighed. Professor Moore was reminding me of our original mission, to get an outside investigation. Since it looked like it wasn't going to happen through the Senate and the Subcommittee on Manpower and Personnel, we had to find another way. That battle might have been lost, but the war was not over yet.

The next day, I returned to Congressman Downey's office to discover Congressman Downey had set a date for a hearing of his own for Wednesday, August 4. I was put to work drafting a letter to the superintendent of West Point from Mr. Downey, requesting officers and cadets' presence for the hearing. To me, the fight was to be won or lost in Washington. Due to the hearing on August 4, I felt, again, a glimmer of hope.

CHAPTER 29
TIME FOR A COMPROMISE

I CALLED CAPTAIN LINCOLN TO inform him of the August 4 meeting.

"Good morning, Captain Lincoln. Cadet Ringgold here."

"Good morning, what may I do for you?"

"Well, I wanted to update you on the activity in Washington," I said.

"Good, I'm glad you called."

"Thank you, sir. To start, the Senate Subcommittee of Manpower and Personnel has ceased hearings to my disappointment. However, Congressman Downey has decided to hold his own hearing, scheduled August 4. I thought you'd like to attend," I said, hopefully. "I know you may not be able to leave West Point at this time, sir, but possibly . . ."

"Ringgold, I will very much consider it. Let me update you with what's been happening here."

"Please do. I'm listening, sir."

"Did you hear about the thirty-seven cadets that asked the Military Court of Appeals to stop the Officers Boards?"

"Yes, I'd heard. Do you think they have a chance in court?"

"Likely not, but the Internal Review Panels are not going well. It's obvious that there is bias to those being accused. I don't expect any cadets to be cleared. None. The Honor Boards had twelve members, and the cadets needed a unanimous vote to be found guilty. When the panels took over, they were made up of only two officers and one cadet, diminishing the chances of an acquittal severely. Recently, however, the panels have included no cadets! Secondly, they aren't keeping formal records of their hearings, so we can assume they aren't following protocol."

"Really?" I asked, surprised by the boldness of not keeping records.

"West Point keeps changing the procedure. As you know, all Cadet Honor Boards are tape-recorded and stored, but not so with the panels. Even more horrendous is the fact some cadets are not receiving notice to appear at their own hearing. So for you, you may not get a notice at all to appear at your July thirtieth hearing, especially since you haven't been charged—just scheduled. Some cadets have even been led to believe that they were being brought before the panel as witnesses against other cadets only to discover that they were on trial themselves!"

"Now that's rough," I said, sincerely.

"There's a lot of intimidation happening right now, too. Your classmates are being treated like criminals."

"Tell me something I don't know."

"Well, one thing you might not know is how they turned things around. When you were living in Transient Barracks, do you remember noticing the guys not caring about their appearance?"

"I sure do. I disagreed with that. I felt that presenting ourselves well was important."

"Then you'll surely smile to know that this group of accused are getting haircuts, shining their shoes and brass, and holding their heads up high again. They're not willing to feel disgraced.

They're not willing to feel humiliated."

"Wow, that's great. It sounds like they've improved not only their appearance, but their attitude."

"Exactly."

"Well, I'm glad to hear it. Thank you for sharing," I said, sincerely.

"Another thing that's happened is your classmates have been advised that they have a right to remain silent, to only be told later that they were required to testify and that if they remained silent that it meant they were guilty."

"Oh geez. Sounds like Captain Burt's in charge of the prosecution," I said.

"You got that right. Here we are, working day and night to give our cadets a good defense, only to find out that some cadets had to suffer through their own hearings without counsel in an effort to speed up the hearings! They're also trying to get the cadets to incriminate themselves. It is outrageous!"

"I've heard that some cadets are being retried by the panel after being acquitted by their Honor Board."

"Yes. That unfortunately is completely true. Cadet Harms has gone public concerning his own double jeopardy."

"I'd heard about him, too." I sighed. "What a mess that keeps growing. Do you currently know how many cadets have been accused?" I asked, hoping for an update.

"I think we are up to one hundred and eighty-two cadets," he said, sighing. "New names are added every week."

"I'm hoping you could come down to DC to testify for the August 4 hearing. Would that be possible?" I said, eagerly.

"Maybe. I'll certainly try. I'll speak to the other attorneys, too, and let you know if any of them can come as well."

"That'd be great. Thank you, sir, and good luck."

"We need it, Ringgold. Stay strong in Washington. I'll talk to you soon. Bye for now."

"Okay, sir. Thanks again. Bye."

On Friday, July 23, a group of West Point cadets held a news conference in the Thayer Hotel where hundreds of accused cadets filled the audience. I was grateful to hear that they had gone public. Better late than never. Their news conference shined light on the illegal actions by the Internal Review Panel. Michael T. Rose, the new civilian attorney for some of my classmates, had been hard at work trying to convince the secretary of the Army to consider a lesser penalty than expulsion. It really felt like the pressure was building and some sort of compromise needed to be found.

Captain Lincoln informed me that my name had been taken off the list of names for the Officers Board, so that battle ceased, and I didn't forget to call my mom to let her know. For whatever reason, the commandant decided not to reopen my case, so I was still considered in good standing within the Corps of Cadets. As surprising as that was, I was not given a summer assignment which allowed me to continue my work in Washington.

AUGUST 1976

CHAPTER 30
CONGRESSMAN DOWNEY'S
AD HOC HEARING

THE PUBLIC FORUM TOOK PLACE in 2118 Rayburn, the gigantic hearing room that is home to the House Armed Services Committee, on Wednesday, August 4, at 2:00 P.M. Forty members of Congress attended.

Four Law professors were present including Captain Daniel H. Sharphorn, Captain Victor S. Carter, Captain Burk E. Bishop, and Captain Arthur F. Lincoln, Jr. I was really glad Captain Lincoln was able to come down to Washington, DC to see firsthand what was happening, as well as have an opportunity to testify. I knew the Law professors were risking their futures in the Army by being here.

I noticed Cadet Tom Lagarenne in the audience. A few months ago Cadet Lagarenne had threatened to fight me because he was angry that I'd gone public about West Point. I had heard he had been pulled into the scandal and had been found guilty of cheating. Whatever his motivation for being there, I was glad to have his support for the hearing.

Father Curley was also here. He was willing to take a public stand, despite the backlash he was receiving within the Catholic community. He had been my confidant, and I drew strength from his presence. With God on our side, I was feeling rather hopeful that today's hearing had the potential of being victorious.

Congressman Downey opened the public forum.

"Good afternoon, everyone. Thank you for your presence. West Point is now contending with the most serious honor scandal in its one-hundred-and-seventy-four-year history. More than two hundred cadets have been formally charged with cheating and scores more remain under investigation.

"In June, I testified before the Senate Armed Services Committee's Subcommittee on Manpower and Personnel concerning my findings after investigating West Point in May with my assistant, Fred Kass. West Point's superintendent, General Berry, testified, as did Rear Admiral McKee, the Naval Academy's superintendent. No one has been able to explain why this cheating scandal occurred. I did ask General Berry to attend today's forum, but he declined. Overall, the voice of the administration has been heard. Now is the time to hear first-hand from the cadets themselves, as well as from the military attorneys representing them.

"To begin, Cadet Timothy D. Ringgold will share his personal account."

It was finally my time to testify. I knew that despite not having had an Officers Board last month as originally scheduled, that I may still not be accepted into the Corps of Cadets in the fall without consequences. Five of my classmates joined me at the table, all of us dressed in our white summer uniforms. I began with the confidence that I knew what to say. I had thought about the most important points over and over, having given my own testimony repeatedly in my mind.

"Good afternoon, members of Congress. Thank you for giving me the opportunity to speak for myself and on behalf of the West Point class of 1977. With me here today are five classmates: Cadet

Betler, Cadet Jacobson, Cadet Figueres, Cadet Ray, and Cadet Lutz, three of whom have been acquitted. Other cadets are in the audience. It's certainly crucial that we have a voice and share the truth of what has been happening at our beloved military academy. To start, I have not come here today in my own self defense, as there are no charges against me, and I have never been charged with cheating. I had, in fact, been found guilty of toleration, a dismissible offense, after speaking openly with the under secretary of the Army, Norman Augustine. I'd expressed my viewpoint to him that cheating, as defined at West Point, is widespread." I paused, gulped, and took a deep breath to calm my nerves.

"The charges against me have since been dropped by the commandant, General Ulmer. I point that out because I'm here on behalf of my classmates who have only done, as I explained to the Army under secretary, more or less what the rest of us have done at one time or another. Let me explain: my classmates had not carried unauthorized notes into an exam, and they did not copy the exam of a student next to them. They collaborated on a take-home assignment.

"This cheating scandal is real and it's serious, but it does not reflect the individuals involved. Rather it reveals the fact that there is a major problem within the administration of the Honor System. I completely support the Honor Code, as my classmates here will also testify. We love West Point and believe that honor must be part of the system, as it has been for many years. However, the Honor System, the Academy's *implementation* of our Honor Code, is corrupt and broken.

"This was revealed to us early in our plebe year, our first year at the Academy, when the honor captain, Cadet Ronald H. Schmidt, the senior who taught my class the ins and outs of the Honor System, was allowed to graduate after being found guilty of an honor violation by his own Honor Committee. His punishment was not having to serve his five-year service obligation in the Army following graduation. Also during our plebe year, the same honor captain had told us plebes to stop turning in our classmates. This set up a dichotomy that we were never able to resolve.

"Concerning the take-home assignment I referenced to earlier, there are those who blatantly cheated, copying verbatim from another classmates' paper. That, however, is not the majority. The take-home assignment was meant to be completed independently, although all previous assignments in this course had encouraged collaboration. I'm not here to tell you by any means that I condone cheating, but rather to reveal and validate that there has been a breakdown of the Honor System the entire three years I have attended West Point. We want a fair and honest system, but there is nothing fair and nothing honest about the current state of honor at West Point. It genuinely pains me to say so.

"Cadets are not perfect, and we make mistakes just like everyone else. The unfortunate situation at West Point is the fact that cadets can be kicked out for a minor offense just like they can get kicked out for a major offense. For example, Cadet James Conner, a first year student and member of the class of 1979, was recently kicked out for lying because he said he did twenty push-ups but had only done eighteen. You have to make the penalty match the nature of the offense. To expel someone is the death penalty, so to speak, to their service career.

"Currently, a number of my classmates are facing separation for minor offenses. Many are being retried by the Academy's Internal Review Panel after having been cleared by their Honor Board. The Internal Review Panels greatly reduce the chance for an acquittal because each panel only consists of three people, two officers and one cadet, whereas an Honor Board consists of twelve Cadet Honor Committee members and only one vote is needed for an acquittal.

"To understand the severity of the current situation, you have to look beyond the two hundred cadets that have been charged.

Within the Honor Code is the toleration clause. To tolerate an honor violation is itself considered an honor violation, as egregious as lying, stealing, or cheating. At the end of June, Captain Bruce Sweeny, a professor of Electrical Engineering, testified before an Officers Boards that in his opinion as many as four hundred of the eight hundred and twenty-three members of my class who took the EE304 homework assignment may have cheated. To include toleration of those that have witnessed the collaboration on the take-home assignment could include the vast majority of our class.

"We have a situation that is beyond repairable by those who run the school. You cannot change the system by the same people who created it. As such, Captain Lincoln, Cadet Steven Verr, along with others, and I have been advocating for an outside investigation. We need someone with a fresh set of eyes, who is not too close to the system, but understands it enough to be able to set things straight. I believe West Point can be an honorable institution again, and that's why we are here. The Academy appears ready to throw the cadets out and keep the system, but I ask you: why not throw out the system and keep the cadets? Thank you."

"Thank you, Cadet Ringgold. Members of Congress, the cadets are open for questioning," Congressman Downey said.

"I have a question." Congressman Patricia Schroeder of Colorado spoke up. "Cadet Ringgold, you've been quoted repeatedly having said that *cheating is widespread*, and yet you hadn't individually reported anyone in the three years you have attended West Point. Is that correct?"

"No, ma'am. During our plebe year, I reported my roommate for an honor violation, something I still feel bad about."

"You feel bad for having reported your roommate, and yet you claimed to the under secretary of the Army in a private meeting that cheating is widespread. Can you please elaborate as to why you make such a claim, but have not reported any other cadets?"

"Yes, ma'am. As I shared, during my plebe year, the honor captain told us to stop turning in our classmates. As much as I took the Honor Code seriously, I did not feel comfortable in the role of reporting suspected honor violations, a feeling shared by many of my classmates. I respect the ideal of toleration, but I found it to be impractical."

"I see. You did say you still feel bad about turning in your roommate, so you have chosen not to replay that experience," Congressman Patricia Schroeder said.

"Yes, ma'am," I said.

"Would you be in favor then of removing the toleration clause from the Honor Code?"

"I do think it should be considered, ma'am. At a minimum, the single punishment of expulsion needs to change, to align the punishment with the severity of the offense and that includes the toleration clause."

"Okay, thank you, Cadet Ringgold. That's all I have."

I answered a handful more questions, but it was mainly to clarify how the Honor System worked. It dawned on me that those who haven't attended one of the service academies were likely not familiar with the intricacies of how the Honor System operated.

★ ★ ★

The Law professors had an opportunity to testify, which took most of the afternoon. I had the profoundest respect for the testimonies given by Captains Daniel Sharphorn, Victor Carter, Burk Bishop, and Arthur Lincoln. Cadets like myself, who challenged the Academy were risking a career that had not yet begun. The Law professors, on the other hand, were risking a career in which they had invested many more years. For example, Captain Lincoln already had ten years of commissioned service, halfway to a twenty-year retirement.

★ ★ ★

Father Curley, too, had the opportunity to testify.

"As one intimately involved with the Corps, I am outraged at some of the distortions that have been allowed to develop. There are not simply *good guys* and *bad guys*. To tolerate such simplification would be the severest of honor violations.

"The Honor System blindly demands and presumes absolute perfection and moves with violence and cruelty against even trivial failings. This Utopian standard of honor appeals to idealistic adolescents who have been brainwashed into identifying this standard as the West Point norm never to be compromised lest *a million ghosts in olive drab, in brown khaki, in blue and gray, would rise from their white crosses* to haunt them."

Father Curley paused. I could tell he was feeling emotional, so he took a deep breath to calm himself. I personally appreciated his passion.

"The sad performance of the Honor Committee this year and the violence directed to new cadet Steven Verr shocked me as few things ever have. Seldom have I witnessed such blind bigotry and prejudice projected in the cause of honor.

"I've been regarding the cheating scandal exposed by the take-home project as less of an honor crisis and more of a leadership crisis within the Corps. I'm not condoning unauthorized collaboration. I'm indicating the multitude of circumstances that should make decent and reasonable men shun from having the cadets carry all the load. I think it is a real management problem. Imagine after encouraging collaboration on electrical engineering problems, suddenly restricting it on a take-home with having little academic value. Who of us is so righteous to claim total immunity if we were found under similar circumstances?

"It is my contention based on firsthand knowledge that the honor violations are much more extensive at West Point than Academy officials seem capable of admitting. I'm less tolerant of the silence of the administration. I have yet to hear our generals accept responsibility for the climate that contributed to the embarrassing situation of so many of these honorable cadets.

"Indeed, I'm forced to conclude the Academy officials are afraid to really look and diagnose the problem. They seem content to purge some bodies, or *bad apples* as I'm told these accused cadets are called. Most of the lawyers I have been associated with are repulsed and use the words *cover up* through selective and limited prosecution. Surely, it is obvious that to isolate individual cadet cases apart from the more glaring structural defects is unjust and outrageous.

"Last June, I wrote to General Berry, asking that justice be tempered by mercy. The cadets are so young and what a lesson could be taught! The example of our commander in chief in granting amnesty to President Nixon stands as a worthy precedent for Academy officials to consider in these critical days. Although, let me be clear, I'm not comparing Nixon's crime to the cadet offenses.

"Congressman Downey and the other members of Congress, I am certain when you understand the complexity and magnitude of the current crisis at West Point, you will not permit some members of the class of '77 to be made scapegoats when greater blame should fall on other shoulders.

"In years past, the Long Gray Line has never failed you; I ask you now not to fail the Long Gray Line. For the cadets' sake and the nation's, I know you will not allow expediency to be substituted for truth. I thank you for listening to me."

Following Father Curley's testimony was loud thunderous applause, including from me. He had stood up for us. He had done the cadets proud.

Mr. Michael T. Rose, the civilian attorney representing some of my classmates, spoke. Congressman Downey introduced him.

"Mr. Rose wrote the book *The Prayer for Relief: The Constitutional Infirmities of the Military Academies' Conduct, Honor and Ethics Systems*, published in 1973 by New York University. As an Air Force Academy graduate, he has direct experience of having lived under an Honor Code as well as having served in the Air Force. He is considered an expert in the administration of the Honor Systems. He is currently representing a majority of the accused at West Point as a civilian attorney. His insight into the scandal is most appreciated."

Mr. Rose walked up to the table with all the microphones facing the members of Congress and gave his testimony. He advocated for graduated penalties instead of the automatic expulsion. He spoke about the Honor Concepts at three other service academies that have graduated penalties and no tolerance clause. He spoke about the lack of due process and the right for cadets to appeal a guilty verdict. At West Point, cadets are pressured not to appeal, that the honor violation will not appear on their record if they do not appeal but does show on their record if they do. Significantly, he argued that the Honor Code is not a separate jurisdiction, that cadets do not own the Honor Code and System; they are part of the US Government, the Constitution, and statutes. The people own the code and the academy; they paid for it and created it through legislation. He advocated to teach cadets how to hold an honor hearing and that intense supervision is required to teach cadets how to administer military justice. Hence, the adults need to be in charge.

I was also blown away by Michael T. Rose's testimony. He appeared to be exactly what my classmates needed in order to save themselves. Afterwards, I had a chance to speak with him.

"Mr. Rose, I personally want to thank you for all you said. I really hope it makes a difference."

"Thank you. I think it will. Keep putting the truth out there and let the public get angry. Public pressure will help change things. Currently, I'm collecting affidavits from my clients and other defense attorneys are doing the same. We're going to have this all documented. But, I have no intention of releasing the documents to the public. Since the cadets trust Father Curley, he's in charge of keeping the affidavits safe. It's simply *the idea* of these affidavits that's going to put pressure on the administration to change because they're not going to want them to go public. I've told my clients that I want every other word out their mouth on campus to be *affidavit, affidavit, affidavit*. We want the administration scared to face the truth and thus forced to change."

"I do understand the value of going public." I nodded. "Captain Lincoln has led the way in supporting his client Steven Verr, and I have followed his lead. As much as I never intended to be a whistleblower, I knew I had to tell the truth of what was happening."

"That's how it happens, Cadet Ringgold. We often find ourselves on a path we didn't consciously choose or rather it feels like it chose us. While I was attending law school, I wrote a law article on the Honor Systems of the five service academies. I had no idea it was going to force me to write a book. Writing a book is time-consuming, expensive, and a hell of a lot of work! But I wrote it because I saw the need for it; it became very apparent to me the majority of the public did not know how the Honor Systems at the military academies worked. Now, here I am considered the *expert* on Honor Systems." He laughed and winked at me.

"Well, it was a smart decision to trust Father Curley with the affidavits. I'm also glad that you were brought on. I really hope you are able to help my classmates."

"It's just a matter of time. West Point is going to be pressured to change. I didn't enjoy calling out the truth on the Air Force Academy, my alma mater, in my book, let me tell you. And from my experience, it's those that run the academies that resist change the most. The higher up, the greater the resistance because they believe it reflects on them since it happened on their watch."

"I understand completely. All summer I've been going from office to office speaking to any senator, congressman, or staff member who'd listen to me. Overall, I've been treated well, except for one office. Want to guess which office?" I asked, rhetorically.

Mr. Rose shrugged his shoulders.

"The only congressman not willing to talk to me has been Representative John Murphy, a Democrat from New York, who is also a West Point graduate."

"Yep, I'm not surprised. Academy graduates think any change is a lessening of their standards, a cheapening of the value of being an academy graduate. But it is not true. Tradition at the academies can best be described as the practice of the past dictating the practice of the future merely because it was the practice of the past. Change is needed and making the system work is the highest form of patriotism," Mr. Rose said.

"I agree. Couldn't have said it better myself."

CHAPTER 31
THE CHEATERS PLUS ONE

ON TUESDAY, AUGUST 10, THE editorial I'd written on July 29 was printed in *The New York Times*.

To the Editor:

For over three months West Point has been beset by the largest cheating scandal in its history, the eighth to strike a service academy in 25 years. The public has been led to believe that the Academy is seeking the facts honestly and responsibly. The accused cadets are portrayed as a disgraceful lot unfit for salvation. These points are simply untrue.

The commandant, General Ulmer, has suggested those cadets facing charges are the only ones who cheated on this exam. Yet, the only charges pending are based on a comparison of exam papers. One congressman, two prosecuting attorneys, two electrical engineering instructors (serving as government expert witnesses) and numerous other officers and cadets have testified that more than 400 of 823 cadets who took the exam collaborated. One attorney testified that he told the superintendent, General Berry, if properly investigated, 300 to 600 cadets could be referred to trial. General Berry's only response has been to stop the most effective means of conducting a proper investigation—the granting of immunity which he had already extended to five cadets and which the commandant has offered to three.

I have never been charged with cheating, but on May 20 I requested through proper channels that General Berry conduct an investigation of my allegations of widespread cheating. I provided him with a list of 74 cadets I suspected. To date General Berry's only response has been to call the allegations, *filth, garbage, and sewage—unhealthy and unproven*. The Academy represented my classmates as moral degenerates. But, even a cursory examination reveals that the involved cadets represent nearly a perfect cross-section of the Corps.

They have worked as hard, have the same desire and dedication that has served the academy, the Army, and the United States for so long. They support the Honor Code as strongly as any cadet, they only ask for the opportunity to learn from their mistakes. If the system is *alive and well* as General Ulmer claims, then surely it can stand some constructive criticism from those who live under it. Before the academy can *dispose* of its *bad apples* surely a full understanding of what has happened is necessary. If the system goes unchanged, it will only be a matter of time before America will be faced with the ninth scandal.

Timothy D. Ringgold
U.S. Military Academy, class of '77

★ ★ ★

I was very pleased with the outcome of the August 4 hearing, and I believed it may be the tipping point. The ironic thing, though, was I felt very sad heading back to West Point in mid August. I drove up to campus with a feeling of dread at the bottom of my stomach. I was here to begin another year at West Point, my very last year. I had unfortunately created a more hostile environment that I could ever have imagined. Every single person at the school, all four thousand cadets along with the administration, knew who I was. I had spent the past two months lobbying in Washington, DC with the hope that something positive would come as a result.

I decided to take my time, park the car, leave my bags and walk up the hill along the Hudson River. It certainly was a breath-taking campus. A few companies of plebes were practicing marching on the Plain. A group of plebes ran by me on the left, the firstie, a classmate, yelling out commands.

It was a beautiful day, the end of summer and still very warm. I found myself walking right to the Catholic chapel. Maybe I was looking for some spiritual inspiration. I went into the chapel and sat down in the back. There were a few other cadets present, but the chapel was quiet with those present deep in thought. I closed my eyes and listened.

"Cadet Ringgold?" I heard a whisper to my left and opened my eyes.

"Hi, Father Curley." I said and smiled.

"Tim, will you come into my office for a moment."

"Of course, Father." I followed him into his modest and clean office and sat down in the chair facing him.

"You've become very famous, Tim. I think your name has even surpassed the mention of Verr's name in the newspaper. It seems you have certainly fought the good fight," he said, grinning at me.

I nodded. "The genie has been let out of the bottle. The Academy can't stuff him back in," I said. That made Father Curley laugh.

"Did you hear about the letter sent to the secretary of defense by thirty defense attorneys requesting an outside investigation?"

"No, I hadn't heard about that yet. Sounds similar to the letter the ten attorneys sent to the secretary of the Army in the middle of May, but was denied? I'm glad to hear it was thirty attorneys this time," I said.

"Correct. There are also rumors of cadets being allowed to resign and reapply in order to return next year. I'm not in favor of that at all. I think it's time for West Point to take some accountability. West Point still remains in the public eye. Any support the Academy had for dismissals is fading fast. It'll be interesting to see how the chips fall," he said.

"I certainly think the external investigation is going to happen; it is only a matter of time. The thing I struggle with, though, is how betrayed I feel by the Academy." I sighed. "I saw the corruption, pointed it out, and in response the Academy retaliated. They put the reputation of West Point before the cadets. We became the proverbial cannon fodder. Those of us who are unhappy with the Honor Code and System have been described as favoring cheating, dishonesty, and lawlessness. It's all horseshit," I said.

"I understand," Father Curley said. "That's the same thinking that if we are against the war, we do not support the troops."

I nodded. "I believe all West Point was interested in doing was to lie, cheat, and steal in order to perpetuate the myth that cadets don't lie, cheat, and steal." I knew I sounded cynical, but I tried to keep my anger under wrap.

"I want to show you something, Tim," Father Curley said, getting up. He walked over to his bookshelf, bent down and reached for something to pull out from behind. I could hear metallic scraping on the floor. He walked back to me and handed me a sign.

I began to laugh. "Where did you get this?" I asked.

"Well, you know how angry and hurt a lot of the cadets in Speed Barracks have been."

Speed Barracks was created after the accused outgrew Transient Barracks. It was actually Summer Provisional Detachment (SPD), also informally known as Special Prisoner Detail, Cheaters Detachment, or Cheater Barracks. Only the accused were permitted in that area of the barracks.

Father Curley continued. "In an effort to calm them down, I occasionally stepped in, afraid that their anger would harm their case. Sometimes they'd listen, but the one thing that irked them was their march to the Mess Hall. They'd pass Colonel Hal Rhyne's little, red MG under that sign, *Special Assistant For Honor*. He was always parked in the same spot, under *that* sign. His car was like a red flag before a bull! They often ranted about how one day they would lift it up and turn it over; I pleaded with them not to do this! It'd simply add fuel to the fire and confirm the contempt so many here have toward them."

I nodded in agreement.

"I'd heard no more of their prank; praise the Lord. Then, last week while I was outside Speed Barracks throwing a baseball with a few of them, one came to me and asked for the keys of my car. I mindlessly handed them over and continued the tossing. Later, as I got back in my car to leave, another cadet told me to look in the trunk of my car when I returned to the rectory. When I did, I found Col. Hal Rhyne's parking sign," he said, grinning. "I can't help but smile and keep the sign with pride," he said, winking at me.

"It's more fitting that you have it, Father," I said, grinning myself.

We sat for some time in silence. It was not an uncomfortable silence for we both felt the intensity of the situation. After a while, I took a deep breath and let it out.

"I don't think I belong here anymore." Father Curley didn't say anything but looked down at his hands. I could tell he wasn't completely surprised by my comment. How many cadets have come to him expressing their pain? "I have seen too much. I've experienced too much." My voice cracked with emotion. "I tried bringing the truth forward. I feel like I have done everything in my power to help my classmates. They're good guys . . ." I said, my voice catching in my throat, "who didn't deserve the treatment they received."

"You're right. They are good guys, and you acted most honorably in your quest to shine the light on the truth. I would be saddened by your departure, but I understand. I think one day, too, the Academy will see it suffered a great loss at its own hands with so many cadets leaving."

"I know I can't stay," I said, definitively acknowledging this truth out loud and to myself. "Since West Point's leadership and their supporters have been willing to destroy our careers over a take-home assignment worth what, five percent of our grade?" I shrugged. "What faith could we have in a serious crisis? I learned firsthand that our leadership would throw us under the bus or waste us in a worthless fight and think nothing of it. They do not care about us in the least. All they care about is protecting a broken system, no matter who gets destroyed in the process."

Father Curley didn't say anything. How could he argue when he himself knew the truth?

"Father, the hypocrisy I see in the Academy, I do not wish to see in myself." I said that statement with such finality that I knew my career as an Army officer was over.

Father Curley stood up and walked behind me, putting his hand on my shoulder. "Tim, like I said, I'd hate to see you go."

I nodded at him. "Thank you, Father Curley."

"Please think it over before you do anything hasty, and my door is always open."

"Hold onto that sign and hang it in your office, instead of hiding it behind the bookshelf. This way you won't forget me and the others."

"I'll always remember, Tim."

I got up, walked out, and went right to my room to type up my conditional resignation letter to get the ball rolling on ending my time at West Point.

UNITED STATES CORPS OF CADETS
West Point, New York 10997

MACC-1   13 August 1976
SUBJECT: Conditional Resignation
THRU: Tactical Officer
           Summer Provisional Detachment
           West Point, New York 10996
TO: Commandant
      United States Corps of Cadets
      West Point, New York 10996

1. I, Timothy D. Ringgold, Company E-1, class of 1977, United States Corps of Cadets, West Point, New York, do hereby voluntarily tender my resignation from the United States Military Academy, because of my unusual involvement in the EE304 cheating scandal. Having never been charged with cheating, I have suffered irrefutable damage to my future as a cadet and potential army officer because of the forthright performance of my duty. For answering a question posed by the undersecretary of the Army, I was subjected to isolation in Transient Barracks, deprived of my rank and position and not permitted to wear my class ring. I was exonerated of all charges by the commandant only to have them reinstated for asking the superintendent to investigate my allegations of widespread cheating. I was forced to testify against my peers in violation of my rights under the Fifth Amendment of the Federal Constitution and

Article 31 of the Uniform Code of Military Justice. I have been threatened with criminal prosecution without any foundation in fact. I have been harassed by Military Academy officials by being allowed to go on leave only to have that leave cancelled within 24 hours and ordered to report back to the Military Academy only to be allowed to continue on leave. My mother received a phone call from someone reporting to be an Academy Official telling her I was AWOL and that I better turn myself in when in fact I was on authorized leave. I have repeatedly petitioned the superintendent for disposition of my case and had my requests go unanswered. I have been relieved of my summer assignment and forced to remain separated from my classmates only to have my charges dropped without explanation. At every opportunity I have tried to inform the Military Academy of the true nature of the problem only to suffer undue harassment and deprivation of my legal rights for my forthright performance of my duty.

2. I understand that if this resignation is accepted, I will not be transferred to any Reserve Component in any status, enlisted, warrant or officer, nor will I be ordered to active duty for any period whatsoever. I acknowledge that the provisions of paragraph 7.08, Academic Credit in cases Involving Cadet Separations Regulations, USMA, apply to my situation.

3. I understand that I may not be appointed in a commissioned grade in a regular component of the United States Army, Navy, Marine Corps, or Air Force, prior to the commissioning date of my current class at the United States Military Academy.

4. I agree to liquidate any indebtedness that I may have to the Treasurer, United States Military Academy, as

soon as possible after my account is settled and a final statement rendered.

5. I am 23 years of age. My mother has knowledge of my resignation.

6. I understand that prior to being forwarded to the Department of the Army, this resignation may only be withdrawn with the approval of Headquarters, Department of the Army.

7. I have retained a copy of this resignation.

> TIMOTHY D. RINGGOLD
> Company E-1
> Class of 1977

When I handed my conditional resignation letter to the secretary for the commandant's office, I sat waiting for an acceptance of the letter. Called back up to the secretary's desk, I was handed my letter back and told that "The commandant is not willing to accept this." Part of me understood that he was not willing to accept what had been written in the letter as fact, but at the same time I was surprised he didn't just want me out of here.

Keeping ever vigilant in what was happening in Washington, DC, I read in *The Times Herald-Record*, dated Tuesday, August 10, 1976, in the article "Downey Urges Cadet Penalty be Suspended" that Congressman Downey wrote a letter to Army Secretary Hoffmann to urge a suspension of the use of the expulsion penalty. The letter was signed by Speaker of the House Carl Albert, Majority Leader Thomas O'Neill, and Armed Services Committee Chairman Melvin Price. They asked Secretary Hoffmann to delay expulsion of any cadets found guilty for a month until the Corps of Cadets voted on a change of the Honor

System. I felt at this point we were beyond needing to collect a vote from the Corps of Cadets to change the Honor System. The Honor System needed to be changed regardless, and I was most certainly an advocate for the penalty to match the crime.

In the same article, it stated that "Sen. Sam Nunn, chairman of a Senate Armed Services subcommittee, called for an immediate investigation of charges that cadets and their lawyers have been intimidated by high Army officials."

In *The New York Times*, James Feron reported in his article "West Point 'Jury' Asks New Inquiry," on August 10 that a board of high-ranking officers at West Point had moved unexpectedly that day, somewhat in the manner of a grand jury, to recommend a major investigation of "widespread cheating."

In the article "Hoffmann Pressed to Name Code Panel" on Thursday, August 12, 1976 in *The Times Herald-Record*, that "173 congressmen have signed a letter strongly urging Hoffmann to name 'a blue ribbon panel' to study the US Military Academy Honor Code and current cheating scandal." That letter, written by Congressman Downey, sounded like the same letter mentioned a few days earlier in that same paper. I was glad Downey was able to get 173 congressmen to sign it! He was certainly receiving the much-needed support from his colleagues that would force the secretary of the Army to form the blue-ribbon panel. It was, without a doubt, only a matter of time, despite General Berry's adamant opposition to form such a panel.

In the same article, however, Frederick W. Smullen, the Academy's spokesman, reported it was "premature and inopportune for any review of the code to be conducted while the current honor hearings are in session."

A few days later, not changing my mind and knowing I would not change my mind, I wrote my official resignation letter.

West Point, New York 10996

MACC-1   17 August 1976

Subject: Resignation of Cadet TIMOTHY D. RINGGOLD, class
of 1977, Company E-1.

Tactical Officer
Co. E. 1st Regt.
United States Corps of Cadets
West Point, New York 10996

1. I, TIMOTHY D. RINGGOLD, do hereby voluntarily tender
    my resignation from the United States Military Academy.
    My reasons for resigning are as follows:
    a. I have suffered irrefutable damage to my future
        as a cadet and potential army officer because of
        my unusual involvement in the EE304 cheating
        controversy.
    b. Even though I was never formally charged with a
        violation of the Cadet Honor Code, I was subjected
        to isolation in Transient Barracks, deprived of my
        rank and position and not permitted to wear my
        class ring.
    c. I was forced to testify against my peers in violation
        of my rights under the Fifth Amendment of
        the Federal Constitution and Article 31 of the
        Uniform Code of Military Justice.
    d. I have been threatened with criminal prosecution
        without any foundation in fact.
    e. At every opportunity I have tried to inform
        the Military Academy of the true nature of
        the EE304 controversy, only to suffer undue

harassment and deprivation of my legal rights for my forthright performance of my duty.

2. I understand that if this resignation is accepted, I may be transferred to The Reserve Component in an enlisted status and ordered to active duty for not less than two years. I request that a waiver of the two year active duty requirement be waived for the above mentioned reasons and because of the expiration of my former 3 year enlistment obligation in the Regular Army.

3. I understand that I may not be appointed to a commissioned grade in a regular component of the United States Army, Navy, Marine Corps, or Air Force, prior to the commissioning date of my current class at the United States Military Academy.

4. I agree to liquidate any indebtedness that I may have to the Treasurer, United States Military Academy, as soon as possible after my account is settled and a final statement rendered.

5. I am 23 years of age. My mother has knowledge of my resignation.

6. I understand that prior to being forwarded to the Department of the Army, this resignation may be withdrawn only with the approval of the superintendent and thereafter with the approval of Headquarters, Department of the Army.

7. I have retained a copy of this resignation.

TIMOTHY D. RINGGOLD
###-###-####
Co. E-1, Class of 1977
United States Corps of Cadets

CHAPTER 32
TRANSCEND THE
LIMITS OF DUALITY

A FEW DAYS AFTER I handed in my resignation letter, I received all the paperwork relieving me of my duties as a member of the Corps of Cadets. Leaving West Point for the last time, I headed home with the intention to arrive before my mother received my resignation letter in the mail.

When I arrived home, I opened the front door and the screen door slammed behind me. I dropped my rucksack on the living room floor and plopped onto the couch.

"Is that you, John?" My mother called from the kitchen.

"No, Mom, it's me."

My mom walked in with a dish towel in her hand and a frown on her face. "I don't understand. Why are you here?" she asked.

I was wearing civilian clothes—a set of shorts and T-shirt from my trunk at school. "I resigned, Mom."

"Oh, Tim. No..." She said, looking heart-stricken.

She came and sat down next to me on the couch, put her arm

around me and sighed. She looked like she might cry. What more could be said? We sat in silence for some time. I could feel my mother processing the multitude of emotions, not of having me back, but of knowing that my long-term goal of becoming an Army officer was over. I wondered in that second if she'd regret having sent me to Staunton Military Academy because of what it cost her.

"So you didn't get kicked out?" she asked, confused.

"No," I replied.

"You resigned?" she asked.

"Yes," I said, nodding.

"Why?" she asked, and then put her hands up to block me answering. "I don't want to know. I don't want to hear another word about it, Tim. This is not happening. This is not an option. You get back into your car and go straight back to the Academy, ya hear? You have just one year left. That's nothing! You're going to finish what you started, Tim. That's all there is to it! We didn't send you to Staunton for nothing. You didn't attend West Point prep school for nothing. You didn't spend three years as a cadet at the most prestigious military academy for nothing!" Her voice started to escalate. "I will not have it! I will not!"

I knew she was scared. I knew she was worried about me, which is why I hadn't called her before I drove across the country to head home.

"Mom, I don't want to be an Army officer anymore. I have no desire to go back to the Army. I'd be interacting with other West Point graduates. It's done," I said, placing my hand on hers.

"Well maybe you can take some time and think on it?" she said, sounding hopeful, but resigned. "You don't just give up, Tim. You're a fighter." Now, she was crying.

I smiled at her words. I certainly am a fighter and like Father Curley said, *I fought the good fight.* "I've spent a lot of time thinking, Mom. I didn't make this decision lightly. They kicked out one hundred and fifty-one of my classmates, and I decided to leave with them," I said, getting choked up; her emotions clearly affecting me.

She nodded. "I don't understand, Tim, but I'm sorry. I really am."

"So I can stay here, right Mom?" I asked, taking her hands in mine.

"Well, I may put you to work now that you're home," she said, a smile reaching her eyes as she wiped away her tears.

"I'm happy to help, Mom. Just tell me what you need done."

The next morning I awoke early, having trouble sleeping. It was so darn quiet. I was so used to barracks being noisy, the echo of voices bouncing off the cement walls and the answering calls of the plebes forced to do chores in the early morning hours.

Where do I go from here? I went to the living room and grabbed my mom's typewriter and took it back to my room. I wrote sometimes to process what I was thinking. Having nothing better to do and wishing to rid my mind of its constant chatter, I began to type.

Hours went by as I clicked on the typewriter and emptied my mind onto pages.

I walked into the kitchen to find some remaining coffee in the pot. As I poured the room-temperature coffee into a cup, the quiet of the house allowed me to remain in my head. I looked in the fridge and realized it had been years since I'd prepared a meal for myself. In Washington, I'd picked up sandwiches or ordered out from Mexican or Chinese restaurants, whatever was cheapest. At West Point, meals were provided in the mess hall or I could grab a snack from my boodle box, a name West Point gave to a cadet's stash of cookies from home. I grabbed a container of cottage cheese from the fridge and an apple from the basket on the kitchen table and headed back to my room.

I typed my thoughts, letting them flow without trying to put them into any semblance of order. After a few more hours passed, I collected the pages I'd written and laid down on my bed to read them. I started to connect the dots to what I had committed to paper.

My initial question was: why? Why would the administration be so hell bent on denying the truth of the situation? Clearly because it happened on their watch, but it felt so much bigger than that. The superintendent was more concerned about protecting the image of West Point than the lives of the cadets themselves. General Westmoreland manipulated the American public with a false image of our success in Vietnam at the cost of American lives, so West Point was doing the same thing at the cost of cadets' careers. It seemed very counterintuitive, like cutting one's nose off to spite the face. The majority of my classmates were good, decent, hard-working young men. They had been class presidents, belonged to academic honor societies, were Eagle Scouts and all-state athletes. They could have gone to any college, but they chose West Point, and West Point threw them out over a homework assignment. To not support their growth, to not help them learn from their mistakes, society lost not only the financial investment, but their years of service that was to come.

As I continued to read my thoughts on paper, I reflected on what had happened. My classmates and I were in high school during the Vietnam War. Every single instructor of mine at West Point was a Vietnam veteran. Even Captain Lincoln had come to West Point directly from Vietnam. My classmates and I entered West Point during an unpopular time to serve. Our country was heartbroken over Vietnam. Our society was split into those who supported the war and those who opposed it. One could argue that the Vietnam War destroyed the Army because not only were we defeated, tens of thousands of soldiers lost their lives, and hundreds of thousands were wounded and traumatized. It's true the Army never lost a battle in Vietnam, but we surely lost the war. Those who did return home were cloaked with shame by the public's animosity who did not honor or understand the sacrifice they had made.

Thus, we were not only a society that needed to heal, but the Army itself needed to heal as well. During these times of loss, we needed to stop and process what just happened. Without taking the time to reflect and process, we risked the danger of repeating our mistakes. It takes courage to acknowledge our pain because it hurts, and we might have to acknowledge our failure.

During the Vietnam War, we were winning the battles, but losing the war way before we decided to withdraw. General Westmoreland's call for more and more troops proved he was willing to waste human life and use force rather than strategy. With guerilla warfare, the game of how war was fought had changed. The mentality during the Vietnam War was reflected by the Academy's handling of the cheating scandal, which was to forge ahead, destroy all that was necessary, and win at all costs, even at the expense of cadets' careers. We truly were cannon fodder. It was devastating.

I think this resulted from the heartache of the administration who wanted to believe what we did in Vietnam was right. The administration did not want to acknowledge the breakdown of the military, essentially the bad things that happened in Vietnam, because if they did, then they would have to know the pain too. Pain is uncomfortable and messy. In order to avoid the pain at all costs, which is what I believed they were doing, they would then need to point their fingers at someone to represent the problem. The cadets became the scapegoats. They represented all that is wrong with the Army because it was too painful for the administration to acknowledge their own heartbreak. This is not to say the cadets were completely innocent, but the punishment often outweighed the crime and thus the burden of reflecting the loss, the pain, the broken-heartedness of the country, fell onto these young men.

If the administration had acknowledged their own heartbreak, then they could have given themselves the much-needed forgiveness for such actions that took place in Vietnam. With the ability to forgive, they could have given grace to the cadets who also made mistakes. If President Nixon can be pardoned, why couldn't my class? At any time, the administration could have paused, forgiven, and rectified the situation. It does not have to be a sign of weakness to show mercy. Still honoring the history and traditions of West Point, along with the awareness of grief and the need for healing, the administration could have re-established some order of sanity. This would have been the ideal leadership. Just as cadets fell short of the honor ideal, the Academy leadership fell short of perfection.

With that realization, I started to see how the cheating scandal had been like a mirror reflecting the Army's unresolved place in the world after Vietnam. West Point is the soul of the Army and the Army was in the midst of licking its wounds. As such, West Point needed the time to pause, reflect and heal; it could not be *business as usual*. The Honor Code was not *alive and well* because the Army was not alive and well. We had to face the fact that we were suffering.

I also think the administration forgot the fact that the college years are of great influence, a time to learn about one's own place in the world and to develop one's own character. The prized cadet years are so special because these are the coming-of-age years that mold and shape a person's life forever. This is where one can develop integrity, honor, and character through experience. A person is not born with patience or courage but has to develop it through experience. It is unrealistic to expect cadets to be perfect, which is exactly what the Honor System required.

The cheating scandal has often been described as a time of

great reflection for the Academy. The world was changing and West Point needed to change with it, but the only way to change was to reflect on what was no longer working. In times of self-reflection, we are given the chance to learn from the past and choose to do things differently, to do things better. We needed to reflect on what was honorable again. Wasn't learning, growing, and forgiving honorable?

The truth was that cadets, like all people, are not just honorable or dishonorable, but fall along the continuum between these two positions. At the end of July, the Cadet Honor Committee formally recommended, for the first time in its history, to not expel a cadet who had been found guilty of violating the Honor Code. The Honor Committee made this recommendation because it perceived that the cadet found guilty of violating the Cadet Honor Code was nevertheless an honorable man and would make a fine officer.

Cadets can still be honorable even if they have violated the Honor Code with the acknowledgment of wrong-doing and growth. Americans can be against the Vietnam War and at the same time support the troops. Cadets can fight the abuses of the Honor System and still support the Honor Code. Both the administration and the accused Cadets can both love and want what is best for West Point. We need to transcend the limits of duality. This is the heart of the matter and brings us to a new awareness that seemingly contradictory thoughts can coexist, but we need to be willing to transcend the limits of black and white thinking.

So, my thoughts led me to the realization that only through acknowledging the pain and suffering caused by the Vietnam War, could we come to understand the reasons behind the cheating scandal.

CHAPTER 33
ONE-YEAR REFLECTION

AFTER UNDERSTANDING MORE FULLY THE intricacies surrounding the cheating scandal, I felt some peace of mind. I was numb, though, not yet feeling the heartbreak that I knew would come over my broken relationship with West Point. To pass the time, I decided to tackle a long-time goal to finally read the book *War and Peace* by Leo Tolstoy. The 1,225 page novel could keep my mind off reality for at least a few days. I really was enjoying this time alone, needing the break, and felt I would decide my next move when it came to me.

Not able to completely disconnect from West Point, I read the newspaper daily. I was aware that Mr. Michael Rose, along with the other civilian and military attorneys, had requested the United States Court of Military Appeals in Washington, DC to reinstate the cadets who had been found guilty during the scandal. The attorneys also asked for a halt in the Academy's proceedings against the accused cadets.

On Monday, August 23, I sat on the couch with my mom and watched the afternoon news to hear Secretary of the Army Martin

Hoffmann testify again before the Subcommittee on Manpower and Personnel of the Senate Armed Services Committee. At 2:39 P.M. Secretary Hoffmann began speaking.

"I had hoped to avoid taking matters out of the hands of the Academy's administration and Cadet Corps, but I recognize the cheating scandal has become beyond the Academy's ability to handle the problem. I recognize, too, that the Academy bears a major responsibility for the breakdown of the Honor System," Hoffmann said.

"Finally!" I retorted.

"Because of the unique situation, cadets in the cheating scandal will be offered a second chance under some rigid conditions. Meaning, cadets found guilty will be put on suspension for one year and must serve either in the Army's enlisted ranks, attend school, or work in an allowable public-service profession. This designated time away from the United States Military Academy should be a time of reflection, a time for the cadet to mature, consider upon his desire for a military career and demonstrate his potential for commissioning. Come spring, these cadets may reapply for admittance. Not all cadets will be accepted back, but most will be.

"Colonel Jack L. Capps, an English professor and graduate from West Point, will be named chairman of the Special Readmission Committee, which will give advice and guidance to cadets interested in the readmission offer. Cadets who are found guilty but choose not to return can simply leave the Academy without having to serve their required two-year enlistment. I believe the concept of the Honor System remains fundamentally sound, but the seriousness of the situation requires extraordinary address to assure that the full health of the system can be restored," Hoffmann declared.

"Did you hear how he said the cadets could reapply, but there was no guarantee of acceptance?" Mom asked.

"Yeah, I heard that loud and clear, Mom, which will not be

fair unless West Point accepts everyone back."

Hoffmann continued, "A special advisory panel will be formed to fully analyze West Point's Honor System. To head this special advisory group will be the distinguished Colonel Frank Borman, a West Point graduate, the president of Eastern Air Lines, and a former astronaut. The public will be impressed with Colonel Borman's stature, dynamism, and inquisitive nature.

"There will also be some academic changes, and the take-home assignments, such as the one that led to the present problem, will be banned."

"How do you feel about the one-year suspension?" Mom looked at me inquisitively.

"Well, I'm not completely surprised. There'd been a rumor recently going around West Point that those found guilty might be able to come back." I sighed. "The thing is, Mom, it sounds like a compromise, but I can't help but wonder if the damage was already done. Those that choose to go back and graduate as part of the class of 1978 will forever have it in their records that they were part of the scandal and there will be a stigma attached to that."

"It's better than getting kicked out. Do you think anyone will be happy with the option though?"

"Maybe. It's just not realistic to think that this won't have an impact on their Army career," I said.

"At least they'll still have a West Point diploma."

"That's true. I also know some of my classmates will likely not return," I said matter-of-factly.

"Has West Point ever done anything like this before?"

"Never. This will be the first time. There's evidence, Mom, that at least half my class cheated, so to only have ten percent punished is unfair. They're essentially scapegoats in a cover-up of the scope of the scandal."

"Oh, I see," she said, wide-eyed and not convinced.

★ ★ ★

Hearing the phone in the kitchen ringing, I debated answering it and was grateful when I heard my mother did.

"Hello? Yes, he is. Who may I say is calling? Okay, one sec, Mr. Flanagan."

I hadn't been in touch with anyone from school.

"Tim? Phone for you," her voice sounded through the hallway.

"Okay, Mom. Be right there."

As I came into the kitchen, I was handed the phone. I took a deep breath before I spoke. "Flanagan, how are you, man?"

"I'm okay, Ringgold. I know you've resigned, and it isn't probably right of me to be calling, but I needed to talk."

"That's what friends are for. What can I help you with?"

"Ringgold, I don't think it was right what happened to our class, and I don't know what to do about it."

"What do you mean? You had plenty of opportunity to speak up the past few months." I didn't mean to sound accusatory; I was just stating the fact.

"Ringgold, it's not that simple."

"What's not simple about that? Whenever we got together and talked about the scandal, you withdrew and remained quiet. Clearly you had no interest in what was happening to our class *then*. It was clear you did not want to be involved."

"Ringgold, I could've been one of them," he admitted. "I could've easily been accused of cheating just like our classmates."

"What are you telling me, Flanagan? Are you trying to say that you are as guilty as the ones being thrown out?"

He cleared his throat and swallowed before answering. "Ringgold, I didn't have a clue what a Zenor Diode was and still don't. It wasn't in the textbook, and I don't remember the professor ever mentioning anything about it, so . . ." He cleared his throat again. "So I went over to a classmate's room. I won't mention who's, but I asked him for help. I asked him what a Zenor

Diode was, and he told me 'it's like a ladder. It either moves up or it moves down.' Once I heard that, I went back and relooked at the question. I was able to figure it out and solved the problem on my own. That's why they weren't able to identify me when they compared the papers."

"I get it. We were all in the same situation. But the fact remains, you asked for help and a classmate gave it. We both know the academic instruction was poor, which was likely part of the problem, but that's another issue. Do you feel better having told me this?" I asked.

"No, not exactly. I wanted to ask you: do you think I cheated?"

"Me? No. But by the Honor Systems' standards, by the philosophy of the current administration at West Point, you *absolutely* cheated."

"Oh my god, Ringgold, don't say that!"

"But that's the whole point, Flanagan. You did no worse or no better than those who've been kicked out or those that resigned to avoid the embarrassment of getting kicked out. Yes, there were some guys who blatantly knew they cheated, but the majority were good guys who didn't deserve to get kicked out and their careers ruined."

"Did you see Secretary Hoffmann's announcement about the suspension?"

"Yes, both my mother and I saw it."

"There were loudspeakers set up all over West Point, in barracks and classrooms, so we all could hear Secretary Hoffmann. He mentioned a ten-day grace period starting Sunday where cadets could come forward, admit their guilt, and take the one-year leave of absence. Do you think I should turn myself in?" Flanagan asked, clearly hoping that I would discourage him.

"Oh Flanagan. You know this is a bunch of bullshit. What purpose would it serve if you turned yourself in? Relieve your conscience for asking a classmate a question?" I sighed. "I know you're trying to do the right thing, and I respect you for that, but the time that you should've acted was months ago. I get it. I understand why you didn't come forward or rather why a lot of our classmates didn't come forward . . . you didn't want to risk your careers. I get it. What happened to choosing the harder right instead of the easier wrong?"

The Cadet Prayer went through my head. *Make us to choose the harder right instead of the easier wrong and never to be content with a half truth when the whole can be won. Endow us with courage that is born of loyalty to all that is noble and worthy, that scorns to compromise with vice and injustice and knows no fear when truth and right are in jeopardy.*

Flanagan remained quiet, so I went on. "Did you think you were alone in this predicament? You weren't. What you did was completely trivial and by all reasonable standards of honor, you are innocent. And a lot of our classmates, who were thrown out or now given this one-year suspension, are also innocent. You and I are friends, and I've always considered you to be an honorable man, so I don't think it would serve any purpose for you to turn yourself in. More than fifteen percent of our class are enough sacrificial lambs."

"I couldn't do what you did, Ringgold," Flanagan said, trying to explain. "I couldn't risk being thrown out. You know my dad was a West Point grad and died last year? If I'd done anything to jeopardize my staying at West Point, I would've broken his heart. I wouldn't have been able to live with myself."

"I understand the complexity of it, Flanagan. I do. I really do, and I'm sorry that you felt trapped. I'm sorry that you felt like you couldn't speak up without the risk."

"I talked to my brother, Brenden, about it. Besides you, he is the only one I've told. He's a yearling, and we both agreed that the situation was beyond our control."

"Listen, I've spent all summer fighting for an outside investigation, and it truly felt outside my control, too. Finish off your last year at West Point and move on. Do some good in this world and don't look back. And in the meantime, don't put any other cadet in the position of having to turn you in or be guilty of an honor violation! That's what you did by talking to your brother. I don't have an obligation to report you, but your brother does. Every cadet does. Feel sorry all you want, but stop sharing with other cadets, okay?"

"Okay, Ringgold, I understand. Thanks for talking."

"Take care of yourself, man. Call me anytime, brother. Bye."

There was one person who was clearly not happy with Secretary Hoffmann's decision. Father Curley felt that the cadets caught up in the cheating scandal had suffered enough. Having possession of the cadet affidavits, Father Curley knew better than any cadet the true extent of honor violations across the Corps. The affidavits included names of up to 700 cadets, as well as graduates who were currently commissioned officers in the Army, about honor violations including individual events, dates, and times. What particularly galled him was the realization that the class of 1977 would be divided into two groups: the cadets found guilty and those not charged. Those who came forward under the amnesty program would forever be labeled *cheaters* and those who, like Tim Flanagan, were equally guilty, but didn't come forward, would be labeled the *honorable* members of the class. As a result, Father Curley removed the affidavits from the safe deposit box in Marine Midland Bank in Highland Falls, and gave them to Congressman Downey to place on President Ford's desk with a letter:

Catholic Chapel of the Most Holy Trinity
United States Military Academy
West Point, New York 10996

3 September 1976

Gerald R. Ford
The President
The White House
Washington, DC 20500

Dear Mr. President:

Embodied in the Cadet Prayer are these essential sentiments: "Make us choose the harder right instead of the easier wrong and never to be content with a half truth when the whole can be won." Over these past months I have been forced to conclude by the developing magnitude of alleged honor violations that there has been a systematic collapse of the Honor Code at West Point. The reasons are varied but the most glaring is the inadequacy of the present honor system. After seeing so much needless hurt and embarrassment inflicted on so many honorable cadets and families, I have repeatedly tried by revealing the scope confidentially to the superintendent to stop this great injustice. Now when we should be seeking reconciliation within the Corps, some cadets have resigned and many more will be separated before the Borman Committee has even diagnosed the problem.

Upon the request of many honorable cadets, I am enclosing affidavits for your review. I ask that you respect these materials in the spirit of the attorney-client relationship in which they were obtained. It is my hope that seeing what should be obvious, you will restrain Secretary Hoffmann from any action until the Borman Committee determines what has been the cause of the current problem.

Two years ago you had the moral courage to act on behalf of Richard Nixon so that the Nation would not be torn apart, a stand which made you unpopular with some. As commander in chief, I beg you to appreciate the magnitude and complexity of the current honor crisis at West Point and not to be content with a half truth when the whole can be won. In years past the Long Gray Line has never failed this Nation. I ask you now, as President, not to fail the Long Gray Line.

Sincerely in the Lord,
Rev. Thomas J. Curley
Catholic Chaplain

President Ford's lawyer, Phillip Buchen, wrote Father Curley back, stating that "it is not appropriate to accept the proffered affidavits under the conditions you have imposed, specifically, that use of the information be subject to the attorney-client privilege," and thus returned them.

SEPTEMBER–DECEMBER
1976

CHAPTER 34

A LETTER FROM
AN ASTRONAUT

HAVING LEFT WEST POINT FOR good, it took weeks before I could reprogram myself to sleep past 5:30 A.M. I constantly felt a sense of urgency during every waking moment. Not having a schedule was both freeing and unnerving; I couldn't help but feel that I had forgotten something or was needed somewhere.

I had difficulty making a decision about the next direction in my life. All I knew was that West Point was behind me, and I was okay with that. Energetically I felt broken into tiny pieces and knew it would take time to put myself back together. For perhaps the first time in my life, I had time to slow down, to think, and to process the recent events. I had time to consider the next phase of my life, as well as time to do nothing—a luxury I'd never experienced.

As part of my newly found freedom, I grew a mustache and let my hair grow, a high contrast to my weekly haircuts. In the fashion of the day, I wore bell-bottom jeans and T-shirts. I continued to jog three to four miles daily to shake off my restlessness. I spent the majority of my time reading, allowing myself to stay within my hermit mindset as long as was needed in order to figure out the next step of my life.

Knowing my appetite was a burden to my mother's weekly paycheck, I got a part-time job at a local farm taking care of the horses. At the horse farm, I shoveled manure, brushed down the horses, and exercised them.

My meager income allowed me to keep the house stocked with red wine, cottage cheese, and canned pineapple, as well as peanut butter and apples, my simple go-to meals.

I did help around the house and cooked occasionally. Using my mom's Betty Crocker cookbook, I made banana pancakes from scratch. My favorite evening meal to prepare was beef burritos and cheese crisps, which always tasted even better reheated. My two older brothers always preferred Mexican food growing up, but my younger brother John liked it when I made chicken stir fry. Mom was happy any evening she didn't have to cook.

It was nice to live such a simplistic lifestyle. Preferring the company of horses over people, I stayed in my solitude, not keeping in touch with anyone still at West Point. There was only one person who I did call and that was Gina. I updated her on the scandal and my departure from school. She was easy to talk to, so I found myself sharing my innermost thoughts about how the cheating scandal was connected to the Vietnam War. She agreed that the scandal reflected a wound in the Army because of society's trauma from the war. She also recommended that I write a book about my experience. I said "no, I can't live in the past. I'm not going that direction. I need to look to the future and figure out what I'm doing and where I'm going."

The months passed by quietly. I was grateful my Mother didn't pressure me about what I was doing, but rather gave me space to figure it out on my own. There had to be a benefit of all those years at military school and in service even if it didn't end in a West Point diploma. I hoped in time I would discover another path.

A few days into December, I was astonished to receive a letter in the mail from Colonel Frank Borman. Pretty much everyone knew who Colonel Frank Borman was, for he was famous for having been commander of Apollo 8, a three-man team that had circled the moon on December 24, 1968. I was fifteen at the time and remembered the pictures of the Blue Marble, showing the Earth from space. I had thought it very smart to put a West Point graduate who was as well-known and highly respected as he was to chair the blue ribbon commission to analyze West Point's Honor System. I knew, with it being December, that the Borman Commission had probably completed its report.

Curious and eager to see what Colonel Borman could possibly have to say to me, I ran to the porch, sat down, and tore open the letter.

For what seemed like an eternity, I sat with the letter clutched to my chest in disbelief.

My mother found me on the porch when she arrived home. Startled by the look on my face, I handed her the letter. After reading it, she said, "Well, ultimately Tim, it is your decision."

"I know. I've allowed myself these months to disconnect from the Academy, but I realize that I may never feel the sense of completion or closure I'm looking for unless I finish what I started," I said, looking at the ground, my right sneakered toe digging into the dirt.

"I like how Colonel Borman validates what you did. He praises your "moral courage and steadfastness in the face of tremendous pressure from Academy officials." He says here it would be a shame if you didn't return and "participate in all the changes" that have been made which you fought so hard for. I can't help but agree with him," she said. I could hear the smile in her words.

"You know, I've never spoken to Colonel Borman. He's never

called me or questioned me in any way nor did any member of his committee. I guess my actions spoke for themselves, and it was clear the role I'd played," I concluded.

"He described being horrified at what they discovered and urged Secretary Hoffmann to have all the cadets reinstated right then and there, so they could graduate with their class," she said, reading from the letter.

"Yes, I agree. I think they should graduate on time even if they missed a semester of school. During World War II, West Point graduated one class a semester early and several that graduated after only three years. Soldiers were needed for the war. If West Point could graduate several classes after only three years, I don't see why they couldn't welcome all of us back to graduate with our class. When we entered West Point in 1973, our superintendent was Lieutenant General William Knowlton. He'd graduated six months early in January 1943. If they could do it then, why couldn't they do it now?"

"That'd certainly be ideal," my mother said. "So there were a hundred and fifty-one cadets that were kicked out or chose to resign because of the cheating scandal?"

"One hundred and fifty-one plus one. Me," I said shyly.

"Wow. How many do you think will reapply in the spring?"

"Your guess is as good as mine. For now, I didn't think I would consider returning. I can hardly believe I'm actually considering it."

"You needed this time away to give you some perspective," she said, sympathetically.

"Maybe so." She kissed me on the head, smiled at me, and went inside the house.

From Colonel Borman's letter, I understood he saw the truth. He was under the opinion that West Point had failed the cadets, not the other way around. He saw the breakdown of the Honor System, that the administration was far more guilty than the cadets themselves. He said the Academy needed a reboot, a fresh start. He knew the damage of having cadets graduate one year later, in a class they didn't know, and how obvious it would be on their record. Borman tried to minimize the impact of the scandal on the cadets by having them graduate with their class. The secretary of the Army disagreed with that recommendation and stuck with the reapply next year requirement.

As I sat there, I quickly realized I would never be happy if I didn't go back and finish what I had started, get my hard-earned West Point diploma, and serve as the Army officer I was destined to be. As jarring as that decision was, I no longer felt so lost.

1977

CHAPTER 35
RETURN TO WEST POINT

IT WAS REASSURING TO READ the *Time* magazine article called "A Barrage Hits West Point's Code," in which a portion of Col. Frank Borman's letter to the secretary of the Army Martin Hoffman, was quoted.

> We believe that education concerning the honor code has been inadequate and the administration of the honor code has been inconsistent and, at times, corrupt. The cadets did cheat but were not solely at fault. Their culpability must be viewed against the unrestrained growth of the "cool-on-honor" subculture at the academy, the gross inadequacies in the honor system, the failure of the academy to act decisively with respect to known honor problems, and other academy shortcomings.

At the end of February, I received a letter from the superintendent sent to all West Point alumni and cadets updating us on the recent changes made to the Academy because of the

Borman report.

In the letter, it stated that of the 151 cadets who were separated from the Academy due to the scandal, 126 cadets had been found to be "tentatively suitable for readmission." They never did include me in the count, which would have brought it to 152. This did not mean we were fully accepted back in; West Point liked to be thorough. Under the readmission protocol, I had to provide a detailed explanation of my activities during my leave. As such, I applied to Arizona State University to attend a few classes since attending school was a valid activity. While I had studied History at West Point, at Arizona State I studied Physics. After the chaos of the cheating scandal, I took refuge in Physics and the search for physical truth. Like the Honor System, the world around us is much more complex than it appears. Since I couldn't find truth in the Honor System, perhaps I could find it in Newton's Laws or the Laws of Thermodynamics. At least the speed of light remained constant.

At the beginning of March, I received a Status Report from Colonel Rhyne, the assistant commandant who had also served as the special assistant to the commandant for honor. His report supported the letter the superintendent had sent earlier. The *Clean Slate* policy allowed readmitted cadets to be forgiven for any honor violation that occurred prior to their separation and readmission.

In early March, I received a personal letter from Colonel Jack Capps, the chairman of the Special Readmissions Committee, asking me to explain the role I played publicly last year and my current feelings on the matter. In *The Arizona Republic*, dated May 14, 1977, I was quoted as saying:

> I feel an obligation to go back. I want to be part of the change. I want to show that the people who left were worth keeping in the first place. I like what he (Borman) had to say. I've calmed down and understand the Academy's side

a lot better now and, frankly, I'm not so sure if I was in the same situation, I wouldn't have reacted the same way the Academy did. All of us who were involved in this fight thought we were fighting to save the Academy because problems were going to persist if West Point did not admit the extent of cheating and accept change. I feel good about the way things have worked out. I want to return to West Point and heal some wounds, as well as pick up my career where it left off.

I received a reply from Colonel Capps about my explanation and reapplication stating, "It will be placed in your readmissions file . . . and will give the Special Readmissions Committee adequate information with which to consider your case." I wasn't in doubt that I would be accepted back in, but there was no guarantee.

By the end of April, I received my acceptance letter to return to West Point and immediately called Gina. She understood my need to go back in order to be able to move on with my life. She was busy teaching and raising her daughter. She wasn't necessarily waiting around for me; it had been almost a year since we had last seen each other. I had no idea when we would have an opportunity to see each other again, but I had this very distinct feeling she would be part of my future.

In preparation of my return to West Point, I was given a Summer Assignment to go to Panama for jungle warfare training before the start of the academic year. I had never been to Panama, but I was excited about being back in uniform. It would give me a month of training and an opportunity to get back in shape, nevertheless. It proved to be more of a culture shock than I had anticipated. One day I was a long-haired college student and a week later I was eating iguana and sleeping on a jungle floor; life was good.

★ ★ ★

I had left West Point mentality brutalized and disheartened at the institution it had become. In choosing to return, I was essentially going to form a new relationship with West Point. Since I had left last August, I knew General Ulmer and General Berry both had been reassigned. Father Curley had left in July. I knew Captain Lincoln had been passed over for routine promotion to major and was told by an unauthorized source that it was because of his defense activities in the scandal. He then left the Army to practice law somewhere in Massachusetts. In fact, all of the defense attorneys, who had also been the Law professors during the scandal, had been transferred.

I was entering a new class, the class of 1978, full of cadets I did not know personally. It was truly going to feel like a new school to me. I really hoped the new West Point would fulfill my childhood dreams of being the school romanticized in the television shows I grew up watching. More importantly, I hoped West Point would live up to its own high standards and that I could find peace in that.

During my year away, I had changed. Feeling humbled and now speaking positively to the press about my return, I was grateful to have a sense of purpose again.

There was new leadership at West Point: General Andrew Jackson Goodpaster, former Supreme Allied Commander in Europe (SACEUR) and onetime staff secretary to President Dwight D. Eisenhower, was from the West Point class of 1939. He was brought out of retirement to replace General Berry as superintendent. The four-star general was a legend within the Army. In 1943, just four years after he graduated West Point, he was a lieutenant colonel commanding an engineer battalion in combat in North Africa and Italy during World War II. He was awarded the nation's second highest award for combat heroism, the Distinguished Service Cross. I was excited about the new leadership at the Academy and confident that General Goodpaster would be the catalyst for internal change it so desperately needed.

Returning to West Point was surreal. I drove up the steep hill along the Hudson, on a clear sunny day. I observed the companies of plebes getting worked out by cadre on the Parade Field. Beast Barracks was in full swing, and I was looking forward to seeing female cadets in uniform for the second year at the Academy. I looked to my left, passing the Catholic chapel and wondered where Father Curley was and how he was doing. To me, attorneys Arthur Lincoln and Daniel Sharphorn, along with Father Curley, were owed a debt that I'd never know how to repay.

Feeling both the familiarity of the place and a slight pang of fear at old memories, I couldn't help asking myself *What the hell am I doing back here?*

Of the 101 who returned, five had already achieved a bachelor's degree during our exile. Of course each would receive another diploma, this one from West Point next June, we hoped.

CHAPTER 36
STEADY MARCH
TO GRADUATION

THE ONE PERSON I DID know in my new class was Cadet Michael Mamer. I had called him when I decided to return and planned to meet him at the hostess office when I arrived on campus.

"Moon Dog!" I called out to him, across the street.

"Ringgold, my hero!"

I rolled my eyes. "Cut the crap. Good to see you, too!" I said.

"So good to see you man. How are you doing?" Mamer asked.

"I'm here. That's all that matters. How was your year away?"

"I was a PFC in an infantry platoon, air cavalry troop of the 3rd Armored Cavalry Regiment at Ft. Bliss, Texas. It was a great year. Where did you serve?" Mamer asked.

"Oh, I didn't. Last fall I didn't think I was coming back, so I took time off, but then attended Arizona State University last semester."

"Oh, I assumed everyone who wanted to reapply had to serve during their time away."

"No. Gratefully not. This is going to be a strange year without Hunt and Flanagan. I'm glad they both graduated without any problems," I said.

"For sure. Have you been in touch with DaRold?"

"Just a little last fall. I really haven't been in touch with anyone since I left, but I know DaRold finished his degree and is applying to medical school. I'm happy for him that he figured out his calling and is going for it," I said.

"Yeah, I am too, but the idea of Doctor DaRold is not exactly comforting," Mamer said, and we laughed. "Hey, plebe. Stop!" Mamer said to a passing cadet. The plebe listened and stood at attention, staring straight ahead with arms pinned to his side. "Plebe, how much water is in the Lusk Reservoir?"

"I don't know, sir," the plebe said, terrified.

"You don't know, plebe? How do you expect to survive here?" Mamer said sternly, feigning anger. "You must remember: There are seventy-eight million gallons when the water is flowing over the spillway."

"Yes, sir."

"How many lights in Cullum Hall?"

"Three hundred and forty, sir!"

"Very good. For that, I'll give you a piece of advice, plebe. In fact, because I'm feeling extra generous today, happy to be at my Academy for my last glorious year after my year away, I'm going to give you two pieces of advice! You ready, plebe?"

"Yes, sir," the plebe said, obviously eager to be on his way.

"First, if you want to hide something that is contraband, use your laundry bag," he said, nodding and circling the plebe in inspection. "Second, a shampoo bottle is great for hiding alcohol, not that I ever did that myself," Mamer said, winking at me. "You got that, plebe?"

"Yes, sir!"

"Good, now give me twenty," Mamer said and turned back to me. The plebe dropped his bag and assumed the push-up position. "I, personally, think this is going to be a great year!"

I couldn't help but shake my head and laugh.

"I'm glad we have each other to finish off this journey together," I said, optimistically to Mamer. "It will be a good year."

"Absolutely, Ringgold. I wouldn't be here if it wasn't for you, man. I'm ready to do this."

One of the changes at West Point was the shuffling of companies. I was not placed back into my original pre-scandal company, E-2, but I really wanted to finish where I started. My former tactical officer, Major Aloysius Greenhouse was still here, so I asked him if I could return to E-2. Major Greenhouse didn't have any issues with me or what I had done the previous year, so he approved of my transfer back to his company.

The Honor System had been wonderfully overhauled. With graduated penalties, cadets were not automatically expelled for violating the Honor Code. This also minimized any use of the silence from bitter cadets concerning cadets that had violated the Honor Code but given a less severe punishment. Due process was now guaranteed, with Army lawyers assigned to represent the defendant and the prosecutor during Honor Boards. Take-home assignments like the one that led to the scandal had been eliminated. The EE304 Electrical Engineering course also disappeared and became part of another course.

It didn't take long to get back into a routine as a cadet. Having attended Staunton Military Academy for two years, then served in the Army for two years, followed by West Point Prep School and three years at West Point, being in uniform felt way more natural to me than the ten months I'd just spent in civilian clothes.

I found out the reasons some of my classmates who'd been mixed up with the scandal did not return. A few got married; some reapplied and when they were accepted back in, turned West Point down to prove a point; and some parents were against their sons returning to West Point. I was pretty sure I was the last person my classmates expected to see return. We'd picked up the nickname *Zenor Boys* because the electrical engineering assignment had been about the Zenor Diode.

One of the first things the returning cadets did was to order our class rings. The tradition of the class ring began at West Point in 1835. Rings were purchased during the second semester of the junior year, and anyone leaving the Academy before graduating had to turn in their class ring before departing.

I'd received a class of 1977 ring in April 1976, just about the time I spoke to Under Secretary Augustine, and my journey through hell began. Gina had attended the Ring Dance as my date as my class celebrated receiving our class ring. When I resigned in August, I was required to turn in my ring. Now, as a new member of the class of 1978, I had the privilege of ordering a new ring. When the Zenor Boys and I received them, there was no declaration or recognition by the Academy. It was kept quiet, as if it really didn't happen—no surprise there.

The class of 1978 was not thrilled to have me or the *cheaters* or *Zenor Boys* in their class. All of us just tried to blend in and stay out of the limelight. Out of the original 152 of us that had left, 101 of us returned which meant we lost 51 classmates officially. I thought it was ironic, too, that we only lost 51 since the start of the scandal, in April of 1976, there were originally 46 cadets pulled out of formation for cheating.

There were those of my classmates that benefited from what I did, and they were very appreciative that they benefitted, but they didn't necessarily appreciate me for having done it. I knew, though, that West Point was able to heal itself because it went through this trauma in ways it would never have done if I, and others like me, hadn't come forward when we did. The corruption would just have perpetuated, but because we forced it out in the open, the Academy was forced to make changes for the better.

My readmitted classmates from the class of 1977 and I were encouraged to speak to the media to say nice things. The administration, under General Goodpaster, realized what had happened, thus the mature adults knew what went awry. It was the immature cadets and officers, with the black and white view of the world, that didn't. At the urging of the Academy officials, I gave a few interviews, all positive and pro-West Point saying, "The academy has really treated us like they ought to treat everyone all the time. It's been less arbitrary than you would expect of a bureaucracy like West Point." I spoke very positively of the changes and of the new Academy leadership.

I tried with varying degrees of success to be the cadet that West Point hoped I would be. How do you walk a thousand miles? You begin with a single step. Not feeling the need to make new friends or to become well-liked, and wanting to keep a low profile, I buried myself in academics. To my delight, I learned that I could get a lot of fulfillment from working hard academically. I knew I carried with me the stigma of the political troublemaker, so some cadets kept their distance, but I made one good friend who knew exactly how it felt to be singled-out and unable to blend in with the crowd.

Her name was Robin. Standing at five feet two inches and weighing less than one hundred pounds, she was a pistol in my mind, fierce, determined and not willing to deal with any bullshit. She also looked about twelve years old in her cadet uniform.

Having been one of the one hundred and nineteen women who had been part of the first class of women during my year away, it was obvious how much crap she dealt with on a daily basis.

"I know exactly who you are," she had told me when we first met.

I nodded, assuming that was the end of our conversation right then and there.

"I think it took a lot of guts to do what you did," she said, sincerely.

"Guts? Maybe. What about you? You decided to break tradition and attend an all-male academy?"

"It's not all-male anymore," she said with her right eyebrow turned up.

"That's true. I was never opposed to integrating women," I said.

"So that is one thing West Point has done right?" she said, sarcastically.

"Absolutely. I always admired how General Berry told the Corps that 'if you have a problem with this, put your resignation on my desk first thing Monday.' Besides, most of us don't get to see females unless they are tourists visiting."

She nodded. "Well, get used to it," she said with a little edge to her tone.

"How was your plebe year? Did the guys treat you respectfully?"

"Ha!" She laughed out loud. "Some did, but most of my classmates ignored me. Then there were the few times they tried to kiss me. Or the moments cadre would whisper in my ear, like he was reaming me out, but he was really telling me he liked my ass." She smirked at me.

I nodded. "Well, you take the good with the bad, right?"

"Yeah, I don't mind that our bathrooms still have urinals in them or that our uniforms still don't fit right. Makes no difference to me; I'm here to stay. I know it's going to take time for people to accept that women belong here," she said, with full conviction. "In one sense, they want us women doing the exact same things the men do, but if we do, then we're Amazons or moose. At the same time, the school wants us to be feminine, but not to use our femininity to our advantage."

"How would you use your femininity to your advantage?" I asked, intrigued.

"I have no idea!" she said, exasperated. "It's not like I could say, excuse me, sir, please don't yell at me today, I have a menstrual headache or sir, the reason I am running slower today is because I have cramps. We have to hide all those things!"

"You could've tried to blend in," I said, sarcastically.

She responded with one eyebrow turned up. "Ringgold, there's nothing I could do to hide the fact I am a woman. I was in the spotlight from the moment I arrived. I was watched during Beast Barracks to see how women were coping. I've been interviewed multiple times. We were the new species at West Point, but thankfully this year every company has women in it!"

I nodded in understanding. "I know the feeling of being in the spotlight."

"And there were those that said to me, 'it was a good morning *until women got here*,'" she said, sticking her tongue at me. "And then there were those that promised me they would run me out of the school." She rolled her eyes. "Somehow, the more cadets threatened me, the more I wanted to stay. I don't know what that says about me . . ." she said and laughed.

I smiled. Hearing her laugh was refreshing.

"Out of curiosity, did the scandal affect your plebe year much?" I asked.

"Well, during Beast Barracks a few of the cadre changed. The company commander changed overnight because he had been charged with cheating."

I nodded.

"And this one time, a firstie called me over and said, *Do you see my hand, Cadet? Yes, sir*, I said. *Do you see what is missing?* he said. *Your ring, sir*, I answered. *I'm not wearing my ring while cheaters are here*, he said."

"Oh geez, and what did you say to that?" I asked.

"I said, *it is a waste of a perfectly good ring, sir*," she said and winked at me.

"Ha! And how do you feel about the Honor System now? Do you think it is working?" I asked, curiously.

"Well, I'm in favor of the Honor System being run by the

Administration because the Honor Committee will abuse its power by using it to run out cadets they dislike," she said, matter-of-factly.

"Yes, I agree. That practice needs to be stopped, and with some adult supervision it should be."

A month before graduation, I was stunned to learn that Colonel Rhyne, the former deputy commandant, and first special assistant to the commandant for honor matters, had died of a heart attack. He was so young, only forty-seven. I'd had a number of interactions with Colonel Rhyne during the honor crisis and developed a lot of respect for him. At the request of General Berry and General Ulmer, Colonel Rhyne had selflessly put his career on hold to remain at West Point for an additional year to help oversee the Honor Committee and Internal Review Panels during the scandal. By staying at West Point, he postponed command of an armor brigade, a prestigious post that was necessary to be considered for promotion to Brigadier General. I'd heard that Colonel Rhyne had put in for an early retirement shortly after the Borman report was released as a protest over the firing of his boss, General Ulmer, who'd been reassigned six months early without a promotion. Thus, Colonel Rhyne's career ended prematurely because of the cheating scandal and doubtless this contributed to his heart attack and premature death.

With a heavy heart, I attended Colonel Rhyne's funeral at the Old Post Chapel at the West Point Cemetery on May 11, 1978, alone. I mean, there were a couple hundred mourners in attendance: his family, West Point classmates, colleagues from his service, as well as current cadets. I was the only returned cadet from the class of '77 who attended his funeral. Mamer and the others hadn't had much interaction with Colonel Rhyne and thus didn't feel compelled to attend his funeral as I did.

With General Berry in Europe and General Ulmer at Fort

Hood, I felt alone in experiencing Colonel Rhyne's passing. Father Curley wasn't there to give a sermon at the funeral. Captain Lincoln wasn't in the audience with me. All were gone. Many of the cadets present were part of the Honor Committee. In reading Colonel Rhyne's obituary, I learned that during the year I had been away, he had been instrumental in administering the changes the Borman Commission had recommended. By all accounts, I agreed with Cadet Mark Irwin's description of Colonel Rhyne during the scandal as the *perfect example of an Army officer*.

My head was lowered as I read the rest of the obituary. I pictured Colonel Rhyne devastated over the events of the scandal, retiring prematurely, and returning home to his wife and four sons. I knew the feeling of loss I had felt myself in leaving West Point in August 1976, for what I thought was the last time. I knew, though, that my feelings of loss couldn't compare to what Colonel Rhyne must have felt as his Army career came to an abrupt halt. I pictured him on his front porch literally rocking himself to death, and the image made me close to tears.

I noticed a few glances my way in the back of the audience; no doubt the cadets were whispering about my presence. They probably thought, as I felt, that I had personally contributed to Colonel Rhyne's passing because of my involvement in the scandal. I swallowed hard, choking back the deep emotion of sadness that was threatening to overtake me. As soon as the funeral came to a close, I walked out, eager to get away from the feeling that I, in some small part, was to blame.

"Ringgold, wait up!"

I heard footsteps behind me. A cadet was literally jogging to catch up to me.

As he approached, I recognized that it was Bucky, General Ulmer's son, who was a cow in the class behind me. I didn't know him personally, but everyone knew who he was. There was no place for a commandant's son to blend in at West Point.

I didn't say anything but waited for him to catch up.

"Hey, Ringgold, I just wanted to see if you were okay."

That took me by surprise. "I'm okay. Thanks for asking."

"Okay, good. I just wanted to make sure," Bucky said, shrugging his shoulders.

I nodded, turned, and continued on my way. I looked back and saw Bucky walk back to the chapel.

I wasn't sure what to make of that interaction but felt nevertheless a little less heart-sick. If Bucky didn't despise me after his dad's reassignment, that meant something. I wondered what General Ulmer had said to his son concerning the scandal, concerning *me*. Maybe he had portrayed that I wasn't the bad guy; maybe he had realized we had all been fighting for the same thing after all.

Father Curley on the veranda of the Catholic Chapel
the exact same spot where Tim Ringgold was commissioned a Second
Lieutenant in the US Army two years later.
Photo taken by Cadet Steven Veer.

Father Curley, far left, marching back from Lake Frederick with New Cadets at the end of summer training.

Father Curley offering Holy Mass in the Catholic Chapel

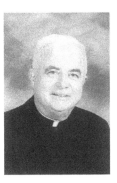

Father Curley today.

*Cadet Tim Ringgold and his favorite date, Gina, at the
Class of 1977 Ring Dance, April 1976.*

Attorney Arthur Lincoln, West Point class of 1966, who selflessly sacrificed his career to expose the injustices of the honor system.

The West Point Law Department, 1976. The four attorneys who testified before Congress in support of the cadets are: 1. Captain Arthur F. Lincoln ('66), 2. CPT Daniel H. Sharphorn ('69), 3. CPT Burk E. Bishop ('67), and 4. Captain Victor S. Carter. Three of the four are West Point graduates.

Peter DaRold outside the Capitol of the United States, June 1976.

Steve Hunt commissioned in June 1977, hours before his graduation with the Class of 1977.

First Classman Tim Ringgold after his return to West Point, October 1977.

In the days immediately before graduation, Tim Ringgold at Trophy Point, May 28, 1978.

Cadet Robin Fenessey, a member of the first class with women, the class of 1980.

Tim Ringgold and his Mother, the day before graduation for the Class of 1978. June 6, 1978.

Tim Ringgold heading to graduation. Behind him is the Plain, Washington Hall, and the Cadet Chapel. June 7, 1978

Cadet Michael Mamer

The morning of graduation day, Tim Ringgold taking the oath as a commissioned officer in the United States Army. The oath was administered by Major Aloysious Greenhouse, his company tactical officer, June 7, 1978.

Tim and Gina Ringgold at their Wedding Reception, 1979.

Arthur Lincoln, center, at Tim and Gina's wedding reception, 1979 with Peter DaRold, bottom right and Tom Wright x-'77.

Tim Ringgold, top right, Peter DaRold, bottom right with two former West Point classmates, Tom Wright, bottom left, and Ken Ryan, top left, at Tim and Gina's wedding reception, 1979.

Destiny & Dad 2016.

EPILOGUE
BY COLONEL TIMOTHY D. RINGGOLD, US ARMY (RET.)

AS AN ARMY CAPTAIN IN 1984, I was assigned to train newly commissioned officers at Fort Benning, Georgia. West Point, ROTC, or the Officer Candidate School had commissioned my students second lieutenants. My job was to make them infantry lieutenants. Coming fresh from five years of troop duty that included command of a forward deployed rifle company, I had a lot of practical experience to share with new lieutenants. For most, this would be their last stop before joining an operational command as infantry platoon leaders.

Late that summer, I was assigned a cohort of newly commissioned officers and given seventeen weeks, eleven of them in the field, to teach these new officers what they needed to know before entrusting them with the responsibility for leading thirty to forty soldiers. Of the forty-three new officers assigned to me, thirty were from the just-graduated West Point class of 1984. This class of cadets had entered West Point immediately after the first class with women graduated in 1980. They never knew a West Point that did not have women graduates, women tactical officers, and women professors. Lieutenant General Andrew Goodpaster was starting his fourth year as Academy Superintendent, having brought stability and credibility back to the institution.

My students and I quickly developed a mentor-protégé relationship as I prepared them to lead infantry soldiers. During field training, it was not unusual to go twenty-four or even thirty-six hours without rest. This was not intentional harassment training, but it was intentionally exhausting. Through training we were making the point that when you are tired, you make stupid mistakes, that your decision-making skills decline rapidly with lack of sleep. Lieutenants, especially new second lieutenants, usually don't need help making stupid mistakes. Our objective was to teach them through their own experiences to rely on their subordinate leaders, that they can't do everything themselves. We were teaching them to be tactical leaders.

All field training was conducted under simulated combat conditions. One evening, two-thirds of the way through the course and as the fourth night of around-the-clock field operations began, we took pity on the exhausted lieutenants—and equally exhausted cadre. We directed the students to move tactically to an administrative assembly area where they could relax their combat posture, get some needed rest, and for the first time during this training cycle, eat a hot meal in the field. We arrived much later in the evening than planned, having moved cross-country on foot in the dark. With a lieutenant leading and another navigating, the one thing we could always count on was the movement from Point A to Point B would be anything but a straight line. After we set up security in the assembly area, chow was brought in. Exhausted myself, I was eager to get a few hours rest before operations began again before first light.

It was a moonless night. Eating in complete darkness to maintain some semblance of tactical discipline, our only light was from a red-filtered flashlight. I settled down under a poncho to get some sleep, surrounded by my forty-three infantry officers-in-training. When I heard a small group chatting about West Point, I moved closer. They were not speaking loudly, but I could hear them clearly in the darkness. As I listened, my interest grew. They spoke with fondness, even reverence, for the institution they had left only four months earlier. It was not so much what they said, but how they said it that grabbed my attention. Like the old grads of decades ago who showed such excitement to be back at the Academy during class reunions, they described a school that was familiar to me, but very different from the West Point I had entered eleven years earlier. Their school was familiar because it was the Academy that I dreamed about attending as a child. It was the Academy reminiscent of the Colonel Red Reeder series of children's books about West Point that I devoured before high school. It was the Academy of the movies and the TV show of the late 1950s that motivated me to seek a life of service in uniform to our nation. How could that be? Their West Point and my West Point seemed so different. Their West Point of the 1980s more closely resembled the West Point of the 1950s and 1960s, the Academy of my childhood dreams, than the reality of my West Point of the 1970s.

How could the few years that separated their West Point journey and my own produce such a different experience? We lived in the same barracks, marched on the same parade ground, wore identical uniforms. We even took some of the same courses in the same classrooms taught by some of the same instructors. Racing through my mind were thoughts of disbelief, confusion, perhaps even envy. The more I heard the adoration in their voices, the more that I wanted to attend *their* school, to experience *their* West Point, not the one I'd found 1973–1978 and had tried since to forget.

Eventually, exhaustion overtook the lieutenants and they drifted off to sleep. While my mind still raced from one thought to another, I asked myself over and over again, *How could it be so different?* Finally, an answer came to me. A student attending University of California at Berkeley during the height of the student anti-war protests of the 1960s likely attended a very different Berkeley than a student of the 1980s—same buildings, same courses, but totally different educational experience. West Point was no different. The West Point of President Eisenhower (class of 1915) was likely far different from the West Point of General Walter Ulmer (class of 1952) or Arthur Lincoln (class of 1966). Was it so different because of Vietnam? My Lai? The unpopularity of the draft? Watergate? The nation's view of military service? Changing cultural values?

Whatever the explanation, the Academy of my time was different from what came before or has come since. As a soldier you learn to deal with the world as you find it, not as you think it's supposed to be or how you want it to be, but the way it is—no rose-colored glasses. As a soldier, you know when the enemy is breaching the wire, it's not the time to complain that Alpha Company was supposed to stop them or the S-2 reported no enemy in the sector. As I finally drifted off to sleep, I repeated to myself, like a mantra: to survive, you must deal with what is. Face facts. Have a clear understanding of what is happening; if you don't like what you find, deal with it first and when the opportunity presents itself, work to change it. In a small way, I guess I already had.

I don't know when I finally fell asleep or for how long. When I awoke, I could sense the movement of soldiers around me. It was still completely dark, but their movements told me it was near first light, time to stand ready and prepare to move out for the day's training. Rather than thinking about what went wrong in my time at West Point, I became curious about what had been done right in the eight years since the EE304 homework assignment destroyed so many careers. What changed the West Point of my day to the West Point my new lieutenants experienced as cadets?

And even more important, what would the West Point of the future turn out to be?

Lieutenant General Sidney Berry, the superintendent, and Brigadier General Walter Ulmer, the commandant, tried to save the Academy from itself, but the familiar paradigm had shifted. The old ways didn't work anymore. Not even an institution as revered as the United States Military Academy could insulate itself from the swift currents of change that ran through the United States and the Army in the aftermath of the Vietnam War and the counterculture undercurrents of the 1960s. The signs were there if they'd known how to identify and understand them. General Berry's Special Study Group on Honor completed its report the year before the honor scandal, finding that the Code required "unattainable human behavior." As if that was not enough of a sign, it found that 73 percent of cadets would not turn in a good friend for an honor violation, itself an honor violation; 77 percent believed the Honor System was used to enforce regulations undermining trust and imposing the single penalty of expulsion for what should have been minor disciplinary problems. Most illuminating, more than one-half of the class of 1977 did not believe the Honor System was fair and just.[1] Observing in hindsight, it was easy to see that the system was a tinderbox just waiting for the spark of the EE304 assignment. The Special Study Group's report should have been the catalyst for change. It wasn't. Regrettably, it was issued at the same time, almost the same hour, that North Vietnamese Army tanks rolled through the gate of the Presidential Palace in Saigon, effectively ending the Vietnam war.

---

1   Report of the Superintendent's Special Study Group on Honor at West Point (often referred to as the "Buckley Report"), May 1975, Appendix 1 (Results of Cadet Honor Questionnaire) to Annex C (Attitudes), items 13, 22, 28. Reprinted in Hearings on the United States Military Academy Honor Code before the Subcommittee on Military Personnel of the Committee on Armed Services, House of Representatives. Hearings Held August 25 and September 1, 1976, Government Printing Office, Washington 1977.

It fell to Congressman Thomas J. Downey, Father Curley, Captain Lincoln, Captain Sharphorn and the other defense attorneys to be that catalyst. As the most junior member of Congress, Mr. Downey and his legislative assistant, Fred Kass, mustered support for the needed independent oversight. Father Curley, Captain Lincoln, Captain Sharphorn and the other attorneys literally put their careers on the line to support the cadets and challenge the inequities of the system. Such support was not without its risks and consequences. The month after I left West Point in 1976, Captain Lincoln was officially passed over for what should have been a routine promotion. His Army career was over. Within days he left the Army that he'd served for more than ten years. Without the support and selfless sacrifices of these courageous men, the cadets had no chance to survive, and frankly, neither did West Point.

Together, Colonel Frank Borman and General Andrew Goodpaster saved West Point. Colonel Borman had the credibility to lead the first independent inquiry. As a West Point graduate himself, it took courage to objectively criticize his alma mater and call for the Academy to acknowledge the "gross inadequacies of the Honor System[2]" and to devote its full energies to rebuilding an improved and strengthened institution. Both Academy and cadets shared responsibility for what happened. In an act of compassion and justice, he called for "reform and regeneration, not retribution.[3]" The Borman Commission and the follow-on Department of the Army study group made more than 230 recommendations of long overdue changes. Without Colonel Borman putting his reputation on the line, it's doubtful the Army Study Group would have been as far-reaching with its own recommendations.

---

2   Report of the Special Commission on the United States Military Academy, 15 December 1976, cover letter signed by Commission Chairman, Frank Borman, un-numbered 2nd page.

3   Ibid.

Recommendations can easily be ignored or implemented half-heartedly. One recommendation that all parties agreed to was that the Honor Code remain unchanged: *A Cadet will not lie, cheat, or steal, nor tolerate those who do.* The focus was on the Honor System and its inadequate and uneven implementation of the Honor Code and its single punishment for even the most trivial offense.

When General Goodpaster agreed to come out of retirement to lead West Point, he accepted the assignment at a grade lower than he had retired, under the condition that he would have the latitude to rebuild the Academy according to his "values" and what he thought was "right for West Point."[4] In the end, he implemented more than 200 of the 230 recommendations. As a soldier-scholar, General Goodpaster revitalized the institution and initiated reforms that have maintained the Military Academy foremost among universities and military colleges worldwide. Not content to focus on the Honor System alone, General Goodpaster looked at the entire institution and initiated reforms in academics, military training, and leader development based on a diversified core curriculum, an academic majors program, a four-class leadership system, and realistic training for the challenges cadets would face in their military careers.

If not for the leadership and values of General Goodpaster, I believe that today, nearly five decades after the incidents described in this book, West Point would be a mediocre institution that had outlived its usefulness. Instead, the Academy that I walked away from in 1976, expecting to never return, was transformed by General Goodpaster to become the preeminent leader development institution in the world. Despite the heartache I personally experienced at West Point, I am proud to be a graduate. I hope in telling the events of this time, readers will see that West

---

4   Association of Graduates, U.S. Military Academy, West Point, NY, Assembly, Volume 45, June 1986, p.33.

Point not only survived a dark period but became stronger for it. For the readers that were involved or affected by West Point's 1976 Cheating Scandal, I hope that by reliving these events, from reading this book, that you experience healing and closure. I know looking back, that if I were to re-experience that time in my life, I would make the same choices. I spoke out then because of my love for West Point and the values it seeks to uphold. May it continue to do so for generations to come.

Colonel Timothy D. Ringgold, US Army (Retired)
The 35,995[th] graduate of the United States Military Academy
West Point class of 1978

REFERENCES

I. https://vault.si.com/vault/2000/11/13/code-breakers-fifty-years-ago-red-blaiks-football-powerhouse-at-army-was-decimated-by-the-loss-of-players-who-violated-the-military-academys-honor-code-but-who-really-acted-dishonorably

II. Feron, James. "West Point Anticipated Turmoil on Honor Code." *The New York Times*, 30 May 1976.; This is quoted from a report over the code in a meeting at West Point on October 1, 1974.

APRIL

Chapter 1:

1. https://www.archives.gov/founding-docs/declaration-transcript
2. https://www.westpoint.edu/
3. https://www.westpoint.edu/admissions/steps-to-admission
4. https://www.theatlantic.com/daily-dish/archive/2007/05/the-west-point-oath/228155/
5. https://en.wikipedia.org/wiki/Paris_Peace_Accords

Chapter 2:

6. https://en.wikipedia.org/wiki/Douglas_MacArthur; https://vault.si.com/vault/2000/11/13/code-breakers-fifty-years-ago-red-blaiks-football-powerhouse-at-army-was-decimated-by-the-loss-of-players-who-violated-the-military-academys-honor-code-but-who-really-acted-dishonorably.
7. Walton, Mary. "The shame at West Point: It's more than cheating, and it cuts deep." *Philadelphia Inquirer*, 12 April 1976.
8. Feron, James. "Honor Code at West Point Focus of Renewed Turmoil." *The New York Times*, 16 April 1976.

9. https://en.wikipedia.org/wiki/Pardon_of_Richard_
   Nixon#:***:text=The%20pardon%20of%20Richard%20
   Nixon,Ford%20on%20September%208%2C%201974.

Chapter 3:

10. Berry, General Sidney. Letter to Fellow Graduates and
    Friends at the Military Academy Date unknown, but likely
    March 1976.
11. https://en.wikipedia.org/wiki/Sidney_Bryan_Berry
12. https://www.womensmemorial.org/history/
    detail/?s=women-enter-the-military-academies

Chapter 4:

13. Feron, James. "New Cheating Case Erupts at West Point." *The
    New York Times*, 7 April 1976.
14. Feron, James. "More Than 90 Cadets at West Point Face
    Charges of Cheating on a Test." *The New York Times*, 8 April
    197.
15. Krawetz, Michael. "Some Cadets Cleared." *The Evening News*,
    13 April 1976.
16. Feron, James. "Honor Code at West Point Focus on Renewed
    Turmoil." *The New York Times*, 16 April 1976.

Chapter 5:

17. https://thevietnamwar.info/us-presidents-during-the-viet-
    nam-war/; http://thevietnamwar.info/vietnam-war-draft/
18. https://now.tufts.edu/articles/lessons-living-room-war
19. https://en.wikipedia.org/wiki/Opposition_to_United_
    States_involvement_in_the_Vietnam_War
20. https://docs.google.com/document/d/12NBYvCbjBLDoasH
    MHQTRVlKmwwpW7x7qenHmEVtsQz4/edithttps://docs.
    google.com/document/d/12NBYvCbjBLDoasHMHQTRVl
    KmwwpW7x7qenHmEVtsQz4/edit; http://thevietnamwar.

info/vietnam-war-draft/; https://en.wikipedia.org/wiki/Mu-hammad_Ali#Vietnam_War_and_resistance_to_the_draft

21. https://www.youtube.com/watch?v=BPgWqgpgVRc
22. https://thevietnamwar.info/how-many-people-died-in-the-vietnam-war/
23. http://en.wikipedia.org/wiki/Samuel_W._Koster

Chapter 6:
24. Feron, James. "Tough Academic Regime Blamed by Some Cadets." *The New York Times*, 13 April 1976.
25. "What Price Honor?" *Times Magazine*, 7 June 1976.
26. Feron, James. "More Than 90 Cadets at West Point Face Charges of Cheating on a Test." *The New York Times*, 8 April 1976.
27. Hirst, Don. "Second Scandal Hits West Point." *Army Times*, 26 April 1976.
28. Feron, James. "New Cheating Case Erupts at West Point." *The New York Times*, 7 April 1976, pp.31.

Chapter 7:
29. Walton, Mary. "The shame at West Point: It's more than cheating, and it cuts deep." *Philadelphia Inquirer*, 12 April 1976.

Chapter 8:
30. Feron, James. "Honor Code at West Point Focus of Renewed Turmoil." *The New York Times*, 16 April 1976.

Chapter 9:
31. Ferguson, Fred T. "Most academy honor codes not as rigid as West Point." *The New York Times*, 3 June 1976.
32. Feron, James. "West Point Cadet Faces New Charges; His Congressmen Demand an Inquiry." *The New York Times*, 27 April 1976.

33. Ibid.; Feron, James. "Honor Code at West Point Focus of Renewed Turmoil." *The New York Times*, 16 April 1976.

34. "Honor Committee cadet denies ordering 'silence." *Middletown*. 22 April 1976.

35. "Duty, Honor, Country." *Los Angeles Times*, 10 May 1976.

36. Feron, James. "Cadet Committee at West Point Does Away With 'The Silence'. *The New York Times*, 12 September 1973.

37. Greenhouse, Linda. "Silent Agony Ends for Cadet at Point." *The New York Times*, 7 June, 1973,

38. https://en.wikipedia.org/wiki/The_Silence_(1975_film)#:***:text=During%20his%20junior%20year%20at,imposed%20%E2%80%9Cthe%20Silence%E2%80%9D%20anyway.

MAY

Chapter 10:

39. Ringgold, Timothy D. Letter to Senator Barry Goldwater. 7 May 1976.

40. Cuellar, Jose A. Letter to Timothy D. Ringgold. 6 May 1976.

41. https://en.wikipedia.org/wiki/Miranda_warning

42. Feron, James. "Cadet Who Said Almost All Cheated Faces Expulsion From West Point." *The New York Times*, 12 May 1976.

43. "Honor, yes, but only to a point: Tale of 2 codes." *The Times Herald Record*, 12 May 1976.

Chapter 11:

44. Feron, James. "Lawyer Charges Bribery to 'Fix' Verdicts in Cadet Cheating Cases." *The New York Times*, 4 May 1976.

45. Feron, James. "Reviews Started in Cadet Cheating: 50 Found Guilty and 2 Quit West Point -- Appeals to Begin Next Week." *The New York Times*, 23 April 1976.

46. Hewitt, Richard. "Cadet charged with honor code violation." *The Middletown Record*, 2 May 1976.

Chapter 12:

47. https://www.google.com/search?rlz=1CAEAQE_
    enUS810US811&sxsrf=ALeKk0oERflhNJrTWw5ThlIkR
    hJW_2v2Ig%3A1592501974461&ei=1qbrXpzSG-uLytM
    PoomUqAw&q=times+are+a+changin+lyrics&oq=times
    +are+a+changin+lyrics&gs_lcp=CgZwc3ktYWIQAzICC-
    AAyAggAMgIIADIGCAAQFhAeMgYIABAWEB4yBggAE-
    BYQHjIGCAAQFhAeMgYIABAWEB4yBggAEBYQHjIGC
    AAQFhAeOgQIABBHOgQIABBDOgcIABAUEIcCOgsIL-
    hCLAxCoAxCYAzoNCC4QQxCLAxCoAxCYAzoFCAAQi-
    wM6CwguEIsDEKMDEKgDOggIABAWEAoQHlDOK1j-
    N2DLOWgAcAF4AIABY4gBjAWSAQE3mAEAoAEBqgEHZ-
    3dzLXdpergBAg&sclient=psy-ab&ved=0ahUKEwiclfeT9IvqA
    hXrhXIEHdIEBcUQ4dUDCAw&uact=5

48. Feron, James. "Lawyer Charges Bribery to 'Fix' Verdicts in Cade Cheating Cases." *The New York Times*, 4 May 1976.

49. Feron, James. "Honor Code at West Point Focus of Renewed Turmoil." *The New York Times*, 16 April 1976.

50. New York Times News Service. "Honor code lawyer asked to leave Point." *The Times Herald Record*, 11 May 1976.

51. New York Times News Service. "10 West Point lawyers ask probe of cheating scandal handling." *The Times Herald Record*, 7 May 1976.

52. Feron, James. "West Point Officers Urge Army to Oversee Inquiry on Cheating." *The New York Times*, 7 May 1976.

53. Feron, James. "Honor Code at West Point Focus of Renewed Turmoil." *The New York Times*, 16 April 1976.

Chapter 13:

54. Hirst, Don. "No 'Silence' for Cleared Cadets." *Army Times*, 10 May 1976.

55. Claiborne, William. "'Hypocrisy' at West Point: Stealing, Cheating by Cadets Called Commonplace." *The Washington Post*, 19 May 1976.

56. Walton, Mary. "The shame at West Point: It's more than cheating, and it cuts deep." *Philadelphia Inquirer*, 12 April 1976.

57. "Cadet lawyer's shift called 'not punitive'." *The Stars and Stripes*. 14 May 1976.

58. "Honor at West Point." *The New York Times*, 12 May 1976.

59. Goldwater, Senator Barry. Letter to Cadet Timothy D. Ringgold. 12 May 1976.

60. Ringgold, Cadet Timothy D. Letter to Senator Barry Goldwater. 18 May 1976.

61. ABC Newsclip, March 13, 1976

Chapter 14:

62. Stamell, Marcia. "Honor code under scrutiny: Scandal at the Point." *The Bergen Record*, 17 May 1976.

63. Augustine, Under Secretary Norman R. Letter to Senator Barry Goldwater. 19 May 1976.

Chapter 15:

64. Perry, Robert. "West Point: Cheating inquiry to widen." *The Times Herald Record*, 24 May 1976.

65. Feron, James. "West Point Acknowledges Cheating Is Widespread." *The New York Times*, 24 May 1976.

66. Gale, Reginald. "70 to 90 cadets may face charges." *The Times Herald Record*, 25 May 1976.

67. Feron, James. "Panel Investigating 70 to 90 New Cases of Suspected Cheating at West Point." *The New York Times*, 25 May 1976.

68. Claiborne, William. "Soul-Searching at Military Academy." *The Washington Post*, 23 May 1976.

69. "Cadets Termed Honor Code Unfair, Idealistic." 28 May 1976.

70. Perry, Robert. "Rep. may ask academy to delay appeals hearings." *The Times Herald Record*, 24 May 1976.

71. Gale, Reginald. "Candor gives cadet trouble." *The Times Herald Record*, 13 May 1976.

72. Feron, James. "Cadet Who Said Almost All Cheated Faces Expulsion From West Point." *The New York Times*, 12 May 1976.

73. Feron, James. "West Point Easing Procedures In Administering Honor Code." *The New York Times*, 23 May 1976.

74. Stamell, Marcia. "Scandal at the Point." *Bergen Record*, 17 May 1976.

75. Gale, Reginald. "Honor code under scrutiny: Military honor code at a crossroads." *The Times Herald Record*, 23 May 1976.

76. "City cadet at West Point faces expulsion for 'tolerating' cheats." *The Arizona Republic*, 12 May 1976.

Chapter 16:

77. Feron, James. "Panel Investigating 70 to 90 New Cases of Suspected Cheating at West Point." *The New York Times*, 25 May 1976.

78. Feron, James. "West Point Cadet, Seeking Acquittal Reason, Again Faces Expulsion." *The New York Times*, Wednesday, 26 May 1976.

79. Gale, Reginald. "Point juniors must stay until probe over." *The Times Herald Record*, 27 May 1976.

80. Feron, James. "Study Sought by West Point Legal Staff Is Ruled Out by Secretary of the Army." *The New York Times*, 20 May 1976.

81. "Decision dismays Point lawyers." *The Times Herald Record*, 20 May 1976.

82. Claiborne, William. "'Hypocrisy' at West Point: Stealing, Cheating by Cadets Called Commonplace." *The Washington Post*, 19 May 1976.

83. "West Point Officers: Cadets' Counsels Will Finish Cases." *Army Times*, 24 May 1976.

84. Feron, James. "West Point Acknowledges Cheating Is Widespread." *The New York Times*, 24 May 1976.

85. Feron, James. "Panel Investigating 70 to 90 New Cases of Suspected Cheating at West Point." *The New York Times*, 25 May 1976.

86. N.Y. Times News Service. "Cadet under guard after threats." 23 May 1976.

87. Editorial. "In a word, panache." *The Times Herald Record*, 24 May 1976.

88. Claiborne, William. "Soul-Searching at Military Academy." *The Washington Post*, 23 May 1976.

89. Gale, Reginald. "Military honor code at a crossroads." *The Times Herald Record*, 23 May 1976.

90. Feron, James. "Honor Code at West Point Focus of Renewed Turmoil." *The New York Times*, 16 April 1976.

91. Feron, James. "West Point Easing Procedures In Administering Honor Code." *The New York Times*, 23 May 1976.

92. Gatewood, Dallas. "1975 Study: Cadet Code 'Unrealistic'. 28 May 1976.

93. "Cadets Termed Honor Code Unfair, Idealistic." 28 May 1976.

Chapter 17:

94. Combined News Services. "Cadet Cheating Probers Detain class." 27 May 1976.

95. CBS News, May 27, 1976

96. Claiborne, William. "'Hypocrisy' at West Point: Stealing, Cheating by Cadets Called Commonplace." *The Washington Post*, 19 May 1976.

97. Hewitt, Richard. "Tape may involve more cadets in scandal." *The Times Herald Record*, 30 May 1976.

Chapter 18:

98. https://www.thethayerhotel.com/?gclid=CjwKCAjw88v3BR-BFEiwApwLevUkMJrGjX9DyAtX8Ir32ompRZUEOwXm7cIbu8OuynRZ4GaLckIu5kBoCnRoQAvD_BwE&gclsrc=aw.ds

99. Franker, Susan and Eric Gelman. "The Army: A Point of Honor." *Newsweek*, 24 May 1976.

Chapter 19:

100. Feron, James. "Tough Academic Regime Blamed by Some Cadets." *The New York Times*, 13 April 1976.

101. Farlekas, Chris. "Ex-Point doctor: Some cheating tolerated there." *Times Herald-Record*, 13 April 1976.

102. Feron, James. "Panel Investigating 70 to 90 New Cases of Suspected Cheating at West Point." *The New York Times*, 25 May 1976.

103. Hildebrand, John. "A Point of Honor." *Newsday*, 28 May 1976.

104. Gale, Reginald. "Junior class concerns: High grades, low profiles." *The Times Herald Record*, 27 May 1976.

105. "USMA announces new review board in honor case." *News of the Highlands,* 27 May 1976.

106. "West Point Cheating Scandal Calls Honor Code Into Question." *Baton Rouge Advocate*, 28 May 1976.

107. Editorials. "West Point's Honor Code Isn't Working." *Newsday*, 28 May 1976.

JUNE

Chapter 20:

108. Gale, Reginald. "70 to 90 cadets may face charges." *The Times Herald Record*, 25 May 1976.

109. Hildebrand, John. "A Point of Honor." *Newsday*, 28 May 1976.

110. Feron, James. "West Point Cadet Faces New Charges; His Congressmen Demand an Inquiry." *The New York Times*, 27 April 1976.

111. Carter, Malcolm. "Survival, Honor Code In Conflict." *Evening News*, 1 June 1976.

112. Claiborne, William. "The Long Grey Line: Is its honor tarnished?." *Sports Television,* 28 May 1976.

113. Gale, Reginald. "Pre-trial publicity hangs up first of cheating trials." *The Times Herald Record*, 29 May 1976.

114. Combined News Services. "Cadet Cheating Probers Detain class." 27 May 1976.

115. Feron, James. "Cheating Cases May Involve 250: West Point Officials Given Figure by Army Lawyers." *The New York Times*, 28 May 1976.

116. Feron, James. "Cadets of the Past Return to Cheer Long Gray Line." *The New York Times*, 29 May 1976.

117. Cunningham, Barry. "Scandal Casts Pall Over Cadets' Gala Day." *The New York Post*, 3 Jun 1976. **I changed the date. General Westmoreland actually spoke Friday, May 28, 1976.**

118. Feron, James. "West Point Anticipated Turmoil on Honor Code." *The New York Times*, 30 May 1976.

119. "Somber Spring: Scandal darkens West Point's finest moments." *The Sunday Star-Ledger*, 30 May 1976.

120. https://www.amazon.com/Westmoreland-General-Who-Lost-Vietnam-ebook/dp/B005OCG11Q/ref=sr_1_1?dchild=1&keywords=westmoreland&qid=1598310286&sr=8-1

Chapter 21:

121. Gale, Reginald. "Cadets graduate in scandal's midst." *The Times Herald Record*, 3 June 1976.

122. "Address by The Honorable Martin R. Hoffman, Secretary of the Army at the Graduation Ceremony, United States Military Academy." *News Release*: Office of Assistant Secretary of Defense Public Affairs, Washington, DC, 2 June 1976. (Actual speech given, abbr.)

123. Gale, Reginald. "Judge rejects honor code ban." *The Times Herald Record*, 3 June 1976.

124. Farlekas, Chris. "Chaplain a calm center in storm of Point scandal." *The Middletown Record*, 1 September 1976.

Chapter 22:

125. Feron, James. "Army Secretary Says He's Considering Review of West Point's Honor System." *The New York Times*, 3 June 1976.

126. United Press International. "36 cadets join accused cheaters list." *The Arizona Republic*, 5 June 1976.; "No verdict on 6." *The Times Herald Record*, 4 June 1976.

127. Ottaway News Service. "Rep demands West Point academic probe." *The Times Herald Record*, 4 June 1976.

128. Gale, Reginald. "36 more cadets charges." The *Times Herald Record*, 5 June 1976.

129. https://www.mcmilitarylaw.com/articles-of-ucmj/article-31/#:***:text=The%20statements%20of%20an%20accused,or%20through%20the%20use%20of

130. https://www.mcmilitarylaw.com/articles-of-ucmj/article-92-failure-to-obey-an-order/#:***:text=Article%2092%20defines%20disobeying%20a,orders%2C%20and%20dereliction%20of%20duty.

131. Gale, Reginald. "4 cadets file to block honor code enforcement." *The Times Herald Record*, 2 June 1976.

132. "Challenges honor code: Cadet sues academy." *The Times Herald Record*, 2 June 1976.

133. Feron, James. "34 More Cadets at West Point Are Facing Cheating Charges." *The New York Times*, 8 June 1976.

Chapter 23:

134. Feron, James. "West Point Sued Over Honor Code." *The New York Times*, 2 June 1976.
135. Claiborne, William. "West Point's Code Backed." *The Washington Post*, 22 June 1976.
136. "What Price Honor?" *Times Magazine*, 7 June 1976.
137. Affidavit: Timothy D. Ringgold, 31 May 1976.
138. "Challenges honor code: Cadet sues academy." *The Times Herald Record*, 2 June 1976.
139. Feron, James. "Army Secretary Says He's Considering Review of West Point's Honor System." *The New York Times*, 3 June 1976.
140. "Scandal Hits One Fifth of Cadets." 10 June 1976.
141. Associated Press. "Lawsuit challenges honor code as West Point charges mount." *The Arizona Republic*, 2 June 1976.
142. Gale, Reginald. "4 cadets file to block honor code enforcement." *The Times Herald Record*, 2 June 1976.
143. "No retreat from honor." *Home News*, 2 June 1976.
144. Randazzo, John. "Is the Point's Honor Code Out of Step?" *The Times Herald Record*, 6 June 1976.
145. Carter, Malcolm. "Survival, Honor Code In Conflict." *Evening News*, 1 June 1976.
146. Feron, James. "Decision Is Reserved in Academy Case." *The New York Times*, 10 June 1976.

Chapter 24:

147. Brown, Mark. "Senate panel to probe academy honor code." *The Times Herald Record*, 11 June 1976.
148. Cunningham, Barry. "Scandal Casts Pall Over Cadets' Gala Day." *The New York Post*, 3 June 1976.

149. "Sock, radio, may prove two plebes' undoing." *The Times Herald Record*, 2 June 1976.

150. Cunningham, Barry. "Scandal Casts Pall Over Cadets' Gala Day." *The New York Post*, 3 Jun 1976.

151. United Press International. "36 cadets join accused cheaters list." *The Arizona Republic*, 5 June 1976.

Chapter 25:

152. Gale, Reginald. "46 more cadets charged by panel." *The Times Herald Record*, 2 June 1976.

153. Ottaway News Service. "Rep demands West Point academic probe." *The Times Herald Record, 4 June 1976*.

154. Brown, Mark. "Senate panel to probe academy honor code." *The Times Herald Record*, 11 June 1976.

155. Feron, James. "Civilian-Military Panel on Academy Honor Codes Is Urged in House." *The New York Times*, 19 June 1976.

156. "The Point." Sunday Record, 13 June 1976.

157. Thayer, Frederick. "Out of Step at the Point." *The New York Times*, 16 June 1976.

Chapter 26:

158. Hoffmann, Martin R. "Before the Subcommittee on Manpower and Personnel Committee on Armed Services, U.S. Senate, Second Session, 94th Congress: Honor Codes at the Service Academies." Record Version, 21 June 1976.

Chapter 27:

159. Downey, Thomas J. "Before the Subcommittee on Manpower and Personnel Committee on Armed Services, U.S. Senate, Second Session, 94th Congress: Honor Codes at the Service Academies." Record Version, 22 June 1976.

160. Feron, James. "West Point Easing Procedures In Administering Honor Code." *The New York Times*, 23 May 1976.

161. "What Price Honor?" *Times Magazine*, 7 June 1976.

162. Thayer, Frederick C. "Out of Step at the Point." *The New York Times*, 16 June 1976.

163. Corddry, Charles W. "West Point scandal raises basic issue." *The Sun*, 13 June 1976.

164. Hewitt, Richard. "Point instructor: Half the junior class cheated." *The Times Herald Record*, 25 June 1976.

165. "Army assigns 42 lawyers to work on Point scandals." *The Times Herald Record*, 29 June 1976.

166. Feron, James. "Cadet Loses Fight to Stay at West Point." *The New York Times*, 30 June 1976.

167. Ottaway News Service. "Guilty cadets were acquitted in '75, officer says." *The Times Herald Record*, 30 June 1976.

168. Feron, James. "West Point Given Code Assurance: Senator Nunn Says Change Will Not be Legislated 'From Washington'." *The New York Times*, 1 July 1976.

JULY

Chapter 28:

169. Feron, James. "Cadet Sues West Point for Court-Martial." *The New York Times*, 2 July 1976.

170. "West Point adds 2 in cheating probe." *Newark Star Ledger*, 7 July 1976.

171. Feron, James. "Prosecutors Say West Point Limited Code Cases." *The New York Times*, 12 July 1976.

172. Associated Press. "37 cadets ask court to dismiss West Point cheating charges." *The Arizona Republic*, 14, July 1976.

173. Moore, Robert H. "West Point's provincialism." *Christian Science Monitor*, 13 July 1976.

Chapter 29:

174. Feron, James. "Group of Cadets Accuses Academy." *The New York Times*, 24 July 1976.

175. Feron, James. "West Point Faces New Difficulties." *The New York Times*, 25 July 1976.

176. "Cadets' Offenses Alleged in Court." *Washington Post*, 8 July 2976.

177. "West Pointers claim they were railroaded." *New Brunswick Home News*, 25 July 1976.

178. Feron, James. "West Point is facing administrative and morale problems." *The New York Times*, 30 July 1976.

Chapter 30:

179. Feron, James. "House 'Forum Set on Academy Code." *The New York Times*, 1 August 1976.

180. Brown, Mark. "Cadet decided it was time to start fighting city hall." *The Times Herald Record*, 3 August 1976.

181. Feron, James. "West Point Cadets at House 'Hearing' Ask End of Ouster for Code Violators." *The New York Times*, 5 August, 1976.

182. Feron, James. "Two-thirds of Ousted Cadets Are Returning to West Point." *The New York Times*, 5 June 1977.

183. Downey, Thomas J. and others. Letter to the Congress of the United States House of Representatives concerning Public Forum on West Point Honor Code. 29, July 1976.

184. Curley, Reverend Thomas J. Letter to Congressman Tom Downey. 3 August 1976.

185. Rose, Michael T. "Memorandum About Why West Point Should Not Expel Every Cadet Found Guilty of Violating the Cadet Honor Code." 3 August 1976.

186. https://www.youtube.com/watch?v=5olMq7TwCUw&feature=youtu.be

AUGUST

Chapter 31:

187. Ringgold, Timothy D. "West Point: The System Indicted." *The New York Times*, 10 August 1976.

188. Foster, Paul L. and 29 attorneys. Letter to the secretary of Defense. 2 August 1976.

189. Green, Al. "Army secretary studies request for Point probe." 3 August 1976.

190. Ringgold, Timothy D. Conditional Resignation Letter to Commandant. 13 August 1976.

191. Brown, Mark. "Downey urges cadet penalty be suspended." *The Times Herald Record*, 10 August 1976.

192. Feron, James. "West Point "Jury" Asks New Inquiry." *The New York Times*, 11 August 1976.

193. Perry, Robert. "Hoffman pressed to name code panel." *The Times Herald Record*, 12 August 1976.

Chapter 32:

194. Feron, James. "Group of Cadets Accuses Academy." *The New York Times*, 24 July 1976.

Chapter 33:

195. "Cadets' Lawyers Call for Return Of Men Held Guilty of Cheating." *The New York Times*, 17 August 1976.

196. "Cadets await DC testimony." L.I. Press, 23 August 1976.

197. Gupte, Pranay. "West Point Cites Four As Cheaters." *The New York Times*, 22 August 1976.

198. Corddry, Charles W. "Army to give guilty cadets 2d chance." *Baltimore Sun*, 24 August 1976.

199. Gupte, Pranay. "Cadets ARe Shaken by One-Year 'Expulsion' Plan." *The New York Times*, 24 August 1976.

200. "Army Backs Off on Honor Code: 2d Chance for Cadets WHo Cheat." *New York Daily News*, 24 August 1976.

201. Associated Press. "West Point's automatic expulsion lifted for cheaters." *The Arizona Republic*, 24 August 1976.

202. Feron, James. "Ousted Cadets Offered Chance to Reapply After a Year." *The New York Times*, 24 August 1976.

203. Associated Press. "New West Point hearing planned." *The Arizona Republic*, 25 August 1976.

204. Moneyhun, George. "West Point honor code shifts." *Christian Science Monitor*, 25 August 1976.

205. Feron, James. "House Unit Calls Army Secretary." *The New York Times*, 25 August 1976.

206. Associated Press. "Plan to readmit cadet cheaters questioned." *The Arizona Republic*, 26 August 1976.

207. Curley, Reverend Thomas J. Letter to President Gerald R. Ford. 3 September 1976.

208. Buchen, Philip W. Letter to Rev. Thomas J. Curley. 9 September 1976.

SEPTEMBER - DECEMBER 1976

Chapter 34:

209. Ringgold, Timothy. "Press Conference." 20 August 1986.

210. "Borman Panel Urges Cadets' Readmission." *The New York Times*, 15 December 1976.

211. Associated Press. "West Point blamed in part for cadet cheating." *The Arizona Republic*, 16 December 1976.

Chapter 35:

212. "A Barrage Hits West Point's Code." *Times Magazine*, 27 December 1976.

213. Berry, Sidney B. Letter to Friends of West Point. 18 February 1977.

214. Rhyne, Hal B. Status Report on Honor at West Point. 28 February 1977.

215. Capps, Jack L. Letter to Timothy D. Ringgold. 2 March 1977.

216. "Cadet who resigned going back to Point." *The Arizona Republic*, 14 May 1977.

217. Capps, Jack L. Letter to Timothy D. Ringgold. 14 March 1977.

218. "Retired General Will Head West Point." *The Phoenix Gazette*, 4 April 1977.

219. Feron, James. "West Point Lawyer Who Challenged Academy in Honor-Code Scandal Resigning After Losing Promotion." *The New York Times*, 27 October 1976.

220. Feron, James. "Two-thirds of Ousted Cadets Are Returning to West Point." *The New York Times*, 5 June 1977.

Chapter 36:

221. Feron, James. "Two-thirds of Ousted Cadets Are Returning to West Point." *The New York Times*, 5 June 1977.

222. Feron, James. "West Point '78 Closing Book on '76." *The New York Times*, 5 June 1978.

223. "West Point graduates survivors of scandal." Source unknown, exact date unknown 1978.

ACKNOWLEDGMENTS

FOREMOST, I WANT TO THANK my husband, Jason David Tilton, who selflessly supported my time-consuming mission of writing even when it often interfered with home and family responsibilities.

I wish to thank all the individuals who advised me on the manuscript. My mother, Gina Ringgold, was the first to read my work, primarily to validate whether the main character sounded like Dad. Theresa Tabakelis, a family friend and schoolteacher, and Mr. Michael T. Rose, Esq. voluntarily and graciously gave of their time and expertise to edit the whole manuscript. Steven Hunt, who also contributed authenticity to the storyline, gave me my favorite endorsement because I, too, hope that this story might help others heal from this event.

I wish to thank all the people who endeavored to support me on this project by letting me interview them, as well as provide documents and pictures: Lieutenant General Walter F. Ulmer, Jr. US Army (Ret.), Colonel Frank Borman, US Air Force (Ret.), Dr. Peter DaRold, M.D., Major Michael Mamer US Army (Ret.)

and Steven R. Verr.

I wish to personally thank Timothy Flanagan for his heartfelt honesty and willingness to use his name in the book. After speaking with him, it made me wonder how many other Alumni from the class of 1977 had felt a pang of guilt from not turning themselves in for possibly having broken the Honor Code.

I wish to thank Major Robin Fennesy, US Army (Ret.), who gave me insight into the complex experiences of having been part of the first class of women at West Point. It was truly an honor to interview her.

As a writer, I really felt connected to my characters, especially two that I had the greatest challenge finding: Colonel Arthur Lincoln, US Army (Ret.) and Reverend Thomas Curley. I did not find these two men in real life until the book had already been written. By that time, I felt like I knew them personally, so it was very lovely to finally connect!

I would like to thank Greg Fields, the acquisition editor at Koehler Books Publishing, for connecting with the storyline and for his sincere encouragement of this project. Because of him, I knew Koehler Books Publishing was the right fit. I would also like to thank John Koehler and my editor, Becky Hilliker.

Lastly, I would like to thank my dad, Colonel Timothy Ringgold, US Army (Ret.), for his willingness to open old wounds and share his experiences, as well as to edit and support the telling of this extremely personal story about his past.

APPENDIX

More Than 90 Cadets at West Point
Face Charges of Cheating on a Test

By JAMES FERON
Special to The New York Times

WEST POINT, N. Y., April 7—A United States Military Academy spokesman said today that more than 90 cadets would be charged next week with violating the cadet honor code by cheating on an electrical engineering examination last month.

The suspects, all juniors, face proceedings before 12 - man honor boards. A guilty verdict means resignation or mandatory expulsion, barring an appeal to a board of officers, and two-year Army service starting as a private to fulfill military obligations.

The scandal, which Academy officials initially sought to suppress, is the second most serious such incident in the institution's 174-year history. In 1951, 90 of more than 100 cadets similarly charged eventually resigned or were expelled for cheating.

The Academy spokesman, Lieut. Col. Thomas Garigan, said the 1951 cheating incident, which involved more than 30 members of the football team, including the coach's son, had been "well planned and coordinated." This one, he said, "appears to be a series of separate incidents."

The recommendation that the suspected cadets face honor boards followed all-night interrogation by three-man teams, or subcommittees, of the honor committee. Some cadets were released after having proved that they could produce the work on their own.

Faculty members teaching Electrical Engineering 304, a required course, had given the same assignment to the more than 800 cadets enrolled in the course's 15-student sections to complete on their own during the first two weeks of March.

Col. Harold Rhyne, deputy commandant of cadets and advisor to the honor committee, said that "it involved roughly 10 mathematical problems requiring the use of a computer and an essay question."

Faculty members grading the papers over the one - week spring vacation, which ended last Sunday, began to notice similarities in the "proof" sections of the mathematical answers, prompting a suspicion of unauthorized collaboration, Colonel Rhyne said.

They brought this to the attention of Academy officials, who turned the matter over to the 88-member committee charged with upholding the honor code: "A cadet will not lie, cheat or steal or tolerate those who do."

Cadet William Andesen and his designated successor as chairman of the honor committee, Cadet Michael Ivy, a junior who was among those who took the test, conferred with engineg department instructors on Sunday. The roundup of suspects began the next day.

A caller identifying himself as a cadet telephoned The New York Times last night, one of three to do so in the last two days, to say that they had been held incommunicado for up to 14 hours awaiting interrogation by the subcommittee teams.

Cadet Andersen, who will join the 101st Airborne Division at Fort Campbell, Ky., when he graduates this summer, denied this in part as he answered questions, surrounded by officers, in the couryard of an administration building today.

"Some were held for up to eight or nine hours," he said, "but they had television, food and a place to do their homework." The questioning lasted until 3 or 4 A.M., he said.

Under the cadet honor system, the rapidly organized subcommittees are the equivalent of assistant district attorneys making preliminary investigations. A smaller executive staff of the honor committee, which reviewed the subcommittee's findings today, fills the role of the District Attorney. Cadet Andersen heads that panel.

April 76

The 12-member honor boards, which will begin hearing the suspected cadets and considering other evidence on Monday, function as grand juries. Cadets are permitted to resign or plead not guilty, if the equivalent of an indictment is returned. A single negative vote on an honor board results in dismissal of the charge.

Cadets seeking to challenge the, implied guilty verdict of the honor board can appeal to five-member appeal boards of officers, whose action parallels that of the trial.

Cadet suspects are informed of their rights, as in civilian life, but are not likely to have an opportunity to consult military civilian counsel until well into the proceedings, a practice that has attracted some criticism.

The honor committee also has been charged in recent years with standing as a constant threat and thus a form of abuse and harassment for petty violations.

Cadets who had been exonerated by the appeal board of officers were punished nevertheless, on occasion, through the "silence," a form of shunning by other cadets, until 1973. Although outlawed then, the silence is nevertheless applied, usually without complete success, at the present time, according to some cadets.

DEPARTMENT OF THE ARMY
UNITED STATES MILITARY ACADEMY
WEST POINT, NEW YORK 10996

MAJA   3 May 1976

SUBJECT: Request for Convening of Impartial Board of Inquiry

THRU: LTC Daniel W. Shimek
      Staff Judge Advocate
      United States Military Academy
      West Point, New York 10996

      LTG Sidney B. Berry
      Superintendent
      United States Military Academy
      West Point, New York 10996

      GEN Fred C. Weyand
      Chief of Staff
      United States Army
      Washington, D. C. 20310

TO: Mr. Martin R. Hoffmann
    Secretary of the Army
    Washington, D. C. 20310

1. The undersigned, detailed counsel for approximately 48 cadets at the
United States Military Academy presently charged with violating the Cadet
Honor Code by exchanging information on a homestudy computer problem
respectfully request that a closed Board of Inquiry be convened, at Secretarial
level or higher, prior to administrative elimination hearings now scheduled
for these cadets at West Point. We appreciate that this may be regarded
as a rather unusual request, but we are convinced that it is fully justified
under the circumstances.

2. In relation to this incident, the Superintendent and other high-level
officials at the Military Academy have publicly stated that it is their
judgment that cheating was not widespread, that the Cadet Honor Committee
accomplished its work in a professional manner, and that cadets remain strongly
supportive of the principles of the Honor Code.

MAJ··   3 May 1976
SUBJECT: Request for Convening of Impartial Board of Inquiry

3. In discharging our assigned duties in this case, we have discovered that
cheating was widespread, that the Cadet Honor Committee not only acted
arbitrarily and improperly in some cases but that certain of its members
affirmatively conspired and acted to conceal and cover up violations of the
Cadet Honor Code, and that the gap between the principles of the Honor Code
and the practice of that Code by the United States Corps of Cadets is
incredibly wide. Direct tangible evidence to support these assertions,
principally in the form of sworn affidavits (typical examples attached, with
names masked), is presently in the hands of the undersigned. These voluntary
statements, taken under oath, convincingly establish:

        a. that but a small fraction of those who actually "cheated" on the
homestudy problem in question are being held accountable for their actions.
Estimates of the number of cadets who failed to live up to the letter and
spirit of the Cadet Honor Code in this matter range upwards of 300 members
of the Class of 1977. Several cadets who have admitted that they gave, received
or tolerated the exchange of information pertaining to this homework problem
have indicated that the actual number of those that violated the Honor Code
in this manner is more than twice that figure;

        b. that the Cadet Honor Committee was conspicuously ineffectual in
distinguishing between cadets who did and those who did not violate the Cadet
Honor Code. Unfortunately, their poor performance in ascertaining the truth
of this matter cannot be attributed entirely to good faith mistakes and errors
of judgment. There is tangible evidence that scores if not hundreds of
"cheaters" in the Class of 1977 were never called upon to account for their
actions in this matter and that others escaped the stigma of being "found"
by the Cadet Honor Committee by lying their way through the proceedings.

4. At this point, the precise scope of the problem cannot be determined. It
can be said that the considerable body of evidence presently available to us
directly corroborates those who, notwithstanding contrary pronouncements by
senior Military Academy officials, believe that the Cadet Honor Code has no
special meaning to many if not most members of the Corps of Cadets who regard
it as just another obstacle to be overcome in order to graduate. It is
apparent that this attitude is completely incompatible with what is generally
understood to be the fundamental purpose of the Cadet Honor Code, to instill
the highest possible sense of personal integrity in tomorrow's leaders of the
Regular Army.

5. Particular attention is invited to the "toleration" clause of the Cadet
Honor Code which has had the peculiar effect in these cases of directly
suppressing the truth. That is, countless cadets who violated the Honor Code,
and know of other offenders, have "gone underground" and been restrained from
speaking openly and truthfully about this incident because to do so would
subject them to the single mandatory sanction of expulsion. Accordingly, we
feel that it is absolutely essential that testimonial immunity be granted all
interested cadets at the Board of Inquiry in order that the true facts concerning
the nature and scope of this cheating incident may be ascertained prior to
the time that the extreme sanction of dismissal is considered and perhaps

2

MAJA   3 May 1976
SUBJECT: Request for Convening of Impartial Board of Inquiry

imposed upon a select few.

6. Neither ethically nor professionally can we as Army officers and attorneys understand the logic, wisdom or fairness of existing attempts to "purify" the system by permanently stigmatizing only a few of the many who have transgressed the Cadet Honor Code. Stated differently, the underlying integrity problem within the Class of 1977 and throughout the Corps of Cadets will not be solved by a purge of the 40-50 cadets presently charged. Indeed, such action would tend to vindicate large numbers of accomplished cheaters, and perhaps liars, who remain in good standing within the Cadet Corps. We cannot reconcile the present status and treatment of these cadets with that of our clients who not only face administrative hearings in the near future designed to eliminate them from the service but already have been involuntarily moved to another cadet company, denied varsity athletic privileges, and denied the opportunity to receive and wear their class rings. These "nonpunitive" measures have had the effect of bringing pressure upon these cadets who have elected to ask for an administrative hearing rather than to summarily resign.

7. The urgency and importance of this request, both to the dozens of young men involved and also to the entire officer corps of the United States Army, cannot be overstated. All that we ask is that the Board of Inquiry be truly fair and impartial, that it be convened at the highest possible level above that of the Superintendent, and that testimonial immunity be granted to cadet witnesses so that the true facts surrounding this incident may be brought to light in a responsible, orderly and timely manner. Our request for a hearing before a tribunal which does not report to those presently charged with the administration or supervision of the Cadet Honor System is a carefully considered one. We would emphasize that we seek no special favors for our clients; we simply ask that their treatment at the hands of United States Military Academy and Department of the Army officials be no more unfavorable than that received by innumerable cadets who are similarly situated. Such is not the case at the present time.

8. It is our understanding that the Class of 1977 is expected to provide leadership to the Corps of Cadets when the first group of female cadets is admitted and throughout our Country's Bicentennial Year. That being the case, the resolution of this matter in an expeditious, fair and above-the-board manner would appear to be in the best interests of everyone concerned. Your personal and careful attention to this request would be appreciated.

DANIEL H. SHARPHORN   BURK E. BISHOP
CPT, JAGC   CPT, JAGC
Detailed Counsel for Respondents   Detailed Counsel for Respondents

ARTHUR F. LINCOLN, JR.   JAMES L. OSGARD
CPT, JAGC   CPT, JAGC
Detailed Counsel for Respondents   Detailed Counsel for Respondents

3

MAJA   3 May 1976
SUBJECT: Request for Convening of Impartial Board of Inquiry

PAUL L. FOSTER   DOMINICK J. THOMAS, JR.
CPT, JAGC   CPT, JAGC
Detailed Counsel for Respondents   Detailed Counsel for Respondents

VICTOR S. CARTER, JR.   LE ROY L. DE NOOYER, by DJS, agent
CPT, JAGC   CPT, JAGC
Detailed Counsel for Respondents   Detailed Counsel for Respondents

W. ALEXANDER MELBARDIS   WILLIAM J. HEMMER
CPT, JAGC   MAJ, JAGC
Detailed Counsel for Respondents   Detailed Counsel for Respondents

4 Incls
   1. Affidavit
   2. Affidavit
   3. Affidavit
   4. Affidavit

THE NEW YORK TIMES, WEDNESDAY, MAY 12, 1976   L   49

Cadet Who Said Almost All Cheated Faces Expulsion From West Point

BY JAMES FERON

Special to The New York Times

Norman R. Augustine, Under Secretary of the Army. He was told of the widespread cheating by a cadet at West Point.

WEST POINT, N. Y., May 11 —A cadet faced expulsion today after being found guilty of "tolerating" cheating because he told the Undersecretary of the Army, Norman Augustine, that a cheating scandal at the United States Military Academy was vastly more widespread than officials had acknowledged.

The cadet, Timothy Ringgold, 22 years old, of Phoenix, was transferred to transient barracks, a form of confinement, immediately after he was charged last night by a cadet honor board with a violation of the honor code. He now faces an appeal board of officers.

The honor code, which stems from the origins of the 174-year-old military academy, states that "a cadet will not lie, steal or cheat, or tolerate those who do." Long defended as a source of strength, it has come under increasing criticism as a means of abuse.

Called Cheating Usual

Cadet Ringgold said his allegation that "cheating is widespread" and that the 40 cadets officially charged so far "had done no more than almost every cadet has done at some time in his career" came during a frank discussion with Mr. Augustine on a routine visit in mid-April.

"Five juniors and five sophomores were selected at random," Cadet Ringgold recalled, "and the Secretary even asked the officer accompanying him to leave the room. I gave him an honest answer when he asked about the honor code. I

thought the conversation was privileged."

A few days later, the cadet said, he was called in by Cadet William Andersen, a senior who is chairman of the honor committee and the focus of a growing dispute over the manner in which alleged honor violations are pursued.

"He asked if I knew of any cadets who had cheated and not been investigated," Cadet Ringgold said. "If I said yes, it would be a violation [toleration] and if I said no it would also be a violation [lying], so I refused to answer.

"He said I was not being investigated myself so I could feel free to answer, but that was a lie, because six cadets had already signed statements. Anyway, my lawyer told me not to say anything because 95 percent of the convictions here are based on self-incriminating statements."

Lawyer Asked to Leave

Cadet Ringgold disclosed that he was being defended by Capt. Arthur Lincoln, a member of the judge advocate general's staff who has provided legal support for a number of cadets in controversial cases at the academy. Captain Lincoln was recently asked to leave West Point, although a requested extension of his tour at the Academy was granted two months ago.

"Although I was out on a limb by myself last month," Cadet Ringgold said in a telephone interview, "cadets are now coming forward to support me. They are providing lists of 50, 75, 100 and more names of other cadets who they cheated with."

These disclosures, the cadet confirmed, formed the basis of a letter signed two weeks ago by 10 Army lawyers, or roughly half the staff assigned to West Point, asking the Secretary of the Army, Martin R. Hoffmann, to investigate the manner in which the Academy was investigating its cheating scandal.

Letter to Goldwater

The cadet said he had written to Senator Barry Goldwater—"he's my Senator, he's a member of the Board of [Congressional] Visitors and member of the Senate Armed Services Committee"—asking the Arizona Republican for a full investigation "because the Academy also has been trying to pressure cadets into resigning rather than face appeals boards."

He said that the cadets, all of whom would face two years' duty starting as privates to fulfill military commitments if convictions were upheld, "are being told that they might get assignments of their choice if they resign."

"If not, they could be sent anywhere," he added.

Cadet Ringgold also confirmed allegations by other cadets that honor boards, or juries, had been "fixed" in the series of April hearings that reduced the 101 cadets originally accused of cheating to 32, three of whom have already resigned. The Academy confirmed recently that one cadet had been officially charged with jury tampering.

GIVE FRESH AIR FUND
GIVE REAL GRASS

ky, pro-Israeli zealots are uncovered. Agnew spent nearly two years on the novel and says it was a "therapeutic" exercise that bucked him up when he was down. Sample sex: "He slipped off her slacks and began to explore her body. 'You are ready, aren't you?' he said as her breath began to come in quick, shallow pants." Sample murder: "He placed the sharp point of the [ice] pick above the top, cervical vertebra and, with a strong thrust, drove the full length of the needle upward under the cerebellum and into the medulla oblongata."

Agnew plans to begin writing his memoirs later this year. Playboy Press has already taken 37,000 orders on an advance printing of 50,000 copies of "The Canfield Decision" and laid aside 25,000 more for its book club. "It could make him half a million dollars," predicted Michael Cohn, director of Playboy Press's book division, last week. Not bad for a felon-once-removed.

—TOM MATHEWS

THE ARMY:

A Point of Honor

The U.S. Military Academy's honor code is so much a part of life at West Point that most plebes sign it without hesitation. "A cadet will not lie, cheat or steal," it reads, "or tolerate those who do." The code has frequently been criticized as rigid and arbitrarily enforced, but last week it was under frontal assault in what could become the largest cheating scandal in West Point's 174-year history. Students and lawyers at the Academy report that hundreds of cadets may be involved; last week, NEWSWEEK learned that in a letter requesting the Secretary of the Army to conduct an independent investigation into the scandal, ten Army lawyers stationed at West Point implied that the Academy might be attempting to cover up the extent of the cheating.*

The cheating episode began in March after instructors in an electrical-engineering class noticed similarities in a take-home exam they had given much of the junior class, and alerted the Cadet Honor Committee to investigate. After hearings before the honor boards, 49 cadets were charged with cheating (the penalty for violating the code is expulsion) and 49 others exonerated. The investigation might have ended there, except that in a conversation with Under Secretary of the Army Norman Augustine, who came to West Point on a visit in mid-April, Cadet Timothy Ringgold said the cheating was far more widespread than officials had acknowledged.

When word of Ringgold's statement

*The Air Force Academy is also dealing with cheating charges. Last week, six cadets refused an honor-committee request to resign for cheating. An Academy investigator has been asked to look into the charges.

became known to the Honor Committee, it accused him of "tolerating" cheating (late last week the Academy suddenly dropped all charges against Ringgold because of what it called "new evidence"). At the same time other cadets, worried about Ringgold's allegations, quietly admitted their own violations of the code to Army lawyers and implicated fellow students. NEWSWEEK learned that one of several affidavits sent along with the lawyers' letter to the Pentagon contended that 185 students had committed honor-code violations. Some of the affidavits also detailed instances of tampering with the honor boards—cases in which, according to one lawyer, accused cadets threatened to "drag members of the honor boards with them" unless they were acquitted of violations.

At West Point, one cadet accused of cheating maintained that the Academy had purposely not "expanded the investigation because it would just about collapse if it faced the summer and fall with half the [seniors] missing." Academy officials denied there had been a cover-up; one spokesman said that "the Academy has pursued every lead that has been developed." Army officials, who review all cases of cadets charged with honor violations, refused comment except to say they were "considering" the lawyers' request to conduct a board of inquiry into the scandal.

In the midst of the cheating controversy, Steven Verr, a 19-year-old Illinois plebe, came forward with another story of alleged honor-code violations. During new cadet training last summer (in which hazing is common, though unauthorized), Verr told an upperclassman who had found him crying that his parents had been injured in an accident; in fact Verr's tears had been brought on by weariness

Verr, Lincoln, Ringgold:
In the midst of a cheating scandal, charges of harassment and talk of a cover-up

Photos by Bernard Gotfryd—Newsweek

and hunger caused by denial of food. After the honor committee found him guilty of lying, Verr said fellow students began harassing him. When West Point superintendent Lt. Gen. Sidney Berry overturned the conviction last March—a decision that rankled the cadet honor committee and its chairman, William Andersen—Verr said the abuse stepped up. He reported there had been telephone threats on his life; he also claimed that the honor board hearing his case had originally been sympathetic to him (only one vote is needed to acquit), but that Andersen had improperly pressured it into reaching its 12-0 vote. Andersen last week categorically denied the charge, saying he had spoken only twice during the deliberation to "clarify facts."

Although he made no allegations against Andersen, Verr's attorney, Army Capt. Arthur Lincoln, also went public in defense of his client. The honor committee, he argued, was circulating "false information" about Verr. Last week Lincoln, who has provided legal support for other cadets in controversial cases, revealed that he had been asked by the Pentagon to submit his choices for reassignment next year, even though his request to remain at the Academy a fourth year had been approved two months ago. "It would be a normal request under normal circumstances," he explained. "But we all know why they're doing it."

Verr's harassment and the cheating scandal have both focused attention on a code that has long been a tradition of cadet training. Most students clearly still believe in it. But a growing minority also suspect, as Lincoln does, that West Point's honor code may sometimes do as much to undermine honor as to uphold it.

—SUSAN FRAKER with ERIC GELMAN at West Point, N.Y.

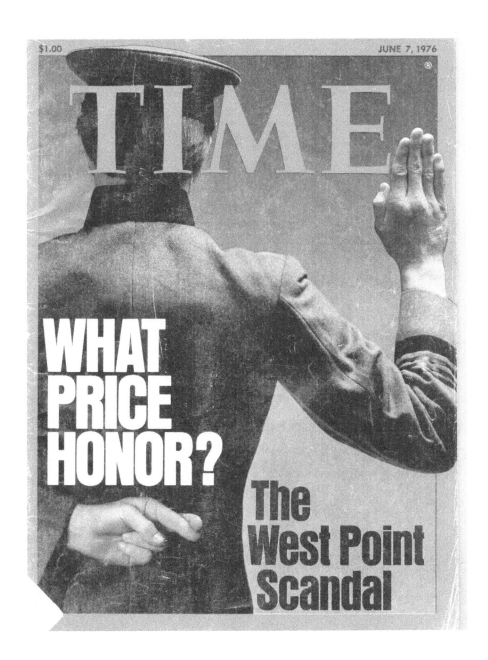

WEST POINT PLEBES WAITING IN FORMATION OUTSIDE MESS HALL

ARMED FORCES/COVER STORY

WHAT PRICE HONOR?

shined his shoes. When he was Secretary of the Army, Howard ("Bo") Callaway complained, "The honor code often deals with trivia." No matter: the trivial could get a cadet "separated"—expelled—as surely and swiftly as the significant.

The current violations grew out of a take-home electrical-engineering examination in March. A total of 823 second classmen—or juniors—took the test. So far, four cadets have resigned after being charged with cheating on the exam. Forty-eight others have been found guilty by honor committees; these cadets are awaiting review of their cases by 13 boards composed of officers. At the same time, instructors are going over the papers submitted by nearly 100 other cadets.

All this would be bad enough, but last week the situation worsened when members of the junior class said they were giving authorities the names of literally hundreds of their classmates who, they claimed, had violated the code. The avowed aim of this rush to judgment: to implicate so many cadets that West Point could not possibly dismiss all the guilty ones without virtually wiping out the entire junior class.

Captain Arthur Lincoln, a lawyer and West Point graduate who represented some of the cadets at one point during the proceedings, estimates that 90% to 95% of all cheating incidents are not reported. Cadet Timothy Ringgold, who is accused of tolerating cheating, claims that "roughly one-third of my junior class cheated, and the other two-thirds tolerated it."

Some cadets are pressing their case against the honor code with astonishing frankness—for West Point. Not only are they appearing on television and granting interviews, but they are also seeking out newsmen who will listen to their stories. Now that campuses elsewhere are quiet, and have been for several years, a wave of delayed-action student revolt is washing over the 174-year-old institution, where the best way to survive has been to conform. Cadets are demanding that they be given the same rights of due process that civilians enjoy under the law. Some young legal officers at West Point are siding with the cadets, claiming that hearings on code violations are often nothing more than kangaroo courts that flout the 14th Amendment.

As the scandal rumbled across West Point, Lieut. General Sidney B. Berry, 50, the academy's superintendent, fought to get the situation under control. A tough, erect veteran of two wars, Berry confessed to TIME, "I've never been in more of a combat situation than I am now. There are things that make me heartsick in the whole situation—so many young men may have violated the honor code. But, by God, I've been heartsick in battle and done what I have to do."

What Berry has done to cope with the scandal and get at its causes is take control of the honor code away from the cadets. Berry gave Colonel Hal B. Rhyne, deputy commandant, a new full-time job: handling honor code questions and issues. He then replaced the cadets' honor committees with an "internal review panel" that will conduct the initial hearings in cases of alleged violations. The panel is made up of three field-grade officers (major and above) and two cadets who next year will be first classmen (seniors). Still not satisfied, Berry created four separate subcommittees to investigate cheating in the junior class, where the scandal is centered. Finally, he ordered the entire junior class to stay

I t is the most traditional of ceremonies at one of the nation's most hallowed shrines. On the broad green plain high above the Hudson River, where Baron von Steuben drilled minutemen 200 years ago, thousands of proud parents and nostalgic graduates will assemble this week to watch the corps of cadets pass in review: 4,400 young men in swallow-tailed gray coats, white trousers and black shakos stepping out with crisp precision while their brilliant regimental flags snap in the breeze.

As always, the Long Gray Line will provide a magnificent and stirring spectacle. But this year the excitement of graduation day at West Point will be marred by doubts, confusion, bitterness and fear. Dozens of the marching cadets may be dismissed from the United States Military Academy within weeks. There is talk that scores, even hundreds of others may be in deep trouble before the current investigations have run their course. The most serious cheating scandal in its history is shaking West Point—a furor that has set cadet against cadet and threatens the basic nature of the institution itself.

The scandal revolves around the honor code of the corps, which states with neither equivocation nor mercy: "A cadet will not lie, cheat or steal, or tolerate those who do." The "toleration clause" includes those who know that others have cheated but have not turned them in. For all found guilty, there is only one punishment: quick and automatic dismissal from the academy. Times may change and values fade, but West Point continues to rely on its uncompromising code, no matter how impossible it may seem to the rest of society.

Honor committees composed of cadets hear 100 or so cases a year. Most are for violations of the code in dealing with absurdly picayune incidents, such as a cadet's lying about having

TIME, JUNE 7, 1976

on at the Point after graduation to be available to testify if necessary.

In the face of accusations that the Point was trying to cover up the whole story, Berry last week assembled 300 members of his staff and declared: "That's a pile of horse manure. It's going to be a long summer. Somehow we've got to get ourselves organized to get this traumatic experience over as quickly as possible. It's a painful thing, but we are paid to do tough things in the soldier business."

What drives Berry to get at the root of the problem is his firm conviction that the honor code is the "archstone" of West Point's stern motto: Duty, Honor, Country. Says he: "I do not think the code is anachronistic. Integrity is essential in the development of leader-soldiers." Indeed, Berry and many other high-ranking officers, including non-West Pointers, agree that the honor code serves an absolutely irreplaceable function, as do the more lenient codes at Annapolis and the Air Force Academy. All three academies accomplish their main purpose: they produce well-trained and dedicated officers.

Graduates of the academies may form only 11% of the corps of commissioned officers on active duty in the armed forces (10% in the Army, 17% in the Navy, 9% in the Air Force), and the military may be getting steadily more democratic. But a man wearing the heavy and instantly recognizable class ring of one of the academies starts with a tremendous advantage. Fully 43% of the Army's generals are West Point "ringknockers"; 56% of the Navy's admirals went to Annapolis; 34% of the Air Force's generals attended one of the academies. Says General Melvin Zais, 60, an ROTC graduate from the University of New Hampshire: "The West Point influence is like a drop of blue ink in a glass of water. It isn't much in volume, but it influences the coloring of the whole glass. West Point permeates our resource."

GRADUATING MIDSHIPMEN TOSSING CAPS INTO AIR IN ANNUAL RITUAL AT ANNAPOLIS
"The honor code was the most important influence on my life, period."

With impressive unanimity, graduates of the three academies agree that the honor codes helped greatly to prepare them for a life in the military. Air Force Colonel Bradley P. Hosmer, top man in the class of 1959 at the Air Force Academy, goes one step further: "The honor code was the most important influence on my life, period. It affects your standards of self, my expectations, and even how I raise my kids." In all three services, academy graduates emphasize the importance of being able to trust the word of a fellow officer.

The honor code that has become so important to West Point —and the U.S. Army—began under Colonel Sylvanus Thayer, superintendent from 1817 to 1833. A Dartmouth man with a backbone of iron, Thayer changed West Point from a humdrum school for the sons of wealthy families into a first-class engineering institution. After studying European military systems, he also imposed on the cadets a kind of Prussian discipline that lingers today. Thayer had strict rules against lying and stealing, and what was called "irregular or immoral practices."

Shortly before the turn of the century, cadets set up their own vigilance committee and conducted covert "trials" of those who breached the code. When he was superintendent in 1922, Brigadier General Douglas MacArthur created the honor system, with an official board of review composed of cadets.

The first major scandal at West Point occurred in 1951, when 90 cadets were forced out for cribbing on examinations, including 37 members of the football team. In 1966, 42 cadets departed after having been accused of cheating. Four years later, West Point's honor code was amended to include the phrase forbidding any cadet to tolerate wrongdoing by another. In 1973, 21 cadets were sacked for cheating or condoning cheating.

The toleration clause has caused severe problems since it was introduced. Admits Brigadier General Walter F. Ulmer Jr., commandant of cadets: "It's not natural for an 18-year-old to tell on his friends. It's something that has to be instilled." Accordingly, cadets get 25 hours of formal instruction in the intricacies of the honor code.

As a prime reason for having an honor code, instructors frequently note that one combat officer must always be able to rely on the word of another. To illustrate this point, the cadets are often told a story—perhaps apocryphal—of a company commander who radioed one of his platoon leaders to move his unit out of a particular area. The platoon leader, deciding that his men were too tired to stir, later radioed back that the maneuver had been completed—but he actually let his troops stay in place. Relying on this false statement, the company commander

PLEBE BEING "BRACED" IN 1957 IN HAZING DRILL, NOW BANNED

SUPERINTENDENT BERRY REVIEWING COLUMNS OF MARCHING CADETS
"I've never been in more of a combat situation."

THE NATION

COLONEL RHYNE

BRIG. GEN. ULMER

CADET ANDERSEN

ordered an artillery unit to open fire on the area. The entire platoon was blasted away.

The present scandal began with an exam that required juniors to design a voltage-regulator circuit. When an instructor began looking over the completed papers, he found a handwritten footnote on one that stated: "I have received assistance on this paper."

Later the same day, the instructor found another test paper with wording identical to the one that bore the footnoted confession. The hunt was on. Soon 117 papers with suspiciously similar phrasing and matching misspellings were discovered. The Honor Committee, composed of 88 cadets from the top two classes, formed seven subcommittees of three students each to study the suspect papers and interview their authors.

After the initial screening, 101 cadets were under deep suspicion. They were next called before boards composed of twelve Honor Committee cadets for further examination. Some appearances lasted three hours, some three days. At the end of a week, the Honor Committee decided that 49 cadets were innocent and 52 guilty.

Four have already resigned (their names are still kept secret); the other 48 are now having their cases reviewed by five-member officer boards, each chaired by a full colonel, which have the power to reverse the findings of the Honor Committee and declare a cadet innocent.

The final court of appeals at West Point is Berry. As superintendent, he has the power to overturn the findings of the review board and decide that a cadet is innocent. But even then, the absolved cadet's classmates may shun him as a pariah. To some zealots who swear by the honor code, the very fact that a cadet is accused of wrongdoing is reason enough to condemn him —a situation that shows how a system designed to develop honor can be warped to foster dishonor.

A case in point, which coincidentally is causing a furor this spring, involves Steven Verr, 19, a slight (5 ft. 9 in., 140 lbs.), mild-mannered fourth classman, or freshman. Verr's troubles began last August while he was attending "Beast Barracks," the summer of rigorous training and hazing given to incoming plebes (a word derived from plebeians). Verr was subjected to a traditional form of harassment: upperclassmen ordered him not to put certain foods on his tray, or made him sit at attention while others ate. After going hungry for two days, Verr had tears in his eyes as he left the dining hall. When an upperclassman demanded, "Mister, what are you crying about?" Verr told a disjointed story about his parents' having been in an automobile accident. Verr's lie was discovered, and he was found guilty of violating the honor code by both the Honor Committee and the officers' reviewing board.

Berry reversed the

PLEBES IN "BEAST BARRACKS" SUBMIT TO INTERROGATION BY AN UPPERCLASSMAN BEFORE BEING PERMITTED TO SHOWER (1957)
Most of the sadistic practices have been abolished, but the pressure remains.

findings, saying that Verr had had "no intent to deceive." But it was an unpopular decision, and Verr's troubles were only beginning. He found himself shunned by many of his classmates, although the practice—known as "the silence"—has been officially banned at West Point since 1973. In that year, wide publicity was given to the case of Cadet James J. Pelosi, who was subjected to this treatment for 19 months after having been reinstated on a legal technicality, although he had been convicted of an honor code violation. Referring to Verr's experience, Cadet William Andersen, the present head of the Honor Committee, issued a statement declaring that "a significant number of us disagree with Berry's decision." Added Andersen, who is considered a zealot and a martinet by a number of cadets as well as officers, and has been accused of conducting vendettas against those who do not measure up to his rigid standards. "While we have no authority or right to infringe on the human dignity [of individuals], we have the right to choose who we associate with and who to speak to."

Verr claims that his mail has been intercepted and his room ransacked, and there have been vague reports that his life has been threatened. The academy has assigned him a bodyguard. Verr has complained to newsmen about his treatment, much to the disgust of some cadets. Says one: "Verr is getting every ounce of publicity he can out of this and is doing the academy a disservice."

The case of Cadet Timothy Ringgold shows how absurd the honor system can be. After the engineering-exam scandal broke, Ringgold, who was not accused of cheating, and other cadets happened to meet with Army Under Secretary Norman R. Augustine. During the talk, which was supposedly off-the-record, Ringgold said he felt cheating was "widespread" at the Point. Another cadet who was present felt duty-bound to charge Ringgold with toleration.

After the incident was publicized, Ringgold was cleared by academy authorities. Ringgold then sought out General Ulmer and asked just why he had been acquitted. Ulmer explained that he had not referred to any specific case in his conversation with Augustine, nor was there any evidence to back up what he had said. According to Ulmer, the outspoken Ringgold then told him the authorities were looking in the wrong place for culprits. Asked Ulmer: "Are you telling me that you have firsthand knowledge of cadets who have violated the honor code apart from what we know?" "Yes, sir," said Ringgold. Ulmer promptly advised him that he would have to go before an honor code review board once again. Ulmer later explained that he was "morally obligated" to turn Ringgold in after the cadet had volunteered the information. Ringgold's case is still pending.

Even as they search for reasons for the mass violations of the honor code, academy officials are convinced there is no basic flaw in the nature of the cadets who are attracted to West Point. Indeed the quality of the cadet corps is impressive, as is the incoming class of 900 men—and for the first time, nearly 100 women—that will attend Beast Barracks this summer.

The typical cadet in the class of 1976, which is graduating this week, had a B+ average in high school. He was a letterman in some sport (33.8% captained a team) and scored 554 on the verbal scholastic aptitude test and 624 on the mathematics test—not up to the average scores of Harvard or Yale, but well within the reach of such excellent schools as the University of Michigan or Georgia Tech. All of the cadets were nominated for a place in the class by authorized officials, notably U.S. Senators and Congressmen. Many had wanted to enter West Point since early in their high school days or even before, and 13.4% had fathers who were career military officers.

The attrition rate at West Point is roughly comparable to that at Ivy League schools: last year's graduating class lost 36% of its members along the way. If they follow the general pattern, some 70% of the class will eventually get an advanced degree. Most West Pointers now stay in the service for 20 years before reentering civilian life (they are required to serve for at least five years after graduating). The cadets get a solid education in mathematics and engineering, though the liberal arts curriculum has been broadened in recent years. Understandably, the cadets who are more at home with the mysteries of hydraulics still far outnumber those with a taste for the imagery of T.S. Eliot.

The pace at the Point can be brutal. Reveille at 6:10 a.m., duties or study at 6:40 a.m., classes from 7:50 a.m. until 11:55 a.m., and on through the day at double time until taps at 11 p.m. For many exhausted cadets, the major recreation is sleeping. There is still some hazing at the Point, such as forcing plebes to know the number of lights in Cullun Hall (340) and the capacity of Luck Reservoir ("Seventy-eight million gallons, sir, when the water is flowing over the spillway"). But the sadistic practices of the past have been abolished—doing deep knee bends over the point of a bayonet or forcing a cadet to run up five floors of the barracks, don a new uniform and get back down in 2½ minutes.

As is the case at many U.S. colleges and universities, there is constant pressure to get good grades *(see following story)*. The "goats," with the low marks, sit at the back of a classroom, while the "engineers" sit up front and get special privileges. Still the electrical engineering exam that is at the root of the current scandal was worth only 5% of the final grade in that course. Indeed the students being hauled before the Honor Committee included good students as well as borderline cases.

West Pointer Berry (class of 1948) suspects that the main rea-

THE NATION

son for the incident has been the rapid expansion of the academy from 2,496 cadets to 4,417 during the turbulent decade from 1964 to 1974 that included Watergate and Viet Nam. In this period, Berry points out, American teen-agers became more questioning and skeptical, including those who enrolled at West Point. "There has been great discussion about integrity in the Army itself, most of it arising out of My Lai," says Berry. "Frankly, this is a terribly difficult time for the academy."

The cadets who violated the honor code by cheating on a

form to hundreds of regulations contained in a manual known as the Blue Book. Life at West Point consists in large part of finding ways around the regulations; if a cadet is caught, he is disciplined. But, strictly speaking, many violations of the regulations could be interpreted as violations of the honor code. A cadet who misses a parade under false pretenses, for example, could be accused of cheating. According to Dr. Richard C. U'Ren, 37, who was chief of psychiatry at West Point from 1970 to 1972, this dichotomy gives cadets an unfortunate point of view: it is all right to violate the regulations as long as you do not lie about it. "Ethics," says U'Ren, "is often divorced from honor at West Point."

U'Ren also argues that the code has such strict penalties that cadets tend to cover up wrongdoing. During his time at West Point, he says he was told that only 10% of the cheating was reported. "It's a rather ironic fact," he says, "that the code weeds out some cadets who are honest enough to report themselves for honor violations."

What is more, says U'Ren, "West Point does everything in its power to develop a sense of cohesiveness among the cadets. They strive to develop a sense of loyalty and belonging—community. And then they ask these men to turn each other in on

CADETS TAKING AN EXAM WHILE THE FUROR OVER THE CHEATING SCANDAL GROWS

"SILENCED" CADET PELOSI GRADUATING IN 1973

relatively insignificant exam knew that West Point graduates had not hesitated to lie in Viet Nam—falsifying body counts, concealing the bombing of Cambodia, covering up My Lai. Indeed the commander of the Americal Division, which included the platoon led by Lieut. William Calley at My Lai, was headed by Major General Samuel Koster, who became superintendent of West Point in 1968. Two years later, Koster resigned after he was accused of taking part in the campaign to cover up the facts about the massacre at My Lai. Koster was demoted, censured and retired in disgrace in 1973.

"All adolescents are skeptical to some extent," says Ulmer, "and the line between skepticism and cynicism is a thin line." There is mounting evidence that many cadets in the junior class—if not in the corps as a whole—are becoming increasingly cynical about the honor code and system.

HARASSED CADET STEVEN VERR
The full treatment.

Part of the reason is the code's extreme rigidity. Part is the growing feeling among some cadets that their fellow students on the Honor Committee are as sternly self-righteous—and occasionally as sadistic—as a Puritan elder in early Massachusetts. Says a high Pentagon official: "We have to moderate their enthusiasm to be inquisitors."

Important as these problems are, many critics of the honor system believe the fundamental fault lies in the nature of the code itself and the way it dovetails with life at West Point. In addition to having to live by the honor code, a cadet has to con-

honor code violations. It really is a terrible bind for the cadets."

What is happening at West Point this spring seems to confirm the findings of a study of the honor code released last October by the Federal Government's General Accounting Office, which acts as an investigating agency for Congress. The G.A.O. study said "the toleration clause" is one of the biggest problems for the members of the corps, and the longer a cadet stays at West Point, the more tolerant he tends to become of wrongdoing. Some cadets felt that maintaining a friendship is more important than reporting a fellow student and that the penalty of banishment from West Point was too harsh for minor offenses.

As the magnitude of the problem becomes more apparent, high Pentagon officials are quietly deciding that perhaps the time has come for West Point to modify the code. When he heard what was going on, Defense Secretary Donald Rumsfeld impatiently asked aides who was administering the system at the Point and whether there was any room for discretion in the system.

If West Point does decide that its present system is unrealistic and unfair, it has two models close at hand to copy. Both Annapolis and the Air Force Academy have systems that differ in important ways from the Point's. At Annapolis, midshipmen are not required to turn each other in for violations. At the Air

Force Academy, the cadets are not supposed to tolerate infractions, but they are encouraged to talk privately with a suspected wrongdoer to learn his side of the incident. If he has a reasonable excuse, the matter can be dropped then and there. Even if the reviewing committees eventually find a cadet guilty, they can mete out punishment short of dismissal.

Although these modified systems seem to be working well, both institutions have had scandals of their own. In 1974 seven midshipmen were forced to resign for cheating on a celestial navigation exam. At Colorado Springs, 109 cadets (including 29 football players) were forced out in 1965 for stealing and selling exams or tolerating the practice; 46 left after handing around test questions in 1967; and 39 were banished for cheating or tolerating those that did in 1972.

Well aware that the honor code and its system of justice were causing problems, West Point's Berry set up a special committee in 1974 to see how the two "could be strengthened and improved." Composed of 14 officers and 16 cadets, the committee produced a two-volume report ten months before the present scandal broke. The academy is already instituting recommended procedural reforms aimed at removing the secrecy of the hearings and improving the individual's right to due process. For example, cadets appearing before an honor committee are now allowed to be present while witnesses are being questioned.

In its most significant recommendation, the committee urged that the system be modified so that dismissal would no longer be automatic for any cadet found guilty of an honor violation. The

PRINCE OF WALES WITH SUPERINTENDENT MacARTHUR IN 1920
Only for those with a true vocation.

committee urged that cadets be punished according to the seriousness of their offenses; if mitigating circumstances were strong enough, a cadet could be let off with no punishment at all. To be put into effect, the reform authorizing discretionary punishment needed to be approved by two-thirds of the cadets; only 54% voted in favor last spring. Academy officials anticipate that the discretionary option will be approved when the proposal is next put to a vote, probably this fall.

The fact that little more than half of the corps voted for a flexible system of punishments shows how strongly the status quo is defended by many cadets, and their elders, despite the difficulties. "An officer who sees a fellow officer commit an atrocity has an obligation to report him, even if he's a friend," says Ulmer. "If you won't do that, you have no business at West Point." Over the decades, the code has helped to make West Point what George Patton Jr. called a "holy place," an institution that Maxwell Taylor describes as "something like the church: it is not for everyone, only for those with a true vocation." Agrees Berry: "The code's a statement of ideals that I think is sound. Imperfect human beings don't measure up to ideals. It's a pretty demanding code. But the battlefield is a pretty demanding place."

No one could quarrel with Berry's contention that West Point has to prepare young men to perform honorably and reliably on the battlefield. The problem that he and the U.S. Army confront is how to revise the code, and the system of justice that goes with it, to foster a sense of honor in the cadets—a system that they can uphold with honor themselves.

28 L AUGUST 10, 1976

The New York Times

Founded in 1851
ADOLPH S. OCHS, *Publisher 1896-1935*
ARTHUR HAYS SULZBERGER, *Publisher 1935-1961*
ORVIL E. DRYFOOS, *Publisher 1961-1963*

Letters to the Editor

West Point: The System Indicted

To the Editor:

For over three months West Point has been beset by the largest cheating scandal in its history, the eighth to strike a service academy in 25 years. The public has been led to believe that the academy is seeking the facts honestly and responsibly. The accused cadets are portrayed as a disgraceful lot unfit for salvation. These points are simply untrue.

The Commandant, General Ulmer, has suggested those cadets facing charges are the only ones who cheated on this exam. Yet, the only charges pending are based on a comparison of exam papers. One Congressman, two prosecuting attorneys, two electrical engineering instructors (serving as government expert witnesses) and numerous other officers and cadets have testified that more than 400 of the 823 cadets who took the exam collaborated. One attorney testified that he told the superintendent, General Berry, if properly investigated, 300 to 600 cadets could be referred to trial. General Berry's only response has been to stop the most effective means of conducting a proper investigation—the grant of immunity which he had already extended to five cadets and which the commandant had offered to three.

I have never been charged with cheating but on May 20 I requested, through proper channels, that General Berry conduct an investigation of my allegations of widespread cheating. I provided him with a list of 74 cadets I suspected. To date General Berry's only response has been to call the allegations, "filth, garbage, sewage-unhealthy and unproven." The Academy represented my classmates as moral degenerates. But, even a cursory examination reveals that the involved cadets represent nearly a perfect cross-section of the corps.

They have worked as hard, have the same desire and dedication that has served the academy, the Army and the United States for so long. They support the Honor Code as strongly as any cadet, they only ask for the opportunity to learn from their mistakes. If the system is "alive and well" as General Ulmer claims, then surely it can stand some constructive criticism from those who live under it. Before the academy can "dispose" of its "bad apples" surely, a full understanding of what has happened is necessary. If the system goes unchanged, it will only be a matter of time before America will be faced with the ninth scandal.

TIMOTHY D. RINGGOLD
U.S. Military Academy, Class of '77
Washington, July 29, 1976

DEPARTMENT OF THE ARMY
UNITED STATES MILITARY ACADEMY
WEST POINT, NEW YORK 10996

MAJA   2 August 1976

SUBJECT: Request for Convening of Impartial Board of Inquiry

THRU: Superintendent
       United States Military Academy
       West Point, New York 10996

       Chief of Staff
       United States Military Academy
       West Point, New York 10996

       Secretary of the Army
       Department of the Army
       Washington, D.C. 20310

TO: Secretary of Defense
       Department of the Army
       Washington, D.C. 20310

1. The undersigned, detailed counsel for approximately 130 cadets at
the United States Military Academy presently charged with violations of
the Cadet Honor Code, request that a complete and open inquiry be conducted,
at Secretarial level or higher to investigate the nature and scope of problems
within the West Point Honor and Academic Systems. We are convinced that
circumstances at West Point demand and justify such an investigatory body
being convened as soon as possible.

2. This request is substantially similar to a request made by ten defense
counsel assigned to West Point on 3 May 1976 (see attachment) yet incorporates
certain necessary changes warranted by interim events occurring at West Point.
It is our opinion that the allegations enumerated in the 3 May 1976 request
have been fully substantiated by those intervening events and now cause
the very roots of the Honor and Academic Systems as they exist at West Point
to be called into question. Sworn testimony by instructors in the Department
of Electrical Engineering before Boards of Officers looking into these matters

MAJA   2 August 1976
SUBJECT: Request for Convening of Impartial Board of Inquiry

indicates that upwards of 400 cadets collaborated on the EE 304 take-home
exam and that West Point is, at best, a second rate engineering school.
Affidavits of cadets currently in the hands of respondents counsel directly
support these assertions as well as isolate many other areas of concern such
as: frequent and systematic cheating in other courses, constant violation
of the toleration doctrine and other, more serious, matters. Testimony of
cadets has indicated that in a substantial number of required courses procedure
and memorization are emphasized to the exclusion of substance and theory
thereby allowing cadets to maintain high grade averages while learning and
retaining little or nothing of the course. These are not allegations newly
raised at this time, yet, contrary to the Secretary of the Army's instructions
in his earlier denial, they have not been acted upon to any significant degree.

3. At this juncture the precise scope of the problem cannot be defined.
It is abundantly clear, however, that the present difficulty is not an isolated
incident stemming from the administration of the EE 304 exam but rather
the result of a festering sore within the system. Failure to discover and
treat the causes of the problem will ultimately lead to a more deep set
infection requiring more radical corrective measures. The cosmetic treatment
applied by formation of the Internal Review Panel has inflamed both those
cadets already pending charges as well as those fearful of being charged
in the immediate future. The resulting polarization of cadets has forced
many cadets to violate the Honor Code in order to survive and remain at West
Point.

4. Failure to act now can only be interpreted as an obvious attempt to
salvage the heretofore good name of the United States Military Academy at
the expense of its most vital asset, the individual cadet. The suspension
of the Honor Committee investigations, the substitution of inquisitorial
Internal Review Panel Hearings, the absence of Constitutional protections
and procedural safeguards, and the animosity and distrust among the cadets
have all tended to undermine the morale and espirit de corps of the cadets.
As Army officers and attorneys we cannot ethically or professionally support
anything less than a complete and thorough search for the causes of the
current dilemma at West Point. Nor can we support the inadequate and selective
procedures employed by the United States Military Academy in purporting to
investigate these matters. Only if the truth is found can the Honor Code
rightfully be returned to the position of respect and faith it once enjoyed
both within and without the Academy.

5. We therefore request that you convene, with all due speed, a panel of
educators, administrators, and citizens, to determine the causes of the problems
at West Point. The alternative must be continued chaos and the ultimate
destruction of all that is good and productive within the United States
Military Academy.

MAJA   2 August 1976
SUBJECT: Request for Convening of Impartial Board of Inquiry

6. The urgency and importance of this request, both to the hundreds of young
men involved and also the entire United States Army and American public,
cannot be overstated. All that we ask is that the panel convened be truly
fair and impartial, that it be convened at the highest possible level above
that of the Superintendent, and that it be convened without delay. Our request
for a hearing before such a tribunal as requested is a carefully considered
one. We seek only to impart to the investigatory process the basic tenets
of American justice which have been previously lacking.

7. The Class of 1977 is expected to provide leadership and instruction
to those classes that follow at West Point. They will also be expected
to shoulder responsibilities as future Army officers and leaders in society.
That being the case, the resolution of this matter in an expeditious, fair
and above-board manner is in the best interest of everyone concerned. Your
personal and careful attention to this request would be appreciated.

PAUL L. FOSTER   ARTHUR F. LINCOLN, JR.   DANIEL. H. SHARPHORN
CPT, JAGC   CPT, JAGC   CPT, JAGC
Counsel for Respondents   Counsel for Respondents   Counsel for Respondents

JAMES L. OSGARD   THOMAS D. FRITZ   JAMES F. LEE, JR.
CPT, JAGC   CPT, JAGC   CPT, JAGC
Counsel for Respondents   Counsel for Respondents   Counsel for Respondents

DOMINICK J. THOMAS   LEROY L. DeNOOYER   BURK E. BISHOP
CPT, JAGC   CPT, JAGC   CPT, JAGC
Counsel for Respondents   Counsel for Respondents   Counsel for Respondents

CLARENCE M. MYER   JAMES M. NORTON   MARTIN J. BOYLE
CPT, JAGC   CPT, JAGC   CPT, JAGC
Counsel for Respondents   Counsel for Respondents   Counsel for Respondents

SIDNEY P. ALEXANDER
CPT, JAGC
Counsel for Respondents

FREDERIC T. BRANDT
CPT, JAGC
Counsel for Respondents

DAVID E. BROCKWAY
CPT, JAGC
Counsel for Respondents

STANLEY BROWN
CPT, JAGC
Counsel for Respondents

FRANK BRUNSON, JR.
CPT, JAGC
Counsel for Respondents

PETER E. CASEY
CPT, JAGC
Counsel for Respondents

JEFFERSON L. DAVIS
CPT, JAGC
Counsel for Respondents

DONALD P. DESONIER
CPT, JAGC
Counsel for Respondents

BROOKS S. DOYLE, JR.
CPT, JAGC
Counsel for Respondents

JAMES D. EARL
CPT, JAGC
Counsel for Respondents

JAN HORBALY
CPT, JAGC
Counsel for Respondents

LARRY HORTON
CPT, JAGC
Counsel for Respondents

JOSEPH R. PRESTON
CPT, JAGC
Counsel for Respondents

WILLIAM B. RAMSEY
CPT, JAGC
Counsel for Respondents

SAMUEL SFERRAZZA
CPT, JAGC
Counsel for Respondents

JAMES L. TOWNSEND
CPT, JAGC
Counsel for Respondents

JOSEPH J. NOLL
CPT, JAGC
Counsel for Respondents

ANDREW C. OLIVO
CPT, JAGC
Counsel for Respondent

The New York Times

NEW YORK, TUESDAY, AUGUST 24, 1976

Lieut. Gen. Sidney B. Berry, left, West Point Superintendent; Maj. Gen. James McLee, Chief of Legislative Liaison, and Martin R. Hoffmann, Secretary of the Army, confer before testifying at Senate hearing in Washington.

Ousted Cadets Offered Chance to Reapply After a Year

By JAMES FERON
Special to The New York Times

WASHINGTON, Aug. 23 — for a military career and demonstrate his potential for commitment in the West Point cheating scandal by offering guilty cadets who have been ousted the chance to reapply for admission after a one-year period short of "reflection," preferably on active service as enlisted men.

Testifying before a Senate Armed Services subcommittee, Mr. Hoffmann said this would ...

Continued on Page 58, Column 8

Some of the West Point cadets accused in honor code scandal listen to televised testimony from Washington with Capt. James Lee, right, an Army defense attorney, in a classroom at Thayer Hall at the academy.

Continued From Page 1, Col. 4

pressed anger and profound dejection, while those uninvolved were divided. Some asked why anyone found guilty should be readmitted, and others said that the accused had already experienced many months of punishment.

Mr. Hoffmann said that he had "stepped in only after great deliberation and some hesitation."

However, "this one-time action," he said, "was necessary in an unusual and extraordinary situation."

There is "objective evidence," he went on, to support the cadets' claim that the "balance" of control over the Honor Code's administration "has shifted away from them."

Ostensibly run entirely by cadets, the Honor Code is carried out under close administration supervision.

The investigation and initial prosecution of the electrical engineering cases were turned over to an internal review panel dominated by officers early in June, when the majority of cadets had gone for the summer. The cadet honor boards, normally responsible for initial action, are back in operation, but not for the current cheating scandal.

Comment on Panel

Mr. Hoffmann said that the Superintendent's appointment of the internal review panel, taken with other cases, "provided the perception that the importance and weight of honor committee findings have been diminished and that the decisive elements of the Honor Code have been assumed by the Administration of the Academy."

The Army Secretary said that that he also agreed with a point raised by Senator Sam Nunn, Democrat of Georgia and chairman of the subcommittee of manpower and personnel, that the cadets and the staff had drifted apart over the years on matters of the Honor Code and system.

Academy officials have been accused of abusing the Honor Code by employing it to enforce Academy regulations. A West Point officer sitting in the hearing room offered an example, saying that "whisky hidden in a hair-oil bottle is a violation of regulations, for which the penalty might be demerits, but lying about it is a code violation, for which the penalty is expulsion."

Faculty members similarly have been charged with abusing the code. Critics use the electrical engineering examination as an example, saying that it was inviting trouble to give 825 cadets two weeks to complete identical tests while working in their barracks rooms.

Mr. Hoffmann said he would work to correct the confusion over regulations. He dismissed charges of a cover-up in the investigation of the cheating scandal, however, and rejected allegations that the Academy had intimidated Army lawyers who were outspoken in their defense of cadets.

General Berry, under rigorous questioning, conceded that "the institution bears part of the blame" for the cheating scandal. Senator Nunn asked him if this did not thus exonerate the cadets.

"Not at all," General Berry replied. "In this extraordinary case, these extraordinary solutions must be used to prevent extraordinary cases in the future."

He said the Academy had not been sufficiently aware of changes in society dealing with reaction to authority.

Cadets at West Point yesterday marching to Mahon Hall, where they were to meet with lawyers and the commandant

Ousted Cadets Offered Chance to Reapply After a Year

A-10 Thur., Dec. 16, '76 The Arizona Republic

West Point blamed in part for cadet cheating

Associated Press

WASHINGTON — An investigative commission said Wednesday that the U.S. Military Academy is as much to blame for its cheating scandal as are the cadets who collaborated on graded homework last spring.

The commission, appointed in September by Army Secretary Martin Hoffmann, unanimously endorsed the academy's honor code but said it was corruptly administered through the honor system. The commission headed by former astronaut Frank Borman recommended that all 151 cadets snared in the scandal be reinstated as soon as possible.

Referring to the homework project undertaken by 823 cadets in an electrical engineering course, the commission said:

"Inadequacies in the honor system, in the academy environment which was to have supported this system, and the administration of the examination combined to make a cheating incident practically inevitable."

The commission said it is "distressingly apparent" that the honor system "had indeed become grossly inadequate by the spring of 1976."

The report continued: "even more disturbing is that this inadequacy was known to academy leadership well before the homework scandal but no decisive action taken."

Hoffmann said at a Pentagon news conference that a plan will be drafted to implement at least the major recommendations by Inauguration Day, when the secretary presumably will be replaced.

"I'm going to press on to take those actions I properly can take," he said. "I will deal with it as if I were going to stay on."

A second report released simultaneously by the Army substantiated some allegations of harassment made by West Point lawyers who defended accused cadets.

The lawyers, outspoken in their belief that cheating was widespread, maintained that their clients were scapegoats.

The second report, prepared by Bland West, deputy general counsel of the Army, and Brig. Gen. Hugh Clausen, chief judge of the Army Court of Military Review, singled out West Point's commandant of cadets.

Brig. Gen. Walter Ulmer's "vocal disapproval of the activities of the defense counsel was improper, not in the best interests of West Point and contrary to Army policy," the report said.

Hoffmann denied that Ulmer's reassignment, six months ahead of schedule and without promotion, stemmed from the cheating scandal or the report.

Hoffman said Ulmer is being transferred to facilitate a smoother transition in light of the scheduled reassignment next year of West Point's superintendent, Lt. Gen. Sidney Berry.

However, a member of the commission, Gen. Harold Johnson, said that when the investigators visited West Point on Nov. 11, Ulmer "felt at that time that everything was in hand. This commission

Frank Borman

"cannot be made until there is an acknowledgement" of the problems.

Hoffmann agreed with Borman's panel that it might be wise to reconstitute a commission next year to assess progress on the recommendations.

The commission report said cheating on homework by "many cadets" had gone undetected. It added:

"The commission is equally persuaded that scores of other violations of the honor code have gone undetected or unpunished and that, during recent years, a substantial number of cadets have been involved in dishonesty, toleration, and, on occasion, misconduct as honor representatives."

Borman told reporters the commission intended to indict no one.

"The commission viewed our actions as therapeutic, looking for the answers for a regeneration or a renewal, not an attempt to go back on a witch-hunt to hand out individual senses of responsibility," he said.

This was in keeping with the recommendation that the Army drop proceedings against cadets still fighting expulsion. The academy's honor code says, "A cadet will not lie, cheat, or steal, nor tolerate those who do."

Under academy rules, expulsion is mandatory for those caught violating the honor code.

The commission also said investigations should be halted in cases arising out of statements made by guilty cadets in an attempt to show pervasive disregard of the honor code.

In that connection, the Army announced that the cases of nine West Point graduates were being turned over to the Army inspector general after preliminary investigation.

"The time has come to end this unfortunate episode," the commission said. "The academy must recognize that it is not treating a disease that can be cured simply by isolating those who have been infected."

The report said that the honor code was being exploited unfairly by the academy; that it was badly understood; and that the officer corps has not shouldered its responsibility to participate in the honor system.

It recommended that cadets be given an option to turning in honor code violators, and that expulsion not be mandatory for violators.

Borman Committee Recommendations

V

RECOMMENDATIONS

A. Cadets involved in EE 304

The Commission has considered its primary responsibility to formulate recommendations concerning the institutional deficiencies it has found to exist. Unlike many other advisory bodies, however, this Commission has undertaken its work during the very crisis studied. It has thus been impossible to ignore the most fundamental question raised by this entire matter--what must be done with respect to the cadets involved in EE 304.

At the outset, we emphasize our strong support for the Secretary of the Army's August 23, 1976 policy to allow readmission of separated cadets. In recognizing the extraordinary nature of the situation, the Secretary, we believe, acted wisely and compassionately. The cadets did cheat, but were not solely at fault. Their culpability must be viewed against the unrestrained growth of the "cool-on-honor" subculture at the Academy, the widespread violations of the Honor Code, the gross inadequacies in the Honor System, the failure of the Academy to act decisively with respect to known honor problems, and the other Academy shortcomings. The Secretary's action did not condone cheating; rather, it recognized that, in light of the grave institutional responsibility, the implicated cadets should be given another opportunity to meet the ideals of the Honor Code.

The time has come to end this unfortunate episode. The Academy must recognize that it is not treating a disease that can be cured simply by isolating those who have been infected. The Academy must now acknowledge the causes of the breakdown and devote its full energies to rebuilding an improved and strengthened institution. We see nothing to be gained by

17

further action against these cadets and much to be lost by continuing with the divisive and unrealistic attempt to purge all who have violated an Honor Code that is perceived in widely differing ways. What is needed are reform and regeneration, not retribution.

Under these circumstances, we must recommend, as to those cadets implicated in connection with the EE 304 incident, that:

    1.   All such cadets who left the Academy should be allowed to return to the Academy as soon as possible;

    2.   All such cadets presently at the Academy, whose separations have not yet been effected, should be allowed to remain at the Academy; and

    3.   All investigations of such cadets based upon allegations in the affidavits should cease.

We stress that the implicated cadets came from a cross section of the Corps; indeed, some had been leaders of their class. We do not believe that the single act of collaborating on the EE 304 examination makes these cadets unworthy of becoming West Point graduates. The Superintendent, speaking to a group of these cadets on August 28, 1976, expressed our feeling:

    "[I]f one has been found to have violated the Honor Code, in this case by cheating on EE 304, I think that was the wrong decision that the individual made; I think that under the terms of the Honor Code it can be called a dishonorable act; but as I look at those of you whom I know, I do not think that that one error in itself means that you are a dishonorable man--not at all."

Moreover, punishment or continued punishment of these persons can no longer be justified knowing, as we do now, that a substantial number of even more culpable cadets have gone undetected or unpunished. As one member of the Cadet Honor Committee perceptively remarked, if the separated

18

cadets are to be "branded," they ought to be branded only as "the ones who got caught."

We recognize that some of the implicated cadets undoubtedly deserved to have been expelled long ago. The Academy, however, has not, in its procedures, distinguished between such cadets and other highly motivated young men who became entangled in this affair. Failure to do justice to some should not be allowed to preclude mercy to others. All of the cadets should have a final opportunity to prove that they are indeed honorable or, conversely for some, to prove that they are not.

B. The Honor Code and System

With respect to the Honor Code and System, the Commission makes the following recommendations:

> 1.   The Honor Code should be retained in its present form: A cadet will not lie, cheat, or steal, nor tolerate those who do."

> 2.   The nontoleration clause should be retained. However, a cadet should have options in addition to reporting an honor violation. A cadet who perceives a violation must counsel, warn, or report the violator. Some action is required, as distinguished from tacit acquiescence.

> 3.   Sanctions other than dismissal should be authorized for violations of the Honor Code. The Cadet Honor Committee and reviewing authorities should be authorized to consider the facts and circumstances of each case to determine an appropriate penalty. Any recommendation less than separation should be fully justified. Cadets who are separated should not be required to serve on active duty as a result of their separation.

> 4.   All officers and cadets at the Academy must understand the fundamentals which underlie the importance of the Honor Code and the health of the Honor System:

> a.   The Honor Code must be viewed as a goal toward which every honorable person aspires, and not as a minimum standard of behavior for cadets alone. Furthermore, its proscriptions do not encompass all forms of dishonorable conduct; the test

of whether conduct is honorable or dishonorable does not depend solely upon whether it is proscribed by the Honor Code.

b. The Honor Code must not be extended beyond its intended purpose of insuring that only honorable individuals become Academy graduates. Nor should it be exploited as a means of enforcing regulations.

c. The Honor Code and Honor System must be considered the joint responsibility of all cadets and all officers at the Academy. It must be understood that the Superintendent has the responsibility of reviewing and, if necessary, reversing cadet honor determinations. No one "owns" the Honor Code. Everyone must work to insure the effectiveness of the Honor System.

5. The Academy should seek ways to insure that the above fundamentals work on a continuing basis. As a minimum, the following should be accomplished:

a. There must be academic instruction which provides an intellectual base for character development. All cadets should be required, early in their careers at West Point, to begin formal ethics study. This study, which must be part of the core curriculum, should include those ethical problems likely to be faced by a military officer. Ethics should be stressed throughout the entire curriculum and by all constituencies at West Point: Academic, Tactical, Athletic, and Administrative.

b. The content of honor instruction must emphasize the spirit of the Honor Code. A "cook book" approach makes the Code equivalent to another regulation.

c. The method of honor instruction and the environment in which it is conducted must be improved.

d. There must be greater participation by all cadets and officers in the operation of the Honor System. Cadet rank should not be awarded for Honor Committee service.

e. The Superintendent's Honor Review Committee should be continued, but its membership should include cadets and alumni. The Committee should meet at least annually with the mission of guarding the Honor Code against misuse, misinterpretation, and inconsistent interpretation. The Committee should have the ultimate power to interpret the Honor Code.

f. An officer should be appointed to advise the Cadet Honor Committee and the Superintendent's Honor Review Committee. This officer should report to the Academic Board (and not the

Commandant alone) concerning all honor matters.   Continuity
is required in this position.

C.   The Environment of West Point

With respect to the environment of the Academy, the Commission makes
the following recommendations:

   1.   A permanent and independent advisory board should be
established to provide the continuing assistance that most
institutions of higher education receive from their boards of
trustees.   Such a board, established by the Secretary of the
Army, should (1) be non-political; (2) include members who
recognize the proper mission of the Academy; (3) convene
often enough to insure current knowledge of the institution;
and (4) report to the Secretary of the Army its observations
and recommendations.

   2.   The West Point mission statement should be revised to
insure that everyone understands the importance of education
in the mission of the Academy. The acquisition of a quality
college education within a military environment must have
first call during the academic year on the time and energies
of a cadet. Everyone must understand that this is the primary
mission of the Academy from September to June.   Military
training should be concentrated in the summer months.

   3.   The Superintendent should have responsibility for all
aspects of the internal administration of the Academy,
including resolving the competing demands made by subordinate
authorities upon individual cadets.   His selection should be
based upon his interest in education and a demonstrated
ability to provide educational and military leadership.   He
should be assigned to the Academy for a minimum of 5 years
and should be consulted as to the selection and length of
service of the Commandant of Cadets and Dean of the Academic
Board.

   4.   Permanent professors should serve on active duty for
no more than 30 years, unless requested to continue on a term
basis by the Superintendent with the approval of the
Secretary of the Army.

   5.   The Professor of Physical Education should be a member
of the Academic Board.

   6.   The Office of Military Leadership, a department
concerned in large part with providing academic instruction
in behavioral sciences, should be transferred to the Academic
Department. The Director of that Office should be a member of
the Academic Board.

21

   7.   There should be an expansion of programs which bring

outside viewpoints to the Academy, e.g., visiting professors
to and from the Academy.

8.   The Academy must reaffirm the role of the tactical
officer as a company commander and ensure that this role is
uniformly adhered to throughout the Tactical Department.

9.   Tactical officers should be selected from officers who
have completed Command and General Staff College or
equivalent education.

10.   The Leadership Evaluation System should be reviewed
to determine whether it is a constructive force in the
cadets' leadership development.

D.   Military Defense Counsel

We are disturbed by allegations that several military defense
counsel suffered harassment and injury to their Army careers because of
their vigorous defense of cadets. Inasmuch as the Secretary of the Army
had commenced an investigation into these charges, we did not review
these allegations in depth.

The defense function places counsel in an adversary relationship with
West Point--the institution that seeks to discipline or otherwise punish
his client. This adversary relationship is too often viewed as an act of
disloyalty. A cadet client should feel secure that the legal defense
presented is in no way compromised by the lawyer's fear of adverse
personnel actions.

The present system of having the same officer teach law and act as
defense counsel places him in the difficult position of attacking the
basic policies of the institution to which he owes allegiance in his role
as a faculty member. As a partial solution the Commission makes the
following recommendations:

22

1.   Judge Advocates who defend cadets should have no teaching duties.

2.   Military leadership courses should include examination of the role of the lawyer as an advisor to the commander and the role of defense counsel in the justice system.

OFFICE OF THE SUPERINTENDENT
UNITED STATES MILITARY ACADEMY
WEST POINT, NEW YORK 10996

MASG

18 February 1977

Dear Friends of West Point:

The period since my last report to you on 26 August 1976 has been one of intense activity at West Point. This letter will give you a report of events since last August, current actions underway at the Military Academy, some general observations concerning the honor situation, and a look to the future.

Secretary of the Army Decisions of 23 August 1976

As I reported to you on August 26th, the Secretary of the Army reaffirmed on August 23rd that cadets who violated the Honor Code would be separated from the Military Academy. To date, all cadets who were found to have violated the Honor Code in the Electrical Engineering 304 incident have been separated except one, who remains at West Point pending the outcome of legal action. The total number of cadets separated as a result of EE 304 related honor violations is 151.

Also on August 23rd, the Secretary announced his decision to permit those cadets who were separated in the EE 304 incident to apply for readmission to the Corps of Cadets in the summer of 1977. A Special Readmissions Committee composed of both officers and cadets was immediately formed to evaluate, consider, and advise those cadets electing to apply for readmission. To date, 126 cadets who were separated and who requested evaluation by the Special Readmissions Committee have been found to be tentatively suitable for readmission. Under the established readmission procedures, applicants were required to present a plan for relevant activity during their absence and to confirm such plans 30 days after their separation from the Corps. Later this spring the Special Readmissions Committee will consider each applicant's formal request for readmission and make recommendations to the Academic Board through the regular Admissions Committee. The Academic Board will consider each case individually, with the principal criteria for readmission being "suitability for commissioning in the United States Army" and an expressed commitment to the standards and principles of the Military Academy, including the Honor Code.

The Secretary of the Army also announced that, as a matter of equity, all honor cases which arose during the 1975-1976 academic year and resulted in separation would be reviewed upon petition. As a result of this review, seven ex-cadets are being considered for readmission.

Another major action announced by the Secretary on August 23rd was the appointment of the Special Commission on the United States Military Academy, chaired by Colonel Frank Borman, to make an assessment of the EE 304 situation and its underlying causes in the context of the Honor Code and Honor System.

Affidavits

Affidavits alleging violations of the Honor Code by an additional 559 cadets were prepared by several cadets implicated in EE 304 honor violations and delivered to the Chairman of the Cadet Honor Committee on 16 September 1976. The Honor Committee, assisted by members of the staff and faculty, immediately commenced a detailed analysis and investigation of

MASG   18 February 1977

the allegations. After investigating all allegations as thoroughly as possible, the Honor
Committee found sufficient evidence in only five cases to forward them for hearings before
full Cadet Honor Boards. The allegations against the remaining 554 cadets were dismissed
for insufficient or unavailable evidence. The implicated cadet submitted the affidavits
purportedly to demonstrate the pervasiveness of Honor Code violations throughout the
Corps. While I believe that the affidavits failed to accomplish this objective, the
existence of the affidavits was further evidence of the seriousness of the problem. Any
affidavits alleging honor violations by recently graduated cadets were forwarded to the
Department of the Army for investigation.

Change in Honor Procedures

Concurrent with the investigations of the allegations contained in the affidavits, the
Cadet Honor Committee continued their efforts to revitalize the Honor Code and improve the
Honor System. Working closely with military legal advisors, they developed and presented
to the Corps of Cadets a broad range of revised Honor Committee procedures designed to
provide increased due process to cadets accused of violating the Honor Code. On
November 9th the Corps voted overwhelmingly to adopt the revised procedures. Specific
changes include the provision of legal counsel for the accused in the proceedings, the
presence of a legal advisor to assist the Cadet Chairman of an Honor Board, and a military
lawyer to assist the Honor Committee in presenting their case. Investigative procedures
have been refined. Members of all classes from the Corps at large may now sit on Honor
Boards. These revised procedures eliminate the requirement for a subsequent Board of
Officers, and I believe they represent a significant improvement and indicate the interest
and concern of the Corps of Cadets in the Honor Code and System. We will work closely
with the Honor Committee and the Corps of Cadets to ensure that they accomplish their
intended purposes as they implement and refine the revised procedures.

Penalty for Violating the Honor Code

Since at least the 1940's there has been at West Point a single sanction or penalty for
cadets who have been found to have violated the Honor Code: mandatory separation from the
Military Academy. During recent years regulations under which the Military Academy is
governed have read that a cadet who violates the Honor Code "shall be separated" from
USMA. Neither the Cadet Honor Committee nor the Superintendent, therefore, have been
authorized to exercise their judgment or discretion on individual cases of honor violations, no matter what the circumstances.

In February 1976 the Honor Committee sponsored within the Corps of Cadets a vote on the
proposition that a penalty other than mandatory separation be considered for honor violations falling within certain narrowly prescribed circumstances. Perceiving this proposition as an important change in the Honor System, the Honor Committee specified that the
proposition would require the support of two-thirds of those voting. The proposition
failed to carry, although 54.6% of the ballots were in favor of the modification.

On 9 December 1976 the Honor Committee again proposed to the Corps of Cadets that the
Honor Committee be given the authority to recommend to the Superintendent an exception to
the sanction of mandatory separation. This concept is commonly referred to as "discretion."
Factors which were to be considered by the Honor Committee when making such a recommendation
included, but were not limited to:

    -- the education and experience of the cadet under the Honor Code

    -- whether the offense was self-reported

MASG 18 February 1977

-- attitude, or an indication that the cadet has truly learned from the experience and demonstrates an understanding of the value of personal honor now and in the future

-- any previous violations of the Honor Code.

As in February 1976, the Honor Committee required a two-thirds affirmation to adopt the proposal. The proposal again failed to carry, but this time by less than one percent. 66.08% of the cadets who voted supported the proposal. Thus, mandatory separation remains as the only penalty the Honor Committee can recommend to the Superintendent until such time as the Corps of Cadets indicates adequate support for an alternative.

On 19 January 1977, Secretary of the Army Hoffmann directed a change to the Regulations for the United States Military Academy pertaining to the penalty for a violation of the Honor Code. He directed that the regulation which reads that a cadet who violates the Honor Code "shall be" separated be amended to read "shall normally be" separated from the Military Academy. The effect of this regulation change is to permit the Superintendent to exercise his judgment (or to use his "discretion") in matters concerning cadet honor violators in the same way in which he previously has been free to use his judgment in the other sensitive and important personnel actions. In separate correspondence, the Secretary directed the Superintendent to exercise his discretion conservatively in accordance with the guidelines proposed by the Honor Committee and supported by 66% of the cadets in the December 1976 vote.

I believe this change is a wise one which will strengthen the Honor Code and Honor System. Rather than watering down the system, I believe that it imparts a necessary degree of comparison and flexibility to a system which, in a few cases, appeared to be Draconian in its severity. A degree of discretion, furthermore, is inextricably linked to one of the most fragile aspects of the Honor Code -- the nontoleration clause. ("A cadet will not lie, cheat, or steal, nor tolerate those who do.") In my opinion, nontoleration is essential to the Honor Code, for it requires that each cadet be an active participant in the Honor System and it inculcates in cadets the higher loyalties and keen sense of duty required by the profession of arms. There are, however, indications that the single sanction of mandatory separation for honor violations has created in some cadets an overwhelming moral dilemma between reporting a close personal friend for what they consider to be a trivial or poorly defined honor violation not deserving mandatory separation or protecting the friendship by tolerating the violation and thereby becoming an accomplice in the violation. The discretion now available to the Superintendent will help to ease that dilemma and to encourage greater participation and growth by cadets under the Honor Code. I intend to exercise this authority prudently and infrequently.

The Special Commission on the United States Military Academy

The Report of the Special Commission on the United States Military Academy, delivered to the Secretary of the Army on 15 December 1976, is an ambitious attempt to deal comprehensively with a dynamic situation and complex set of issues. It is wide-ranging, critical, and thought-provoking. It expresses strong support of the Military Academy as an essential, unique national institution and endorses the Honor Code as it now stands. The Report highlights some areas of concern that were already under study and identifies other areas in which there is the need or potential for strengthening and improving the Military Academy. The introspection, evaluation, and actions resulting from the Commission's investigation and report will continue to be helpful to West Point in the days and years ahead. We are grateful to the members of the Commission for their unselfish efforts and their genuine concern for the health and well being of West Point. You may read the entire Report in the March 1977 issue of ASSEMBLY, our alumni magazine.

After intensive review of the Commission's Report, the Secretary of the Army announced his immediate response on 5 January 1977. A resume of the Commission's major findings and recommendations together with the Secretary of the Army's response follows:

MASG   18 February 1977

        The Commission fully supports the Honor Code as written as a simple statement of essential standards of integrity to which every honorable person aspires. The Honor Code, insofar as it proscribes lying, cheating, and stealing, is supported and indeed treasured by most cadets; however, the Commission found that many cadets do not fully support the nontoleration provision as presently interpreted.

        The Commission found that in its opinion there had been a serious deterioration of the Honor System (the way in which the Code is implemented within the Corps) as a result of a number of factors, among them the continuation of the single sanction of separation, the strict requirements of the nontoleration clause, the context and method of honor instruction, evidence of past corruption within the Honor Committee, the gradual extension and exploitation of the Honor System to enforce regulations, and elements of the cadet environment which were nonsupportive of the Honor Code. The Commission concluded that the number of cadets who had resigned or been separated as a result of the EE 304 incident did not reveal the full extent of honor violations at the Military Academy. While the Commission did not excuse totally the actions of those cadets who collaborated on the EE 304 examination, they concluded that the institution must share responsibility for the incident.

        The Commission recommended that those cadets implicated in connection with the EE 304 incident who had left the Military Academy should be allowed to return as soon as possible. The Secretary of the Army concurred with that recommendation and directed that, in consonance with existing law and academic requirements, cadets qualified for readmission would rejoin the Corps in the summer of 1977.

        The Commission recommended that those implicated cadets who still remained at the Military Academy whose separations had not been effected should be allowed to remain at the Military Academy and that all investigations based on allegations contained in the affidavits should cease. The Secretary rejected those recommendations from the standpoint of equity and directed that the investigations and processing continue.

        The Commission recommended retention of the Honor Code in its present form. The Secretary concurred.

        The Commission recommended there be an improved system of education in the Honor Code to include a four-year program of instruction in ethics and military professionalism and that cadet participation in the Honor System be broadened. The Secretary concurred. The Military Academy has set in motion actions and studies to improve and expand educational programs in honor, ethics and military professionalism. The revised Honor Committee procedures adopted in November 1976 expanded cadet participation in the Honor System.

        The Commission recommended that sanctions other than dismissal should be authorized for violations of the Honor Code and that the nontoleration clause should be retained but that cadets should have options in addition to reporting an honor violation. The Secretary ended the single mandatory sanction of separation by the change in regulations described earlier and directed the Military Academy to evaluate all aspects of the nontoleration clause of the Honor Code. This is being studied by a joint involvement of both cadets and officers.

        The Commission made a variety of recommendations aimed at improving the cadet environment as it relates to the Honor Code. These touched upon nearly all elements of the Military Academy: cadet-officer relationships, academic curriculum, demands on cadet time, organization and functions of the Military Academy, role and composition of the Academic Board, selection and role of tactical officers, the leadership evaluation system, the statement of the mission of the Military Academy, and establishment of evaluative procedures to keep attuned to the role of honor in the Corps of Cadets.

4

MASG 18 February 1977

A significant number of recommendations were already being implemented prior to release of the Commission Report. Examples are the changes to academic procedures adopted by the Academic Board in July 1976, the revitalized program of honor instruction being developed and implemented by the Honor Committee, and the establishment of the officer position of The Commandant's Special Assistant for Honor Matters. Other recommendations being staffed for implementation in the near future are the separation of the Staff Judge Advocate from the Department of Law, revised selection criteria for tactical officers favoring Command and General Staff College graduates, and the change in the composition of the Academic Board to include the addition of the Professor of Physical Education and the Director of the Office of Military Leadership.

Long-term actions are being studied by three internal Department of the Army Study Groups, each having Military Academy representation and input. The Study Groups are: Academic, headed by Major General Hillman Dickinson; Environment, headed by Brigadier General Jack V. Mackmull; and Professional Development, headed by Brigadier General Jack N. Merritt. The unifying theme for the study groups is the determination of the most effective method for inculcating the concepts of duty, honor, and service to country in all activities that influence cadets. The results of these studies will be completed by this summer and will be made available to the Chief of Staff of the Army and the Superintendent for their consideration.

General Observations

Let me make a few general observations which, for the most part, are points made in my letter to you of last August, but which I believe are worthy of reiteration:

-- The great majority of the Corps of Cadets continue to believe in, support, uphold, and be guided in their lives by the spirit of the Honor Code. I am heartened daily by the exceptional quality and high ideals of the young men and women of the Corps of Cadets.

-- The concept that the ultimate responsibility for a person's actions -- to lie or not to lie, to cheat or not to cheat, to steal or not to steal -- rests in the individual's free moral choice, environmental factors notwithstanding. This is and must continue to be a basic tenet of honor at West Point and in the Army.

-- The dedication, professionalism, sensitivity, and genuine concern with which everyone has worked throughout this period to resolve this situation are directly responsible for the survival and ultimate strengthening of the Honor Code and the Military Academy. The Special Commission has given us a hard-hitting appraisal of the situation from a different perspective. Those involved at Department of the Army level, from Secretary Hoffmann on down, have worked with a sense of urgency and love for the Military Academy and everything for which it stands. The United States Military Academy staff and faculty have given selflessly of themselves and their time. Members of the Corps of Cadets have has supported and strengthened the Military Academy in a mature, responsible, disciplined, thoughtful manner. The leadership provided by the Class of 1977 has been firm and effective. Members of the Cadet Honor Committee have worked tirelessly and continuously to develop improved procedures, conduct investigations, educate and train themselves and the Corps, and to preserve and strengthen the Honor Code. Their maturity, sensitivity and determination to pursue what is right have been unfailing. I am grateful for the efforts of all concerned parties.

Other Activities

The normal activities related to the mission of the Military Academy have proceeded remarkably well during this unusual period. The Class of 1980 has taken its place in the Corps of Cadets and has demonstrated great promise and potential. Women cadets have been successfully integrated into the Corps and the institution. Physical and military training programs have gained in effectiveness. Performance of athletic teams has improved and

MASG   18 February 1977

continues to do so, and the women's athletic program is off to a successful start. Having selected the branches of the Army in which they will be commissioned, members of the Class of 1977 look forward to their graduation and joining the Army Officer Corps on 8 June 1977. Applications are high for admittance with the Class of 1981, which will enter the Military Academy on 6 July 1977 about 1425 strong.

In early January 1977 Brigadier General Walter F. Ulmer, who had been Commandant of Cadets since April 1975, departed West Point to become Assistant Commander of the 2d Armored Division at Fort Hood, Texas. As Commandant of Cadets, this superb soldier performed his duties in one of the Army's most consequential brigadier general's assignments in an outstanding manner and under the most challenging circumstances. We are grateful for the contributions made by General Ulmer and his family to the West Point community.

In mid-January Brigadier General John C. Bard assumed duties as Commandant of Cadets. A graduate of the Class of 1954, former Cadet First Captain, Rhodes Scholar, mechanics instructor at West Point, and veteran of two tours of combat duty in Vietnam, General Bard is eminently qualified to serve as Commandant of Cadets. We are pleased to have him and his family with us.

A Summing Up

This is an unusually important time in the life of the Military Academy. It is a time of challenging, questioning, and testing of basic assumptions, values, standards, traditions, practices, procedures, and systems. It is a time of institutional and individual soul-searching, analysis, study, appraisal, and reflection. It is a time for reaffirmation of that which is sound and helpful for the future, for discard or modification of that which is faulty, illogical, or outmoded, and for renewal of commitment to the values, ideals, standards, and quality of service expected of West Point and its cadets and graduates. What is needed now is objectivity to recognize both current strengths and past mistakes, foresight to identify requirements of the future, determination to bring about constructive change, and intelligence and sensitivity enough to accomplish this in consonance with the mission of the Military Academy and the best interests of the Army and the Nation.

I am optimistic about the future of West Point. The institution is sound, strong, and enduring. It is dedicated to the principles of duty, honor, and service to country and has reaffirmed its conviction that integrity is absolutely essential to soldiers and to military institutions. I believe that, as one compares March 1977 with March 1976, the Military Academy is stronger and healthier, the spirit of honor is heightened, and the Honor System more realistic and effective. Much remains to be done, and many difficult decisions lie ahead; but we are on the right track and moving in the right direction. I believe that we will achieve the right objectives.

The Department of the Army has described the purpose of West Point in the following words:

> "The mission of the United States Military Academy is to educate, train, and motivate the Corps of Cadets so that each graduate shall have the character, leadership, and other attributes essential to progressive and continuing development throughout a career of exemplary service to the nation as an officer in the Regular Army."

This mission is our guide as we work to strengthen and improve the United States Military Academy.

Sincerely,

SIDNEY B. BERRY
Lieutenant General, U.S. Army
Superintendent

HEADQUARTERS UNITED STATES MILITARY ACADEMY
Office of the Commandant of Cadets
West Point, New York 10996

MACC-H   28 February 1977

MEMORANDUM FOR: CHAIRMAN, SPECIAL READMISSIONS COMMITTEE

SUBJECT: Status Report on Honor at West Point

This memorandum describes the major issues related to honor that
have been addressed this academic year.

    1. <u>The Honor Code</u>. The Corps, the Staff and Faculty, and
the Borman Commission reaffirmed the Honor Code exactly as stated:
"A cadet will not lie, cheat or steal, nor tolerate those who do."

    2. <u>New Academic Procedures</u>. In September 1976 the Dean of
the Academic Board announced the following new academic procedures:

       a. Background.

       (1) On 18 May 1976 the Superintendent appointed a Special
Study Group to recommend ways to improve academic procedures govern-
ing themes, daily writs, written partial reviews, term-end examinations, design problems, laboratory exercises and homework. On
24 July the Academic Board approved the changes recommended by the
Study Group, to be effective in Academic Year 1976-1977. The effect
of these changes will enlarge the possibilities of academic discussion
outside the classroom.

       (2) Intellectual growth is ultimately dependent on indidivdual
effort. Cadets must develop a sense of personal responsibility for
the attainment of academic competence. Work copied from another con-
tributes little to the learning process. While the learning process
benefits from the use of extensive resources and the criticism of
others, both honorable conduct and accepted academic practice require
that the work of others be clearly and unambiguously acknowledged
when used in the preparation of any paper or problem which is submitted
as one's own work. To do otherwise is at best misleading and at worst
outright theft of another's work.

       b. Discussion of Classwork. Cadets are authorized unres-
tricted discussion of anything that occurred in a class or examination
as soon as they are dismissed from the classroom. Discussion may be
with anyone, whether that individual has attended that particular
session or not.

    c. Discussion of Homework. Because discussion is a
healthy and essential part of learning, cadets are encouraged
to enter into full and free discussion of all homework assignments, graded or ungraded, to include themes, research papers,
laboratory reports, design problems and homework problems. This
unrestricted discussion is subject to the requirement that cadets
document any references and assistance used and degree of that
usage, in accordance with instructions contained in The Style
Manual, July 1976.

    (1) In the past discussion was permitted up to the point
when writing began on any outline, preliminary draft or final
paper which the cadet was to submit as his own product. Under
the new procedures full and free discussion is permitted throughout preparation, subject to the requirement that all assistance
contributing to the final product must be documented.

    (2) Discussions and assistance of a general nature are
to be documented in an acknowledgement statement preceding the
signature on each homework submission. If the discussion or the
assistance can be identified with a specific portion of the paper,
documentation should be in the form of a footnote.

    3. New Procedures for Processing Alleged Honor Violations.

    a. On 9 November 1976 the Corps of Cadets, 85 per cent
voting in favor, adopted new procedures for processing alleged
honor violations. The new procedures are outlined below:

    (1) An accused cadet is now warned formally that he is
not required to make any statements and that he has the right to
consult with counsel during the preliminary investigation. Previously this step was not a requirement.

    (2) If a subcommittee is convened it will consist of two
honor representatives and three cadets from the Corps-at-large
who are from the same class as the accused. A majority vote of
subcommittee members is required to forward the alleged violation
to a Full Honor Board. Previously an affirmative vote of one of
three honor representatives was sufficient to forward the case.

    (3) A Full Honor Board now consists of four honor rep-
resentatives and eight cadets from the Corps-at-large. These
eight cadets are selected randomly from the Corps. At least
three classes with two cadets each must be represented among the
eight cadets from each class in the Corps. The accused cadet may
choose to eliminate one class from board representation and
distribute those two vacancies to the other three classes in
whatever manner he so chooses.

MACC-H   28 February 1977
SUBJECT: Status Report on Honor at West Point

(4) The Full Honor Board membership also includes a
Legal Advisor, Government Recorder, and counsel for the accused.
All three are military lawyers appointed from the Department of
Law. Note that the accused is <u>represented</u> by counsel at the Full
Honor Board. The new structure provides the due process require-
ments of the courts and eliminates the need for a Board of Officers
in the Honor process.

(5) After hearing all evidence, the Full Honor Board
will vote by secret written ballot. A guilty vote of 10 of the
12 members is required to forward the case to the Commandant for
review.

(6) The record of the Cadet Honor Board Proceedings is
subject to review by the Commandant, Superintendent, and Secretary of the Army.

b. On 9 December 1976 the Honor Committee asked the Corps
to approve a proposal to allow Full Honor Boards to retain a cadet
in the Corps. The proposal specified narrowly defined criteria
for retention to ensure that it remain the exception rather than
the rule. The Corps failed to adopt this proposal, thus leaving
separation as the only sanction under Honor Committee Procedures.
The Secretary of the Army, in response to the Borman Commission
Report, changed USMA Regulations to read that a cadet "who violates
the Honor Code shall normally be separated." This change will
allow the Superintendent to exercise discretionary punishment
under identical criteria considered by the Corps on 9 December
1976. The Superintendent plans to use his discretion carefully
and infrequently.

4. The "Clean Slate" Policy. The Honor Committee has completed
its investigation of cadets named in affidavits. Those cadets who
had departed the USMA were not investigated further. On 14 December
1976 the Secretary of the Army approved a "clean slate" policy for
cadets who return to the Military Academy under his plan of 23
August 1976. This policy states that readmitted cadets will be
forgiven for any honor violation which occurred prior to their
separation and subsequent readmission.

                         HAL B. RHYNE
                         Colonel, Armor
                         Special Assistant to Commandant
                             for Honor

3

Retired General Will Head West Point

The Phoenix Gazette □ April 4, 1977 A.

WASHINGTON (AP) – Defense Secretary Harold Brown today announced reassignment of Lt. Gen. Sidney B. Berry, superintendent of scandal-marred West Point, and the recall of retired Gen. Andrew J. Goodpaster to replace him.

The Army said Berry will complete a normal three-year tour as superintendent of the U.S. Military Academy in June. His new assignment will be announced later.

Selection of a retired general to head the U.S. Military Academy is unprecedented, officials said.

BROWN SAID that Goodpaster, former supreme allied commander in Europe and onetime staff secretary to President Dwight D. Eisenhower, "possesses the unique blend of military and educational background and experience deemed necessary for the superintendency today."

The defense secretary also said that Goodpaster, who will serve as a lieutenant general when he comes back on active duty, "reflects the best qualified individual available to the Army at this time."

Martin R. Hoffman, who was Army secretary during the recent cheating scandal, which involved 151 cadets, said late last year the new superintendent's authority would be strengthened and that he would remain in the post up to eight years.

HOFFMAN said at the time that Berry would leave on schedule this spring.

Berry, who had been regarded as one of the Army's outstanding generals and a potential chief of staff, faces an uncertain future.

Although he was not singled out for specific blame in follow-up investigations of the worst scandal in West Point history, many Pentagon officials say they fear his future prospects might be adversely affected because it happened during his tour of duty.

BROWN'S announcement that Goodpaster would replace Berry in June said the Army chose the retired general after considering a recommendation by the Borman Commission that the new superintendent meet the criterion of "a demonstrated ability to provide educational and military leadership."

That commission, named by Hoffman to look into the scandal, was chaired by Frank Borman, the former astronaut who now heads Eastern Airlines. The Borman Commission last December recommended changes in enforcement of the cadet honor code and reinstatement as soon as possible of the cadets implicated in the cheating.

GOODPASTER, a 1939 West Point graduate, holds a bachelor's degree and a Ph.D. degree in international relations from Princeton as well as a master's degree in engineering.

He served as commandant of the National War College from July 1967 to June 1968 and, after retiring from the Army in 1974, was a senior fellow at the Smithsonian Institute's Woodrow Wilson International Center for Scholars.

As NATO commander from July 1969 until December 1974, Goodpaster supervised the defenses of Western Europe.

In the past, the Army has always chosen active-duty general officers as superintendents at West Point.

The New York Times

JUNE 5, 1978

West Point '78 Closing Book on Cheating '76

By James Feron
Special to the New York Times

WEST POINT - The largest class in the history of the United States Military Academy is preparing for graduation this week, a ceremony that the Superintendent, Lieut. Gen. Andrew J Goodpaster, says will "close the curtain" on the 1976 cheating scandal.

The ranks of the 990 graduates include 92 readmitted cadets who accepted a Pentagon amnesty requiring a year of "useful service" away from the Academy. More than 60 others also accused of cheating on a take-home examination declined the offer, with the majority continuing their education elsewhere.

Although the readmitted cadets will be indistinguishable in the long, grey line of graduates receiving their diplomas and commissions as second lieutenants in Michie Stadium on Wednesday, the institution they leave behind has changed drastically.

Reforms introduced in the wake of what became West Point's worst cheating scandal include a restructuring of the entire academic program, major changes in military training and an overhaul of the cadet honor system.

General Goddpaser, the former NATO commander who came out of retirement to oversee the reforms, said in an interview that "Something like the cheating scandal does not happen by accident - there must be underlying causes." The goal, therefore, was to "find the remedies."

They have been far-reaching, producing what may be the most comprehensive changes in the institutions 176-year history. In fact, some cadets, including at least one who was involved in the cheating episode, feel they may be too radical.

Cadet Timothy Ringgold, who became a central figure in the scandal for having told a visiting Assistant Secretary of the Army that the situation was worse than the Academy was admitting, said he endorsed the academic changes with their "emphasis on excellence rather than simply passing" but felt also that "the Academy may have gone overboard on easing military discipline."

Cadet Ringgold, accused of "tolerating " cheating but never tried on the charge, resigned when the others were dismissed and returned to West Point when they did. He said, "It's possible the academy learned the wrong lessons. It's not that you shouldn't throw cadets out - some are not suited for this environment - but that you weigh each case on its merits. Some of those who left deserved another chance, or at lest a fair trail."

But "things are working out," he said. "The academy is trying . It was reflexing two years ago, not thinking. It didn't want to know what the problems was. Now it's saying we have a problem." he said, emphasizing the "we", and "maybe that explains their unwillingness now to throw guys out."

General Goodpaster indicated that the most significant changes were being made in the academic area. "We've changed our entire curriculum, a tremendous undertaking." The changes include shortening classes from 80 minutes to 60 minutes, reducing re-   Continued on page D9

Cadet Timothy Ringgold at West Point

Lieut. Gen. Andrew J. Goodpaster

West Point '78 Is Closing Book on the Cheating of '76

Continued from Page B1

quired courses from 48 to 40 and increasing electives from 7 to 10.

Cadets will be taking more philosophy, for example, and they will probably be required to sign up for a new course, "The Institution of the American Society," or how the military relates to other institutions, including the press and Government.

New Curriculum Described

Ironically, one of the courses that will disappear—it will become part of another course—is EE304, the electrical-engineering class in which 152 cadets were eventually accused of collaboration on a take-home exam although more than twice that number were widely believed to have been involved.

The new curriculum, General Goodpaster said, also recognizes that "with the higher disciplines of a modern army it is no longer possible to reach a high level of competence across the board." West Pointers will be graduating in the future with specialties, or "high performance in a particular area of concentration."

The grading system has also been scrapped, to be replaced by one that is more precise, a B-plus and a B-minus as well as the simple B of before. Also discarded is the general order of merit, ranking an entire class from No. 1 to the infamous last man, or "goat."

"We want to recognize that each individual here has his own academic profile, doing well in some and not so well in others," General Goodpaster said. "I do not want to stereotype or categorize a man according to a single number. Everyone has more dimensions than that," he said.

Shouted Instructions Ended

Training and discipline also have been reformed. The face-to-face shouted instructions by upperclassmen to plebes, which General Goodpaster said

"was mistakenly confused with leadership," have been eliminated "although we still have eyeball-to-eyeball instructing in a firm voice," he added.

Cadets agreed that, as one put it, "the place is a lot quieter." The "stress theory" of plebe year continues, however, "with true military demands remaining high," General Goodpaster said. "The pressure," he noted, "should not take the form of harassment and abuse."

This includes a change in "cadet knowledge," required of plebes, with the elimination of such impractical but time-honored questions as "How many lights in Cullum Hall (340, sir)" or "How much water is in Lusk Reservoir (78 million gallons, sir, when the water is flowing over the spillway.)" Acceptable queries now deal with identification and location of army divisions, for example.

The cadet honor system, formed over the years around the honor code that "a cadet will not lie, cheat or steal, or tolerate those who do," also has been changed, largely to protect those charged with arbitrary investigations and decisions.

Defendants Get Lawyers

The pool of potential cadet jurors has been broadened and due process has been included in the initial stage, with Army lawyers assigned to represent the defendant and the prosecutor as well as the honor board itself. Lawyers had entered the case in the past only when a board of officers have conducted later hearings.

The Superintendent, similarly, now has the Pentagon's approval to impose penalties less severe than dismissal, which was the only punishment open to him in the past. To avoid dismissing a cadet he would have had to over turn the cadet board's findings, an action that led to cadet retaliation through "the silence," or shunning, of an accused cadet.

All these changes have come in the

last year or are scheduled for the next academic year. General Goodpaster conceded however that cadets were resisting some of them. He said that a first-classman (senior) had asked his tactical officer "Why all the explaining? In the Army you just tell somebody to do something and you don't have to explain it."

Women Cadets Opposed

The tactical officer replied that, on the contrary, " 'You'll be telling them what has to be done and then explaining why and how to do it,' " General Goodpaster said.

If there is resistance to change at West Point, in fact, it appears to be concentrated on the admission of women, which still rankles many cadets and officers, rather than on the alterations in academic training or ethical areas.

There are now 163 women cadets at the academy of the 223 who entered in the last two years. Their dropout rate is roughly equivalent to that of the men, but they remain far from universally accepted.

"It's difficult to explain the cadets' own interpretation," one graduating cadet said. "They want the women to do the same things the men do, but if they do, then they're Amazons or mooses. They want them to be feminine, but then they accuse them of using their femininity."

General Goodpaster provided little consolation for those officers and alumni who would like to see the women disappear. "It comes down to the question of how do you provide leadership in an army that has both men and women in it. This institution is committed to the proposition of integrating the services of men and women on a professional basis.

"I understand that there will be resistance, but we are going to hold our officers to professional standards. If they really don't like it, then they're in the wrong line of work."

409 North Fairfax Street
Alexandria, Virginia 22314

August 12, 1986

Mr. Timothy D. Ringgold
118 West Gay Street
West Chester, Pennsylvania 19380

Dear Mr. Ringgold:

President Ford asked me to return to West Point in
1977 because the institution was in turmoil following
the 1976 honor scandal. At that time I learned the
extent of the problem and I am confident that it has
been fixed.

In your letter of August 4, you asked me to comment
on your conduct during those difficult days ten years
ago. Everything I know about your involvement in the
events of that time leads me to the conclusion that
your actions were selfless, honorable, and in the
best interests of West Point.

If you think it necessary, I will be glad to try to
remember and comment on specific events.

Sincerely,

Andrew J. Goodpaster

THE
EISENHOWER
INSTITUTE

Andrew J. Goodpaster, General, USA (Ret.)
Senior Fellow
goodpaster@eisenhowerinstitute.org

918 Fifteenth Street, NW Eighth Floor Washington, DC 20005-2311
(202) 628-4444 Fax (202) 628-4445
www.eisenhowerinstitute.org